Social Research and Disability

Social Research and Disability argues that the contemporary rules of sociological methods outlined in numerous research methods texts make a number of assumptions concerning the researcher including ambulance, sight, hearing and speech. In short, the disabled researcher is not considered when outlining the requirements of particular methods. Drawing upon these considerations, the volume emphasizes how disabled researchers negotiate the empirical process, in light of disability, whilst retaining the scientific rigour of the method. It also considers the negative consequences arising from disabled researchers' attempts at "passing" and the benefits that can emerge from a reflexive approach to the method.

This innovative and original text will, for the first time, bring together research-active academics, who identify as being disabled, to consider experiences of being disabled within a largely ableist academy, as well as strategies employed and issues faced when conducting empirical research. The driving force of this volume is to provide the blueprints for bringing how we conduct social research to the same standards and vision as to how the social world is understood: multi-faceted and intersectional. To this end, this edited collection advocates for a sociological future that values the presence of disabled researchers and normalizes research methods that are inclusive and accessible.

The interdisciplinary focus of *Social Research and Disability* offers a uniquely broad primary market. This volume will be of interest not only to the student market but also to established academics within the social sciences.

Ciaran Burke is an Associate Professor of Higher Education at the University of the West of England. His research focuses on access to higher education and graduate employment pathways. Adopting a Bourdieusian theoretical lens, he has published extensively on issues including graduate employment, social justice and social theory.

Bronagh Byrne is Co-Director of the Centre for Children's Rights and Co-Founder of the Disability Research Network at Queen's University Belfast, Northern Ireland. Her research focuses on the rights of disabled children and young people. She has published widely on inclusive education and the implementation of international disability rights law and children's rights law.

Sociological Futures

Series Editors:
Eileen Green, Professor Emerita, Teesside University
John Horne, Waseda University, Japan
Caroline Oliver, Associate Professor of Sociology, UCL Institute of Education
Louise Ryan, Professor of Sociology, University of Sheffield, Vice Chair of the BSA

Sociological Futures aims to be a flagship for new and innovative theories, methods and approaches to sociological issues and debates, and 'the social' in the 21st century. This series of monographs and edited collections was inspired by the vibrant wealth of the British Sociological Association (BSA) symposia on a wide variety of sociological themes. Edited by a team of experienced sociological researchers, and supported by the BSA, it covers a wide range of topics related to sociology and sociological research and features contemporary work that is theoretically and methodologically innovative, has local or global reach, as well as work that engages or reengages with classic debates in sociology bringing new perspectives to important and relevant topics.

The BSA is the professional association for sociologists and sociological research in the United Kingdom, having an extensive network of members, study groups and forums, and a dynamic programme of events. The Association engages with topics ranging from auto/biography to youth, climate change to violence against women, alcohol to sport, and Bourdieu to Weber. This book series represents the fruits of sociological enquiry, reaching a global audience, and offering a publication outlet for sociologists at all career and publishing stages, from the well-established to emerging sociologists, BSA or non-BSA members, from all parts of the world.

What is Food?
Researching a Topic with Many Meanings
Edited by Ulla Gustafsson, Rebecca O'Connell, Alizon Draper and Andrea Tonner

Social Research and Disability
Developing Inclusive Research Spaces for Disabled Researchers
Edited by Ciaran Burke and Bronagh Byrne

For more information about this series, please visit: www.routledge.com/Sociological-Futures/book-series/SOCFUT

Social Research and Disability

Developing Inclusive Research Spaces for Disabled Researchers

Edited by
Ciaran Burke and Bronagh Byrne

Routledge
Taylor & Francis Group
LONDON AND NEW YORK

First published 2021
by Routledge
2 Park Square, Milton Park, Abingdon, Oxon OX14 4RN

and by Routledge
52 Vanderbilt Avenue, New York, NY 10017

Routledge is an imprint of the Taylor & Francis Group, an informa business

British Library Cataloguing-in-Publication Data
A catalogue record for this book is available from the British Library

Library of Congress Cataloging-in-Publication Data
A catalog record has been requested for this book

ISBN: 978-1-138-38765-2 (hbk)
ISBN: 978-0-429-42612-4 (ebk)

Typeset in Goudy
by codeMantra

To all the disabled researchers out there fighting the good fight and laying the ground for those that follow

Contents

Figures

Tables

Acknowledgments

We would like to thank all the contributors to this collection, they have shown patience, scholarship and honesty in the pursuit of making life better for the next generation. In addition, we'd like to thank all the folks at BSA and Routledge for getting us to this stage.

Ciaran – I'd like to extend a special thanks to my co-editor Bronagh Byrne for coming with me on this journey, Gray Burke and Alison Danforth for her kindness and support. Last, I'd like to thank Paul Burke, my dad; he has spent his life trying to make life fairer for those who are forgotten and he is the inspiration for this book.

Bronagh – A huge thanks to Ciaran Burke for approaching me with the initial idea for this book. It's been a pleasure to be able to give voice to an issue that is so close to my heart. Here's hoping this book encourages others to challenge the taken for granted. I'd like to thank my family and friends for their ongoing support. Finally, I'd like to thank Laura Lundy for her never-ending words of wisdom and encouragement as I negotiate academia.

Notes on the contributors

Cynthia Bruce, PhD is a blind activist educator and researcher in the School of Education at Acadia University in Nova Scotia, Canada. She works locally, provincially and nationally to build commitment and capacity around equitable access to education and employment for disabled people. She has worked with all levels of government to implement accessibility legislation and ratify international disability rights agendas, and she consults with communities and organizations to promote an ethic of equity and inclusion. Her research activities aim to generate meaningful inclusion by exposing the systemic and institutional policies and practices that work against the realization of disability rights for disabled students and faculty.

Ciaran Burke is an Associate Professor of Higher Education in the Department of Education and Childhood, University of the West of England. His research has mostly focused on social inequalities within higher education and graduate labour market and the relationship between social theory and method. Ciaran has published widely on these topics and has authored and edited several books including, *Culture Class and Graduate Futures: Degrees of Class*, (Routledge), and *Social Theory and the Politics of Higher Education*, (Bloomsbury).

Bronagh Byrne is a Senior Lecturer in Social Policy in the School of Social Sciences, Education and Social Work, Queen's University Belfast. She is Co-Director of the Centre on Children's Rights and Co-Founder of the Disability Research Network. Bronagh has published widely on disability rights, children's rights and inclusive education. She is co-editor of 'Valuing Disabled Children and Young People' (Routledge) and has led on a range of projects with children and young people as well as Deaf and disabled people using rights-based approaches.

Dr Louise Byrne is a service user researcher focused on peer/lived experience employment. Louise is employed as a Senior Research Fellow at RMIT University, Australia. Louise has previously been awarded a Fulbright Fellowship to conduct research on peer employment in the United States, based at Yale University.

Vera Chouinard is a Professor in the School of Earth, Environment and Society at McMaster University. Becoming disabled early in her career, she experienced a lengthy struggle for reasonable accommodation of her work-related needs. A geographer by training, her work has been concerned with marginalization and struggles for social justice. Her recent publications address topics such as disability activism and disability issues in the Global South.

Anita Z Goldschmied is a PhD candidate in contemporary theory and research. She is a registered social worker, learning disability nurse, and university lecturer. Her main teaching and research interests have centered on several aspects of autism, intellectual disability and mental health, particularly with respect to complexity, as connected, temporal and non-linear emergent performances.

Nancy Hansen, PhD is an Associate Professor and Director of the Interdisciplinary Master's Program in Disability Studies at the University of Manitoba. Her research interests include, disability in spaces of culture education, history, literacy, employment, healthcare and conflict. She is co-editor of the Routledge History of Disability and Untold Stories: A Canadian Disability History Reader. Nancy has contributed to various international academic journals.

Wendy Merchant is a British mother-activist and nurse who focuses on actively contesting the othering of our 'disabled' children and ourselves. She worked on the 'Getting Things Changed' project at the University of Bristol, and her own auto-ethnographic research 'Caring for disabled children in hospital: Mothers and nurses experiences' at UWE, Bristol.

Caroline Miles is an activist researcher and qualified solicitor. She was previously employed as a Research Associate at the Norah Fry Centre for Disability Studies, University of Bristol, and was involved in the 'Getting Things Changed' research programme.

Karen Mogendorff is a Dutch anthropologist and communication professional with a PhD in the Social Sciences. Her current work focuses on empowering disabled people to tell their stories, and on structurally enabling participation of disabled people in education and research on ageing with a disability. Karen works for both academic institutions and disability organizations and initiatives.

Stuart Read is a disabled person and activist, and Research Fellow at Bath Spa University. Prior to joining Bath Spa University, he worked as a Senior Research Associate on the 'Getting Things Changed' research project at the University of Bristol.

Helena Roennfeldt is a lived experience researcher and academic, specializing in critical and alternative perspectives in mental health. She is currently completing her PhD on subjective experiences of mental health crisis and alternatives to emergency departments. Helena has a Masters of Suicidology; Mental Health; Forensic Mental Health and Social Work.

Michael Schwartz is an Associate Professor of Law and Director of the Disability Rights Clinic in the Office of Clinical Legal Education, Syracuse University College of Law. Michael's research projects have focused on the experiences of deaf patients in the healthcare field, with a particular focus on mental health services, and access to justice for Deaf people. Michael helped to establish the Tangata Group, a non-governmental organization which provides education and training on disability rights.

Dr Annmaree Watharow is a former General Practitioner, specializing in clinical mental health, turned PhD candidate at the University of Technology, Sydney. Dr Watharow is deafblind due to Usher Syndrome and is in the final months of completing her thesis on the hospital experiences of people who are deafblind or have dual sensory impairments.

Introduction

Ciaran Burke and Bronagh Byrne

Emerging from ivory shadows

Life as a disabled academic is somewhat reminiscent of an academic version of the film "The Hunger Games": power, discrimination, inequality, measurements of ability and where attempts to circumvent the rules are seen as rebellious acts. The origins of this edited collection come in part from the editors' personal experiences of being academics, presumed disabled by impairment, but fundamentally disabled through the interaction between impairment and the endemic visible and invisible barriers that arise through the assumed rules, norms, procedures and practices of "academic" research methods. Our initial discussions of the issues, and frustrations with being expected to conform to the taken for granted expectations and assumptions of academia, slowly turned to shock which gave way to anger that a book such as this does not already exist. In short, at the apparent invisibility of disabled academics like us. This book is a response to those frustrations. It is a means of making visible the challenges that disabled academics across the globe are forced to navigate when undertaking research. In bringing our distinct experiences as researchers to the forefront, we seek to create spaces where creative discussions and inclusive responses are determined. Most of all, we want to support disabled researchers like us to emerge from the ivory shadows, take up their proverbial pens and shout out that "these rules [of research] are fundamentally oppressive!"

This book is not a typical "scholarly" work. Understanding the challenges of sociological research – and its need to evolve – requires insider engagement with the subject matter. It necessitates listening to our experiences and recognising that the "personal is political" (Morris 1992) is inherently academic, and at times, of academic making. The book switches the spotlight on how sociological research can be used, not only as a critical tool to uncover the systemic oppression that disabled people experience in society but how, in doing so, the socially constructed – and often subtle – structures, rules and methods associated with that tool oppresses those doing the uncovering. In doing so we wanted to make the book as accessible as possible. It is a coming together of academics sharing (often deeply personal) experiences and strategies, culminating in our call for a more inclusive sociological future. As editors, it is our intention that this edited collection begins to create a space for disabled academics in the future of Sociology and articulate the richness that such perspectives can provide. To begin the process of cementing our place in future research and future debates, we speak through personal experience and often personal frustrations. The relative ease with which the chapters in this book can be read should not be construed as reflecting insignificance of the issues. But rather, as the opposite – that it is of such significance that disabled academics have invoked a personal gaze to lay bare the extent of the challenges encountered.

Disrupting the rules of sociological research

The history of the method within sociological research can be traced to two foundational texts; Durkheim's *The Rules of Sociological Method* (1896) and Weber's *Objectivity in Social Science and Social Policy* (1904). Both men, here, set out the priorities and conditions of sound and valid sociological research. Durkheim guided by the concept of "social facts" developed the Positivist position to establish a set of rules to explain social phenomena. In an effort to maintain the legitimacy of the discipline, as a form of scientific endeavour, Durkheim's rules echoed that of the natural sciences. Similarly, Weber's contribution outlines an approach to understanding social phenomena or *Verstehen*. Echoing Durkheim, Weber provides his readers with a set of procedures and tools including means-end continuum, focus on probability, value neutrality and his most recognised concept – ideal types.

The theme throughout both Durkheim and Weber's work is that to establish and retain legitimacy and authority, the social scientist must adopt if not the methods then the principles of the natural scientist. As Sociology progressed through the 20th century, there has been a number of significant additions – in particular, the establishment of qualitative methods, first through the ethnographic work of Malinowski or Mead and the work of the Chicago School. However, while the qualitative tradition is seen as an alternative route for social research, it is still bound to a series of rules as outlined in numerous research methods texts (Mason, 1996; Silverman, 2006; Bryman, 2015) to increase legitimacy and authority. Also, the criteria on which qualitative research is judged is based on positivist principles of validity and reliability. Where qualitative research has attempted to move beyond these criteria, such as Lewis and Ritchie's (2003) assertion that we can understand "reliability" as "sustainability" or "validity" as meaning "well-grounded" or Hammersley's (1992b) concept of "consistency" and Lincoln and Guba's (1985) combination of "credibility, transferability, dependability, and confirmability", the long shadow of positivist criteria is quite evident. In order for a research project to be legitimate or for research to meet an assessment criteria in undergraduate or postgraduate study, research must conduct itself in a particular way – in other words, by following a prescriptive set of rules.

One notable exception of the persistence of scientific principles – in particular, objectivity – in social science research is standpoint epistemology. Here, we see a position toward research areas and generation of knowledge as politically driven and emancipatory in conclusion. It is within these well-established and rule-based approaches to empirical research which this edited collection takes as its point of departure. We assert that the contemporary rules of sociological methods make a number of assumptions concerning the researcher, including mobility, sight, hearing, speech and a normative understanding of mental health. In short, the disabled researcher is not considered when outlining the requirements of particular methods nor in the criteria for assessing "successful" research. To date, many research methods texts (Barnes and Mercer, 1997; Moore, Beazley and Maelzer 2009; Shakespeare, 2015) have reflected and discussed issues of respondents with particular disabilities; however, the same attention has not been given toward the researcher, who appears bound by ableist norms. There are a few exceptions to this: Berger and Lorenz's (2015) academic text *Disability and Qualitative Inquiry* introduces readers to a range of issues involved in doing qualitative research with disabled people and includes contributions from disabled researchers themselves, however, the latter is not the focus. Elsewhere, Dolmage (2017) in *Academic Ableism: Disability and Higher Education* provides, at times, a personal account of how ableism is woven throughout higher education through campus architecture, curriculum design and general attitude toward disability. His point is very clear: disability has been the focus of academic research while excluding disabled academics. Dolmage, reflecting on Foucault's position that power is not hierarchical but rather is all around, argues that this power and recognition need to be captured to address ableism in academia. His starting point is greater collaboration and shifting away from exclusively understanding disability as an object of research. This edited collection pushes these arguments forward by going beyond the benefits of collaboration and focusing specifically on empirical research.

This edited collection takes the rules of research as faced by the researcher as its point of departure. It brings together a number of disabled researchers and

- Outlines ableist systems and procedures within academia;
- Uncovers the ableist assumptions made by "traditional" methods texts;
- Discusses, and gives legitimacy, to the myriad ways in which disabled researchers negotiate the empirical process, whilst retaining the scientific rigour of the method;
- Considers the negative consequences arising from disabled researchers' attempts at "passing" and the benefits that can emerge from a reflexive approach to method.

In so doing, this book seeks to create a space which finally gives voice to those researchers worldwide who have been marginalised from the sociological *able*stream. To this end, we desire a sociological future that values the presence of disabled researchers and normalises research methods that are inclusive and accessible.

This collection is written by a range of self-identifying disabled researchers with impairments across the spectrum, including physical disability, visual impairment, deafness, deaf-blindness, chronic health conditions and psychosocial disability. Contributors to this collection are at different points in their academic careers, contrasting national contexts and occupying a range of disciplines within the social sciences. While not all contributors come from a sociology background, the issues that arise and the arguments made speak to wider sociological themes; not least the extent to which unequal power relations between a majority non-disabled population and minority disabled population, are deeply embedded across the academy. Yet as editors we are deeply mindful that the book is not fully inclusive of all impairments: there are no contributors with intellectual impairments, for example; nor are there contributors from the Global South. However, this book can only ever be a starting point.

Merely "being" or "making it" as a researcher or academic is insufficient. Rather, barriers abound. This collection is about method; however, it is about how we as disabled researchers conduct research, and as such, it is our voice which at times may appear highly personal, passionate or angry to the reader but goes to the heart of our argument, to move beyond sanitised approaches to research.

Navigating the academy

The underrepresentation of "disadvantaged groups" in higher education is a well-established issue including gender, class and race and ethnicity (The Res-Sisters, 2017; Bhopal, 2019). Unsurprisingly a similar pattern is clear concerning disabled academics (Brown and Leigh, 2018). In the UK context, despite small gains in representation of disabled academics, Brown and Leigh argue that this level of representation falls below working-age adults with disabilities and crucially university undergraduates registered as disabled. Brown and Leigh suggest that one influence on these trends is that disabled academics are required to work extra to illustrate parity with "able-bodied" colleagues, in other words, taking on additional labour in order to "pass". The reluctance to disclose a disability is amplified within the high performance/neo-liberal culture of contemporary higher education despite policies and legislation in place such as the Equality Act 2010 in Great Britain, and the Access to Work programme. As Brown and Leigh (2018) suggest, the focus and priority of universities when supporting disabilities has been toward students, rather than staff. These priorities include policies such as reasonable adjustments, support plans and, in the UK context, a requirement for universities to reduce barriers to participation for disadvantaged groups including disabled students.

The first section of this edited collection "Navigating the Academy" brings to the foreground the practical barriers disabled researchers experience often driven by institutional policies and ableist assumptions. This section begins with Annmaree Watharow's "Owning My Room: Building a Safe, Accessible and Productive Space for Student Researchers with Complex Communication Disabilities".

Here, Watharow recounts the challenges she faced as a doctoral student with deaf-blindness. In the absence of policies and support mechanisms in place to address her particular disability, Watharow was required to chart her own path through her institution. Building and reflecting on this experience, Watharow provides a framework for how reasonable adjustments can be made for the disabled researcher, focusing on areas including communications; safe spaces; supervisors; digital; training; cultural, social life and care of the self; time; research output; and dissemination. In the next chapter, "On the Outside Looking In?: reflections on being a disabled social and feminist geographer", Chouinard provides a reflective account of her career as a social geographer navigating an ableist academy. Here, Chouinard considers the array of challenges disabled academics face including conducting/disseminating research, teaching and securing grant income. Chouinard offers an account of everyday life as a disabled academic accounting for the taken for granted systems in higher education which present distinct challenges. Through reflecting both on her privilege as a white academic from the Global North, Chouinard also outlines the intersections of disability and gender and how an ableist academy "disables" disabled researchers. Chouinard concludes by discussing how academia can provide a much more supportive and generative space for disabled academics and in particular the need to abandon a one size fits all approach to performance and scholarship, to see difference in an effort to reduce the additional labour required to match our colleagues.

The combination of practical barriers and both discipline-specific and general academics' expectations can have a lasting impact on the development and maintenance of the disabled researcher's career. In her chapter "Disability in Academia: a closer look at "wheelchair" Ethnography" Karen Mogendorff considers what she terms the unique barriers and also the opportunities anthropology affords the disabled researcher. Mogendorff's point here is that, while anthropology celebrates "positionality", the nature of the fieldwork demands that the researcher be flexible. Reflecting on both personal experience and secondary analysis of disabled academics' reflective writings, Mogendorff discusses some of the strategies that academics employ, including physically painful attempts at passing, refocusing of the empirical area to reflect disability and opting for less prestigious sub-fields due to the nature of a disability. Mogendorff goes on to suggest that these strategies can be mediated by a status within a university, as such senior academics' (who are more likely to be white men and therefore open to other privileges) roles will change from front-line teaching and research to facilitating and strategy, but their academic standing remains at a similar level. For those disabled academics that do "make it" there is an assumption that these academics can navigate their disability or have a less pronounced disability – here Mogendorff uses Seymour's (2007) concept of "disappearing disability phenomenon". As a result of such attitudes or assumptions toward disabled academics a similar pattern of inequality that affects other minority groups is evident such as income gaps, glass ceiling and sense of anxiety.

In contrast to the absence of support mechanisms as discussed by Watharow and Chouinard and the strategic decisions researchers are forced to make as outlined by Mogendorff, this section concludes with Read et al.'s "Dilemmas of Identity Disclosure and Provision of Disability Support". Here the authors discuss the friction between Access to Work policies in the UK and the need for the disabled employee – in this case, an academic – to self-identify and actively request support. This requirement, the authors argue, risks rebalancing how an institution views the individual, that is, as a "disabled" person rather than a professional academic. Drawing from research findings, personal experiences of members of their university "Staff Disability Forum", the authors unpack the dilemma that disabled academics face when accessing university support systems. Also, this chapter outlines how, through collective action by disabled academics, they can question the assumptions within university policy and managerial practices which reproduce ableist dynamics within the academy.

The first section of this edited collection "Navigating the Academy" provides first-hand accounts of the significant barriers that disabled researchers face when negotiating barriers that their non-disabled fellow students, colleagues, supervisors and line managers etc are not required to even consider, let alone navigate. In an effort to move beyond a culture of "earning your stripes" authors provide frameworks to address these issues and create a more supportive environment for future disabled researchers. There are clear impacts from these barriers on how researchers create and navigate the academy requiring researchers to adopt particular policies. Even in the context of greater official support, there can still be barriers and dangers to professional identity which need to be taken into consideration moving forward. Both the intended and unintended barriers that researchers face, not limited to disabled researchers, and how frameworks and communities of practice can alleviate some of these issues should be a central focus point for sociology moving forward.

Conducting research in the field

In contrast to the "value neutral" preconditions of some approaches to social research, collaboration is a defining feature of related emancipatory research positions such as critical disability studies, critical autism studies, feminist research and critical race theory. As Reinhartz (1992) argues, concerning feminist methodology, this commitment to collaboration is to provide a more equitable process for the research participants, address power inequalities within the researcher/researched dynamic, create an opportunity to observe highly nuanced experiences or attitudes and, crucially, to give a voice to a marginalised or forgotten social group. We continue this tradition in the edited collection by considering the benefits of collaborative research.

The second section of this edited collection "Conducting Research in the Field" is opened by Nancy Hansen's chapter "The Continuing Adventures of a four-Legged Female Academic". Here Hansen provides a context in which she sees the gradual shifting of established patterns and practices toward disabled academics. Hansen both documents and celebrates the strategies required to navigate academic identity, research partners and the empirical process itself, which, through a shifting recognition of marginalised groups, offers an opportunity for a collaborative research process. In so doing she highlights the subtle and, at times, not so subtle normative cues that dictate who belongs and is expected in research space and how these manifest in the field. In continuing the shift away from the merits of a "neutral" researcher, Anita Goldschmied's chapter "10 Affects of Hidden, Mental Dis/Abilities and the Act of Disclosure" considers the implications of having similar invisible disabilities to the participants she routinely researches. She highlights the opportunities and rich findings that situated knowledge can provide. This "thick description" is captured through sharing a tacit understanding of invisible disabilities with her respondents. This position allows for an appreciation of invisible disabilities and also articulates reflexive and hidden experiences which often remain unexamined. The final chapter in this section discusses the benefits and barriers to collaboration between disabled researchers when combining situated knowledge and empirical research. In "Lived Experience researchers: Opportunities and challenges in mental health", Helena Roennfeldt and Louise Byrne provide an account of "Lived Experience" research. Structured as an informal conversation between two researchers (the two authors) this chapter provides both quotations from a recorded dialogue between the authors and then the reflections on this dialogue. Through this collaborative chapter, Roennfeldt and Byrne unpack the gap and friction between definitions of disability and contemporary models of mental health. Building on the potential "concealed" nature of mental health, the authors consider potential strategies of "passing" and equally, as they describe, the Catch 22 of shifting ableist assumptions via direct experience of discrimination. In a bid to address the lack of fit between the often subjective constructions of meaning sitting behind mental health and the external and narrow systems in which higher education institutions operate, the authors call for meaningful co-production between colleagues.

Chapters within the second section of this edited collection "Conducting Research in the Field" centre around the principle of collaborative research. Chapters discussed how patterns of representations and assumptions toward disabled academics have changed and the potential consequences for collaborative work. Alongside this, discussions have illustrated that collaborative research (cemented by disclosing shared "invisible" disabilities) provide greater opportunities to understand participants and amplify their voice. Collaboration comes in many different forms, while the forms discussed here push against the concept of the neutral researcher to a more or lesser degree, the rich data and situated knowledge which can come from such approaches are clear.

Shifting methodologies?

The final section of this edited collection is "Shifting Methodologies", these three chapters consider the flexibility required during the empirical process and question the conditions of rigour as being fundamentally ableist. To return to arguments presented at the beginning of this introductory chapter, we maintain that the majority of methods within sociology (including related disciplines) share a set of ableist assumptions/demands of researchers. As a consequence of not meeting these empirical demands, the very rigour and validity of research are cast into doubt. Again, emancipatory approaches such as feminism, critical disability studies and critical race theory largely attempted to break the mould and provide a very different way of examining and reporting on the social world. Feminist standpoint epistemology (Collins, 1990; Sutton, 2010) has adopted a range of qualitative methods such as (auto)ethnography, semi-structured interviews, participant observation to achieve its epistemological goal. While feminist standpoint epistemology has been heavily critiqued by Hammersley (1992a) on the grounds that it does not take the necessary (read traditional) approaches to ensure rigour, feminist standpoint epistemology has enjoyed sustained application throughout the social sciences.

An issue that the final section of this edited collection addresses, further illustrating its contribution, is the priorities of standpoint epistemologies. Emancipatory approaches such as feminist research, critical race theory and indeed disability studies come to research with a political ontology concerning power distribution within social space. A key priority for many of these approaches is situated knowledge, defined by Haraway (1988) as knowledge which is partial, local and critical. For Haraway, situated knowledge allows us to push back against reductionism and reduce amplifying the most dominant voices within that context. It is dangerous, Haraway argues, to seek out universal truths, writing "the moral is simple: only partial perspective promises objective vision" (1988: 583). In a bid to reject reductionism and not get trapped in relativism, situated knowledge should be both recognised and embraced as complicated and messy. This edited collection is attempting to rise to Haraway's challenge: "I am arguing for the view from the body … versus the view from above, from nowhere, from simplicity" (1988: 589). Reflecting on Haraway's comments on the danger of reductionism and amplification of dominance and, we would add, privileged voices, there is still a danger of reductionism within standpoint positions in terms of alignment to established rigour and the protection that this provides. In other words, methodological approaches such as these still operate within a safety net, while they may be seen by some as pushing boundaries the application of recognised qualitative methods allows these researchers to claim epistemic authority and rigour.

The chapters in this final section consider the impact when that safety net is removed due to having to conduct research while navigating a disability. The considerations that researchers such as these authors have to make have not fully been accounted for in previous emancipatory approaches and as such appear to have been left behind in the development of methods. The final section of this edited collection opens with, "Unsettling Ableism in Research Traditions: Toward Establishing Blind Methodologies", from Cynthia Bruce. In this chapter, Bruce discusses the ableist hurdles blind researchers must pass when conducting qualitative analysis. Despite significant developments in qualitative analysis software, qualitative analysis is still based on heavy assumptions of sightedness; most of these software developments still rely on sight to identify tools such as colour coding. Here, Bruce outlines the analytical framework she developed, assisted by a creative application of assistive technologies, to draw on blind ways of working while retaining rigour.

In the next chapter "Deaf Research Methodologies? Confronting epistemological silences and challenges in qualitative research", Bronagh Byrne and Michael Schwartz consider their experiences as deaf academics who either use sign language or hearing aids and lip reading. This chapter discusses the challenges that deaf academics face when conducting qualitative research with disabled and non-disabled respondents, and, in particular, the assumption and expectation of fluency. The authors reflect on the positive or negative symbolic capital they have based on their disability and the constant absence of a neutral identity. They conclude by outlining strategies to overcome these ableist assumptions and ways to promote greater inclusive practices for deaf researchers.

Our edited collection concludes with, "Repeat After Me": Gestalt, fluency and biographical research", by Ciaran Burke. Here, Burke reflects on the challenges that speech dysfluency – in particular, stammering – poses on qualitative research. Burke outlines the Sociological literature concerning stammering and the theoretical explanations of the stigma associated with stammering. Burke argues that the largely prescriptive rules of qualitative data collection, exemplified through the particular mechanisms of the biographical narrative interview method, reinforce ableist assumptions about the research – in particular, fluency of speech. Burke concludes by outlining both ways forward for qualitative research in general and options to navigate biographical research which includes researchers who stammer.

Chapters within the final section of this edited collection "Shifting Methodologies" have outlined the rigidness and the subsequent dangerous requirements of method, such pre-conditions which may be seen as "normal" or at the very least unproblematic by non-disabled colleagues. Chapters in this section illustrate the ableist challenges disabled academics are required to negotiate irrespective of technological developments. Contributors comment on the pressures they feel to conform and the damage this can cause in terms of identity and integrity in the pursuit of rigour. This final trio of chapters, like many of their predecessors, provide new ways of thinking about and doing research which questions and surpasses ableist lines of inquiry.

The need for an inclusive sociological future

Discussions in this book amplify the need for an inclusive sociological future. This need has been further demonstrated in the context of the Covid-19 lockdown. Disabled researchers who had long highlighted the need to work from home due to inaccessible workplaces or to conserve energy are now finally able to do so. Working from home has become legitimised as never before. The shift to online methods and the use of online communication platforms for research may be a positive experience for some disabled researchers. For others it replaces one type of inaccessibility with another. As with research in physical spaces, research in the online world also emphasises seeing, hearing and speaking. In forcing us to consider new ways of conducting research, we should be using the pandemic as an opportunity to consider how accessible these "new" or less used ways of doing research are from the outset. Now is the time to address this before initially inaccessible methods – consider platforms like Zoom without captions or sign language interpreters for d/Deaf people, for example – become entrenched and complicit in conforming to existing sociological rules.

In his article *Expanding Ableism*, Wolbring (2012) pushes us to consider what "abilities" are considered essential and positive. Within social science research these include speech, sight, hearing, mobility and normative understanding of mental health. These are perceived as required in terms of maintaining a competitive edge in a high-performance culture and also to carry out research which is seen as authentic. As such, there is pressure for disabled academics to "pass" – whether this is overt or covert. We dedicate additional labour to not highlight any perceived weakness. Ableism has been used throughout history as a means to "reasonably" discriminate against members of society; Wolbring cites the rationale for denying women the right to vote until the early 20th century. As an academy we are of the assumption that we are beyond such practices and that such ableism is part of our sociological/academic past. However, as Chouinard argues in her chapter "On the Outside Looking In?: Reflections on being a disabled social and feminist geographer", these assumptions come about through privilege and the absence of a reflexive understanding of the everyday experience of disabled academics. Privilege adopts many guises, but in academia (like in many related social spaces) privilege can be understood in terms of disability and also gender, class and race and ethnicity. Chapters in this edited collection have clearly articulated the intersectional nature of inequalities and the need to consider the consequences of inequalities in isolation and also when combined. In other words, it is time to once again make the familiar strange and question why and how we treat colleagues, conduct research and assess its procedure and findings. Despite university commitments, reasonable adjustments and social charters ableism remains not only in our policies but in our practice and is very much an issue today, one that needs to be addressed for an equitable future for Sociology.

References

Barnes, C. and Mercer, G. (1997) *Doing Disability Research*. Leeds: The Disability Press.

Berger, R.J. and Lorenz, L.S. (2015) *Disability and Qualitative Inquiry: Methods for Rethinking an Ableist World*. Oxon: Routledge.

Bhopal, K. (2019) "Success against the Odds: The Effect of Mentoring on the Careers of Senior Black and Minority Ethnic Academics in the UK", *British Journal of Educational*

Studies (online early view) available from: https://www.tandfonline.com/doi/abs/10.1080/00071005.2019.1581127?journalCode=rbje20

Brown, N. and Leigh, J. (2018) "Ableism in Academia: Where Are the Disabled and Ill Academics?", *Disability and Society*, 33(6), 985–989.

Bryman, A. (2015) *Social Research Methods*. Oxford: Oxford University Press.

Collins, P.H. (1990) *Black Feminist Thought: Knowledge, Consciousness, and Politics of Empowerment*. Boston: Unwin Hyman.

Dolmage, J. (2017) *Academic Ableism: Disability and Higher Education*. Ann Arbor: University of Michigan Press.

Durkheim, E. (1896/1982) "The Rules of Sociological Method", In: Lukes, S. (ed.) *The Rules of Sociological Method and Selected Texts on Sociology and Its Method*. New York: Free Press. pp. 31–163.

Hammersley, M. (1992a) "On Feminist Methodology", *Sociology*, 26(2), 187–206.

Hammersley, M. (1992b) *What's Wrong with Ethnography?* London: Routledge.

Haraway, D. (1988), "Situated Knowledges: The Science Question in Feminism and the Privilege of Partial Perspective", *Feminist Studies*, 14(3), 575–599.

Lewis, J. and Ritchie, J. (2003) "Generalising from Qualitative Research", In: Ritchie, J. and Lewis, J. (eds) *Qualitative Research Practice: A Guide for Social Science Students and Researchers*. London: Sage. pp. 63–286.

Lincoln, Y.S. and Guba, E.G. (1985) *Naturalistic Inquiry*. Newbury Park: Sage Publications.

Mason, J. (1996) *Qualitative Researching*. London: Sage Publications.

Moore, Beazley, S. and Maelzer, J. (2009) *Researching Disability Issues*. Maidenhead: Open University Press.

Morris, J. (1992) "Personal and Political: A Feminist Perspective on Researching Physical Disability", *Disability, Handicap & Society*, 7(2), 157–166.

Reinharz, S. (1992) *Feminist Methods in Social Research*. London: Routledge and Kegan Paul.

Seymour, W. (2007). "Exhuming the Body: Revisiting the Role of the Visible Body in Ethnographic Research", *Qualitative Health Research*, 17(9), 1188–1197.

Shakespeare, T. (2015) *Disability Research Today: International Perspectives*. London: Routledge.

Silverman, D. (2006) *Interpreting Qualitative Data: Methods for Analyzing Talk, Text and Interaction* (3rd ed.). London: Sage Publications.

Sutton, B. (2010) *Bodies in Crisis: Culture, Violence and Women's Resistance in Neo-liberal Argentina*. New Brunswick: Rutgers University Press.

The Res-Sisters (2017) "'I'm an Early Career Feminist Academic: Get Me Out of Here? Encountering and Resisting the Neoliberal Academy", In: Thwaites, R. and Pressland, A. (eds) *Being an Early Career Feminist Academic: Global Perspectives, Experiences, and Challenges*. London: Palgrave. pp. 267–285.

Weber, M. (1904) "'Objectivity' in Social Science and Social Policy", In: Shils, E.A. and Finch, H.A. (eds) *The Methodology of the Social Sciences*. New York: Free Press. pp. 50–113.

Wolbring, G. (2012) "Expanding Ableism: Taking Down the Ghettoisation of Impact of Disability Studies Scholars", *Societies*, 2, 75–83.

Part I

Navigating the academy

Chapter 1

Owning my room

Building a safe, accessible and productive space for student researchers with complex communication disabilities

Annmaree Watharow

Introduction

> DeafBlind people can do anything. The question is not whether or not we can or should do something, but *how* we are going to do it—John Lee Clark, *Where I Stand* 2014.
>
> (Kindle version, Handtype Press, location no: 1698 of 2094)

This chapter seeks to explore how to make a research degree possible for a student with dual sensory impairment, examining what reasonable adjustments can be made and also how many of them might be needed. In short, it aims to provide a practical resource for students (and their potential supervisors), whilst acknowledging that the heterogeneity of interests, abilities, residual hearing and vision, and life course of each student is different. Attitudinal change is needed. The questions *what accommodations are reasonable* and *how much is it going to cost?* ought to be recast as *what does this student need for success?*

There are negligible narrative accounts available to people with deafblindness enrolling as doctoral students; there are also hardly any resources, including research, for deafblind scholars. The following reflections, from my experience as a student postgraduate researcher at the University of Technology, Sydney (UTS)—and from a decade of study in total in Australian tertiary institutions before that—provide one foundation layer (of many to come, I hope) in enabling deafblind students to succeed. In this chapter, as well as reflecting on personal experience, I distil the scant literature on students with deafblindness/dual sensory impairments/disabilities for insight. The subtext is: *I can do this and so can you—but it will be difficult*, because the steps to learning and knowledge production are steep and uneven—as detailed in Figure 1.1. I remind readers that I am in the middle of this process and not yet in a position to survey with hindsight how I arrived here, what forces were at play and what the significance of my research into the communication, access and mobility experiences of deafblind patients is.

A tertiary institution, like the society it is a part of, is slow to provide what the disabled *need* for success in a natural, forthcoming manner. My years at several universities in Australia have been one of favour (you are lucky we are doing this), invisibility (we have no services for people like you), unwanted visibility (whoever shouts loudest often gets more), privilege (I am white, literate and loud), and omnipresent aggressions, assumptions and discrimination. These aggressions, assumptions and discrimination weaken both institutions and individuals. Disabled students are required to *rise above it all, be resilient* and *toughen up*—to work harder for longer for less. If we succeed, we are regarded as amazing: role models, *inspo porn* for the able (well, if they without legs/arms/hearing/sight etc. can do it, why can't you?). And if we fail, that is to be expected. Low expectations abound for people with disabilities in general and for people with deafblindness in particular.

In addition, there are implications of unfair benefits—after accommodations granted following a doctor's visit to certify disabilities (we wouldn't want there to be any fraudulent claims for accessibility provisions) and the granting of what is deemed *reasonable*—many students and academics persist in believing that these confer unfair advantage to the disabled student. The concept of *reasonable adjustments* is a legal, moral and educational ambiguity that can fuel disputes over the cost, the need, the method, the provision and the legitimacy of accommodations. If access to learning and research were indeed equitable, institutions would simply provide everything that was needed for success quickly, without judgement, as directed by *the expert* in their disabilities, the student herself. But our universities (and society) have yet to become truly inclusive and welcoming. This makes climbing the steep steps to learning and knowledge production fraught and challenging.

Tertiary institutions are obliged by legal and moral frameworks in Australia—specifically, the *Anti-Discrimination Act* (1977) and *Australian Disability Services Act* (1986), as well as by international law, specifically, the *United Nations Convention on the Rights of People with Disabilities* (2008) to provide equitable and supported education to students with disabilities. Dr Sev Ozdowski, the Disability Discrimination Commissioner of the Australian Human Rights Commission (-2000–2005) affirms that equitable access to communication is a fundamental human right, ratified by the *Universal Declaration of Human Rights* (1948) and other legally binding treaties such as the *International Covenant on Civil and Political Rights* (1966), all formally confirmed by Australia. He states:

> These are rights which the Australian government has agreed to respect and ensure for all people within Australia. That means all people, not just people who do not have a disability affecting communication … Equitable access to communication is essential if deafblind people are to have any prospect of equality of opportunity and access in education, employment, access to citizenship rights including voting, access to services such as health care or transport; and other areas of social and economic participation … It is one thing to declare human rights in theory. It is another to achieve them in practice … *The Disability Discrimination Act* [Commonwealth, 1992] … is one tool for working towards equality for people with disabilities. It makes discrimination unlawful in employment; education; provision of goods and services among other areas.
> (Ozdowski 2002)

This chapter operates on a social relational understanding of disability; that is, that we are disabled by our bodies and society (Shakespeare 2014). Unfortunately, ableism in academia creates barriers and difficulties in learning spaces for students with disabilities (Dolmage 2017). Furthermore, students with disability do not benefit from policies that prescribe for them as a homogenous group. Nor do students flourish when there are gaps between policies and practice that impact adversely on the provision of supports to students (Mutanga 2017).

The enormous heterogeneity of disability means that a co-creation approach to individuals with diverse learning and support needs is vital to the success of pathfinder students. Students with disabilities themselves possess vast and detailed knowledge of their conditions and needs; they are *expert-knowers* (Barnes & Mercer 1997). Social relational methodology accepts that no model suffices to explicate every disability experience in every person in every culture so, while my focus is on personal experience, this chapter is designed to be read and used as needed by deafblind students and other readers. My experience is that of an Australian postgraduate student with deafblindness in the late teens of this century.

Many terms are used to describe people with dual sensory impairment, but for the purposes of this chapter, I have chosen to use deafblindness to encompass both deafblindness and dual sensory impairment/losses to discuss all students with combined impairments of vision and hearing. At times, I have also used these terms interchangeably; so, this chapter will provide an overview of the term deafblindness using the 2016 Nordic definition as a lynchpin. While this first part of the chapter provides information on deafblindness globally and within an Australian context, it also briefly mentions Usher syndrome and discusses the presence of residual vision and/or hearing among deafblind individuals.

I then outline my subject position as a deafblind PhD student to indicate how my unique requirements, background and education shape my research question, methodologies and practices. I also provide critical information and gaps in relation to studying as a deafblind researcher. This profile includes documenting personal and research data on the steps to learning, knowledge and research production. There are ten steps detailed in Figure 1.1, which are then elaborated on, including: (1) Preparation limbo, (2) Safe conduct, (3) Access and communication, (4) Digital spaces, (5) Pedagogy and supervisors, (6) Unsafe spaces, (7) Knowledge building about disability, (8) Methodological anxieties and tensions, (9) Vicissitudes of life, and (10) Time—this last step is a significant obstacle in my work. The section of Access and Communication includes a table (Table 1.1) that outlines specific Access and Communication Problems/Barriers and their solutions. The section on time includes a table (Table 1.2) that compares the time I take to complete "writing a journal article activities" against the time estimated for a majority of researchers. The intention of sharing this detailed account of my experiences at one institution is to provide a resource that I hope will prove useful to others.

Deafblindness: an overview

Deafblindness research is a nascent field. There are data gaps, invisible subpopulations, and diverse definitions and terminologies to contend with (Wittich et al. 2013; Dammeyer 2014; Larsen and Damen 2014; Simcock 2017; Jaiswal et al.

2018). For the purposes of this work, the Nordic definition and a summary of explanatory comments will be the underpinning definition:

> Deafblindness is a distinct disability. Deafblindness is a combined vision and hearing disability. It limits activities of a person and restricts full participation in society to such a degree that society is required to facilitate specific services, environmental alterations and/or technology.[1]
>
> (Nordic Centre for Welfare and Social Issues 2016)

This 2016 Nordic definition addresses many of the intricacies of life with dual sensory impairments. In brief, the key complexities, drawn from the explanatory comments, are as follows:

1. Distinct and complex disability
2. Hard for each sense to compensate for the other
3. Time-consuming
4. Energy draining
5. Information is received in fragments.
6. Activities are limited.
7. Participation is reduced.
8. Communication, access to information and mobility are affected.
9. Tactile sense is critical as a conduit of information.
10. Communication technology, assistive devices, interpreters and adaptions to the environment may be required.
11. Despite the above, human assistance and support is necessary to provide access to information, mobility and safety.
12. Society is responsible for support and barrier removal.

Research is difficult in this population because of (a) rarity/low prevalence, (b) geographical spread, (c) heterogeneity of the population and (d) vast permutation of communication methods (Luckner, Bruce & Ferrell 2016).

The *World Federation of the Deafblind (WFDB) Report* is a collaboration that seeks to gather data and estimate the global prevalence of deafblindness. Covering 97 million people across 22 nations (a mix of high-, middle- and low-income countries), it was completed in 2018. Significant findings from the report include

- Of the world's population, 0.2–2% live with deafblindness (where deafblindness is used as an umbrella term for all dual sensory impairment) (p. 10).
- The majority of people with deafblindness are over 65 years, so the number of persons with deafblindness increases with age (p. 16).
- Deafblindness often coexists with other disabilities: "Between 20% and 75% of persons with deafblindness" have additional disabilities (p. 33).

Australian data is difficult to ascertain. In 2013, it was estimated that 100,000 Australians lived with deafblindness/dual sensory impairment. Of these, 13,700 were under the age of 60 living with significant disability from the combination of vision and hearing loss (Dyke 2013, p. 1). Deafblindness occurring before the age of 65 is uncommon (Schneider, Gopinath & McMahon 2012; Dammeyer 2014). Usher syndrome accounts for half of all these cases (Wittich et al. 2012) with an incidence of 4–10 per 100,000.

Usher syndrome is both congenital and acquired. In brief, Usher syndrome is an autosomal recessive inherited condition that can impact three major senses in the body: vision (progressive vision loss over time), hearing (loss varying in severity, usually present at birth and may decline), and balance (present in some subtypes of Usher syndrome, but not a universal feature). Sixteen loci have been identified that are either causative or modifier genes (Mathur & Yang 2015). This is what I have.

Few with deafblindness have no sight and no hearing at all; most have limited residual vision and/or residual hearing. Measures to maximise and support these residuals are usually needed for university and research success. The deafblind are, therefore, a small population with high communication, access and mobility support needs.

The research: identifying critical information and gaps

As stated in the introduction, there is a dearth of scholarly work on deafblindness generally (Dammeyer 2014; Larsen & Damen 2014) and on both university and postgraduate experiences specifically (Arndt 2010; Chanock, Stevens & Freeman 2010, 2011; Wolsey 2017).

In the absence of data on deafblind PhD students, I located five papers related to undergraduate student experiences (Arndt 2011; Chanock 2010; Chanock, Stevens & Freeman 2010, 2011; Wolsey 2017). These papers found that strong academic and learning support led to success, while Arndt (2011) and Wolsey (2017) acknowledged the widespread exclusion experienced by many of the students interviewed. A number of the authors advocate the benefits of transition planning and preparation in the months prior to attending college or university.

An exhaustive search has not revealed Australian data on the percentage of Australians with deafblindness at universities. American data relate that only 3.5% of people with deafblindness attend university (Chanock 2010, p. 5). In 1995, Everson and Enos from the Helen Keller National Center in the United States of America (USA) wrote of the few students with deafblindness/dual sensory impairments in universities: "their exclusion appears to have less to do with type or severity of disability than with programmatic and personal barriers in educational programs" (Everson & Enos 1995, p. 2). Given the paucity of literature on deafblindness in particular, and the comprehensive listing of disability literature in Karen Mogendorff's chapter, "A closer look at 'wheelchair' anthropology/sociology" in this volume, this essay reviews literature within the context of my experience.

My position

I am a second-year PhD student with deafblindness and Usher syndrome. At this time, I have profound deafness (>90-decibel loss in both ears) and one degree of central vision in the left eye. There is no usable vision in the right eye, owing to an unrelated (very unlucky) retinal hole and failed surgery. Consequently, I have a wide-ranging, high-impact communication, access and mobility disability that poses significant challenges to the university and myself during my candidature. And it continues to worsen. Despite being born with severe hearing loss and the onset of vision loss at the age of 15, I completed medical school in Sydney, Australia. At this university, I made herculean efforts to normalise. No supports were offered or available (this was in the 1980s) but, surprisingly, my peers were incredibly helpful, sharing notes and assisting with practical tasks. This was difficult labour because I had to make my own support network, support myself financially and work to make up for what I was missing in lectures with additional reading. But graduate I did.

My career has been one of adjustments, and I undertook a Masters in Psychological Medicine so as to move into mental health. I undertook this at a different university, which was accommodating with notes, extra time and clinical placements close to home. These accommodations arose not because of the disability, but because I had a new-born baby and a toddler. As progressivity supervened, I eventually gave up practising but not before becoming concerned at how a number of my patients with single and dual sensory loss were treated in hospital. One had measurable adversity as a result of communication failure and several had anxiety or early post-traumatic stress disorder (PTSD) as a consequence of events during hospitalisation. And so, I began to think, not only "this could me" but what can we do, collectively, and individually, to bolster our defences against communication and care failures in hospital.

I met with representatives from the Department of Health, New South Wales, Australia, who said, "we are unaware that this is a problem, you will need to prove it". This proof-getting entails undertaking a PhD (Can it even be done? I'm thinking as I struggle to get a proposal together, fill in the requisite online forms and get the necessary proofs of disablement). I am the first student with deafblindness at UTS.

I seek to challenge stereotypes: my disability does not equal no ability—I need support to succeed. I offer this account to the scant canon of deafblind literature to show I don't desire simply to participate and be included, I want success. This brings me to the necessity of countering the notion born of the social model of disability, that removing all barriers levels the playing fields and confers an equal advantage. There are "insurmountable realities" (Vehmas & Watson 2014, p. 642) with my circumstances and impairment. Communication for me will always take longer (as well as all other activities of daily living). This is well documented in the literature (see Moller 2003). The university space will, for some time yet, be an occasionally hostile space for people with disabilities with obstacles at seemingly every turn, yet whilst acknowledging this, I want to be solution-focused, salutogenic and successful.

My obstacles

I take the metaphor of *the steep steps to the ivory tower*, which underpins Dolmage's (2017) book *Academic Ableism*, illustrating them below (Figure 1.1) to show the specific obstacles I face in terms of individual stairs: With my aggregation of difficulties, the element of temporality is by far the most vexing hurdle to completing studies, research processes and the actual writing of a dissertation. By reflecting and writing on the obstacles and strategies in a step-wise fashion, I hope to provide a resource detailing what I need and what I found helpful, so that others can

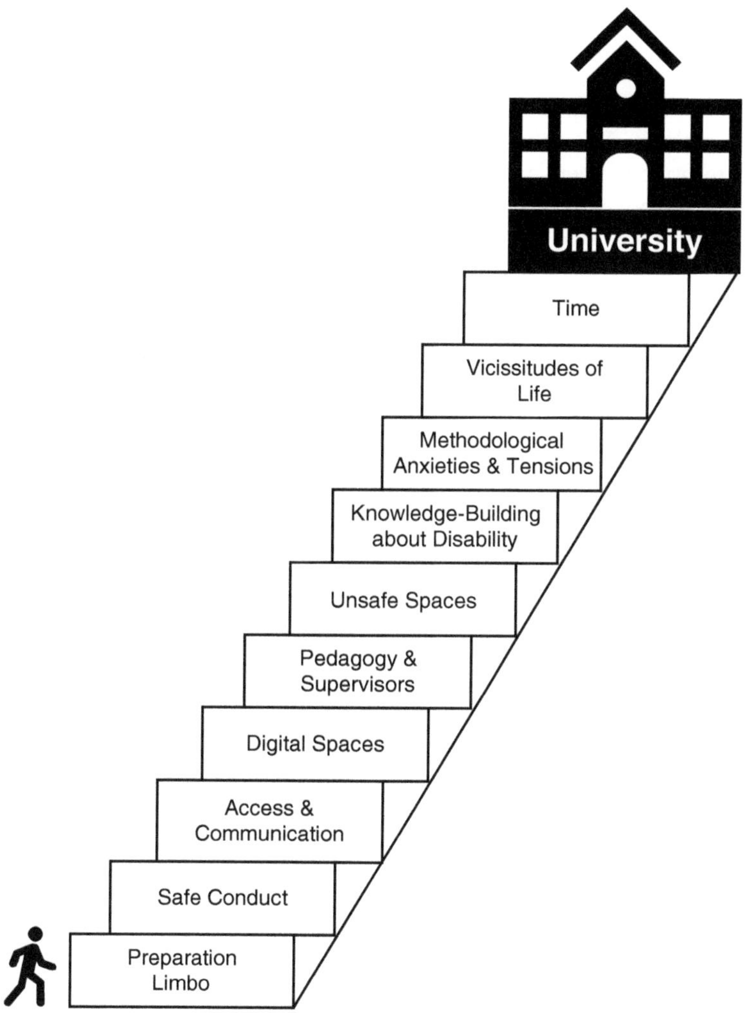

Figure 1.1 Steep steps to learning and knowledge production.

refine and expand, amend and adjust—retaining what works for them, with their specific constellation of needs. In short, these are descriptive examples, taken from personal experience, and are not a prescriptive listing. Through these examples, I will demonstrate that complex communication disabilities do not prevent students from being safe and successful in their studies and research. Notwithstanding this salutogenic approach, I will also demonstrate that both society and universities can do better.

To elaborate on each *step*:

Preparation limbo

Transition planning is offered in the USA as a compulsory component to Information Education Plans (IEP) (Center for Disabilities, Sanford School of Medicine n.d.). I was unable to meet with either the Accessibility team or my supervisors prior to commencement. As a result of a catch-22, I had an initial meeting with an Accessibility Consultant but, not being an enrolled student, I was not informed of her departure from UTS. Nor could she (or anyone in her position) book services or meetings for me until my enrolment. Enrolment itself was limited to a short period before actually starting. Thus, there is a limbo during the planning period. This means many services and meetings occur after enrolment, eroding what should be research preparation time. Universities need to acknowledge this anomaly and adjust their approach to include supported planning.

I suggest prospective disabled student researchers start planning six months before their start dates to map out accessibility needs and funding, and to examine potential pitfalls. Expect delays; expect to encounter some kind but essentially unhelpful staff. Expect to have to justify needs: large and small. Expect to expend significant time on red tape: procedures, filling in non-accessible forms, meetings and the like, none of which concerns your research but involves your access. Without access, there is no research.

Safe conduct

Physical environmental barriers exist aplenty at tertiary institutions for students with any disability (Dolmage 2017). An important early consideration is ensuring a safe space in which to undertake learning and research. The university provides me with a small office contained within the Higher Degree Research student area. This means I am safe, and people know where I can be found (even firewardens in emergencies and drills). In addition, my assistive equipment and human Accessibility Assistants (AAs) have a secure home base. There are locked cabinets and a lockable door, for the expensive assistive devices I use to maximise residual hearing and vision.

Sighted guiding is imperative for my safe conduct, as for many deafblind people, throughout the campus (I detail this in Table 1.1 below). The AAs and I have all learned social haptic touch signals. These were systematically designed and depicted by Lahtinen and Palmer, and are not a language but a way of describing environments by drawing or touching parts of the body, such as the upper arm or back (Lahtinen & Palmer, 2016). Haptic touch signals, therefore, are used by the AAs to alert me to stairs, obstacles, emergencies and instances are more fully described in Table 1.1's section of navigating the physical environment, below. The learning curve about the importance of the physical environment has been experienced not only by myself and my AAs, but also my supervisors, who have become aware of the need to choose accessible meeting locations with easy ingress, good lighting (not too bright and not too dim) and low ambient/background noise levels.

Access and communication

Accommodation is thought of as something that always needs to be created, something that has a cost. This underlines the inherent inaccessibility of nearly all of society: seemingly nothing is ever designed to be accessible in the first place (Dolmage 2017, p. 53).

Ozdowski positions communication support and accessibility to information as central to the flourishing of the deafblind individual and communities, stating in his 2002 keynote address at the 6th National Deafblind Conference:

> Communication is central to our identity as human beings—for all of us as individuals, and as members of communities. … Almost every day there seems to be some new development in information and communications technology. … One exciting aspect of this is that digital technologies have opened up new possibilities for access to information and communication for people with disabilities … technology is not and cannot be the answer to all communication requirements. … Some deafblind people will still need intensive, one on one human assistance to achieve effective communication, whatever developments in technology there are. … But there is a clear message, from experts, advocates and the deafblind community, that deafblind people can communicate effectively—if they have access to appropriate assistance and supports. … It is also clear that many people are not getting this assistance and support sufficiently or even at all …

Accessibility is entwined with this PhD and research process, because without it, progress, participation, inclusion, understanding and research outcomes cannot be achieved. There is no success without access. Communication support for people with deafblindness is imperative. But who is the specialist on individual student needs? Students must be treated as experts when choosing accommodations. They know the most about what works for them and, as Chanock, Stevens and Freeman write, succeeding as a deafblind will be a team sport.

> For people who are Deaf-blind to undertake university study requires the involvement of a wide range of people, including (in addition to their subject

> lecturers) technicians who provide texts in an accessible form, sign language interpreters, librarians, and, if possible, academic skills advisers to help with composing and editing.
>
> (Chanock, Stevens & Freeman 2011, p. 1)

Enablers of positive higher education experiences for deafblind students from five studies include:

- Support from family and friends
- Engaged academic and/or non-academic staff
- Quality, appropriate disability support staff (Arndt 2010; Chanock, Stevens & Freeman 2010, 2011; Wolsey 2017; Chanock 2010).
- The literature acknowledges that adding the accessibility support for a deaf student to the support for a blind person does not aggregate to covering the needs of the deafblind (Spiers & Hammett 1995). Despite the absence of a validated measure or tool, it is often described that dual sensory impairment is not merely the consequence of adding one impairment to another; as Dammeyer notes: "1 + 1 = 3 …. it is a condition more disabling than the sum of its parts" (2014, p. 555).

Therefore, support consists of maximising any residual sight and hearing; using assistive technology and interpreters; and providing human accessibility assistance to bridge gaps, act as eyes and ears, ensure personal safety, and promote inclusion. Each research student with sensory impairments is an individual with diverse needs. The approach to providing services and support, therefore, cannot be homogenous, because there is no one-size-fits-all suite of solutions. As I maintain above, the student is an expert in their own condition and disability (Spiers & Hammett 1995, p. 2; Arndt 2010) and should be an integral part of co-producing support plans and systems; universities need to ask *what is needed for this student to be successful at this time in this place?*

Like many people with deafblindness, I depend on human assistance to make the world safe and understandable. Without this, I am unable to attempt most of the PhD and research tasks. My university ensures 35 hours a week of human accessibility assistance to bridge the gap between software and assistive devices, and the research work I attempt. The advocacy of my supervisors in the early months for the hours I needed meant that I could progress from being able to achieve little to beginning the literature review. The Accessibility Unit, my first assistant Sophie Hopkins and I co-created a new position, as noted above in the "Safe Conduct" section: the AAs. "AAs work closely with people with disability to identify barriers and develop creative solutions in order to improve access for the person with disability" (Hopkins 2018, personal communication, 2nd August). See Table 1.1 for examples of specific access barriers and solutions developed by Accessibility staff, the AAs and me—UTS is investing in my success.

Table 1.1 Specific access barriers and solutions developed by accessibility staff, the AAs and me

Communication/ access area	*Problem/barrier*	*Solution*
Lecture/ seminar/ tutorial	Unable to follow what is being said and taught.	Siemens MiniTek Bluetooth FM System: Speaker wears a microphone that transmits sound to hearing aids. GoogleDocs: Accessibility Assistant (AA) transcribes on digital document, which student has access to on their own device. Social haptics: Give student cues using social haptics to signal time to speak, contribute, work independently and so on.
Literature	Databases not accessible, resulting in barriers to searching for and finding literature. Literature not accessible (font too small).	Human assistance: Conduct database searches with AA. Student will tell AA what they want to be included and excluded from the search. AA will read out search results. The student will tell AA if they require the source. Document conversion: Literature, which is usually obtained as a PDF will be sent to the university's library conversion service. Alternatively, AAs will use Adobe Acrobat DC's "Export PDF" tool to convert PDF to Microsoft Word document. The font of the text will then be increased to Arial 32.
Navigating the physical environment		Social haptics/sighted guiding: Student holds AA's arm above the elbow. AA walks with a straight arm. When navigating a narrow space, the AA will put their guiding arm behind their back, student will move to behind the AA; alternatively, the AA will clamp their guiding arm to their body and shuffle through the space, student will follow AA's direction and take smaller steps. When there is a change in terrain, the AA will tap their guiding arm against their body two times—indicating to the student there is a step or slope. When the AA takes a step up or down, the student will feel the movement and understand the terrain. When the terrain returns to normal—for example, the stairs are finished and the ground is flat—the AA will again tap their guiding arm against their body two times. The AA may tap the back of the student's hand and guide to an object they need—for example, a handrail, a pen, their phone or computer—or to show the student what is around them—what is on their desk.

(*Continued*)

Communication/ access area	*Problem/barrier*	*Solution*
Phone calls	Cannot hear person at the other end of the phone.	Voice interpreting: AA will notify person on the phone of student's deafblindness/dual sensory impairment and that they will be repeating what is said to student. AA will repeat what is said by person on phone by facing student and ensuring pronunciation. Student will respond through speech.
Email	Font of email is too small.	Zoom in on the screen of phone, tablet or laptop to increase font size. Human assistance: AA may dictate the email to student. Student will dictate to AA and AA will type up email. The email is read back to the student before it is sent.
University's online learning platform	Size of font is not big enough for the student to read. Difficult to navigate with use of zoom text software. In addition, the platform does not utilise contrast.	Zoom in on the screen of the phone, tablet or laptop to increase font size. Human assistance: AA may dictate the information that is on the online platform to the student. Student will then advise what they want to access. Student will ask AA to find a document or information available on the online learning platform. The AA will then convert this to an accessible format.
Writing	Difficulty using Microsoft Word and finding cursor on screen.	Student will write on paper with a thick black pen (Pentel Sign Pen, Black); this is then typed up on Microsoft Word in Arial 32 by AAs. Typed documents will then be printed for the student to make changes. These changes will be made by AAs on a new version of the document, which will be printed for the student to make further changes.
Editing	Unable to see punctuation marks, or spelling and grammatical errors. Unable to visualise structure and progression of writing.	Professional editor: pieces of written material are sent to a professional editor for editing and re-editing. Punctuation, spelling and grammar mistakes are amended. Significant word changes and comments are made in text in capital letters. In addition, the editor writes out a list of the changes that have been made. The editor ensures writing is appropriately formatted. The editor also attends to student's concerns regarding the shape and structure of the work, and assists in redrafting the writing, following the student's directions.

Communication/ access area	*Problem/barrier*	*Solution*
Field trips and interviews	Difficulty navigating physical environment, and planning and organising resources. Unable to hear interviewee.	Social haptics/sighted guiding: AAs use social haptics and sighted guiding to help the student navigate the environment (see above, "Navigating the physical environment"). Development of system of research social haptic touch signals, for example, pinching movement on upper arm to signify interviewee is talking. Social haptics may also need to be used to notify the student of the time, when the interviewee is talking or signing and so on. Human assistance: The student will advise AAs what they require to conduct the interview. AAs will be required to book a quiet room for the interview. AAs may also be required to organise appropriate interpreters for the interviewee because participants in this student's research project are deafblind or have a dual sensory impairment. Voice interpreting: AAs interpret and communicate what the interviewee has said—either themselves or through the interpreter—to the research student/interviewer. The AA will situate the student with the light behind them (to improve the student's vision), they will face the student and repeat what has been said.
Social engagement with peers	Difficulty recognising peers faces or voices. Often unable to hear what peers are saying.	Human assistance: AA notifies the research student when someone comes up to speak to them. If the AA knows the name of the peer speaking to the research student, they will notify the research student verbally. Alternatively, the AA will ask the peer's name and how they know the student, before notifying the student. Voice interpreting: As detailed in the section above.
Ethics application	Ethics application is online and is not accessible to the visually impaired. In addition, the form's questions are dependent on the answers supplied throughout the form.	Human assistance: An Ethics Officer from the student's university read the questions to the student and the student dictated their answers. Answers were repeated by the Ethics Officer and approved by the student before submitting.

(*Continued*)

Communication/ access area	*Problem/barrier*	*Solution*
Coding	Excel and NVivo are not accessible for the student.	Human assistance: Research student's co-supervisor has agreed to assist.
Other	Student's vision deteriorating (natural progression of degenerative disorder).	All AAs and the student are learning tactile sign language.

Digital spaces

It is impossible for research students to avoid interaction with online learning platforms and search engines. Yet, there is little research on how inclusive these are for students with sensory impairments. There have been many anecdotal reports to impairment support organisations, stating that online access barriers have prevented blind and vision-impaired students from completing their studies (Vision Australia 2018). Information exclusion is, therefore, an issue for research students with sensory impairments. Few tertiary platforms come with accessibility features. Restrepo and Garcia, in their article on fighting "info-exclusion", state that the following must be offered in order to be "Triple A Level" accessible for all:

- Captions
- Audio description
- Transcription
- Sign language

(Restrepo & Garcia 2016, p. 121)

As often happens, what is accessible for one, info-excludes another (Restrepo & Garcia 2016, p. 120). Subtitles for the deaf and hearing-impaired "may be annoying to those that can see them, but do not need them" (Restrepo & Garcia 2016, pp. 120–21).

Transcripts are often helpful, but are rarely provided by platform or multimedia designers; they can be requested from university access services, but take many weeks to deliver and prove expensive. Another example of what is accessible for one (widespread use of blue-coloured text) is not accessible for another (I can't see the blue text used by the university learning platform UTSOnline/Blackboard). I also struggle to understand the voices of virtual assistants on JAWS and ZoomText. This last problem is solved by using AAs with clear voices and occasional haptics and tactile sign language to read digital communications, so providing a mechanism every page or so for feedback to check that I have understood the content. I have a journal club of volunteers who read articles to me, slowly and clearly, while I make notes of relevant material. These are then typed in 32 Arial Font for review. AAs provide voice interpreting and audio description of multimedia content, which allows me access to the information contained therein.

Pedagogy and supervisors

There is scant material in the literature providing information and practical strategies for academic teaching staff and supervisors when dealing with deafblind students and researchers. While there are some accounts by academics of learning support that they provided for a single undergraduate (Chanock 2010; Chanock, Stevens & Freeman 2010, 2011), I could find none that specifically provide guidance to supervisors of deafblind student researchers. In addition, postgraduates are often expected to teach or be offered tutoring/lecturing opportunities. I find that the AAs are invaluable in enabling me to be visible and valued in student learning at all levels. I have guest-lectured at my own and other universities.

Lived experience reports, primarily of undergraduates, give voice to the lack of embedded disability support and practices in academia (Arndt 2010; Stoffel 2012; Wolsey 2017). Stoffel's contributors in *Deafblind Reality* have poor experiences with non-compliant lecturers and positive, enriching ones with engaged teaching staff. One study cited in Mutanga (2017) showed an example of an institution that has a top-down climate of inclusion and commitment to deaf students and education, which results *in high rates of academic success.*

UTS, where I am enrolled, has a committed disability inclusion culture. My experiences of lecturers, however, has proven inconsistent, demonstrating that individual academic ableism is present and incorrect. I have experienced disempowering and time-consuming situations, necessitating meetings to engage the university hierarchy in supporting behavioural change. Luckily, I find most academics encountered (like my supervisors) are supportive, innovative and creative, resulting in positive experiences of inclusion and success. Most academics I encounter consider creating safe learning and sharing spaces for their students as an integral part of the job. In their rooms, I am learning. I am productive.

We, therefore, lack accounts in the literature about what staff are learning from students with deafblindness (Chanock, Stevens & Freeman 2011, p. 1). While I write this chapter, focusing on my convoluted journey up the treacherous steps to produce new knowledge via research, my supervisors write and talk about their experiences with me at this institution, and more broadly, in blogs and at conferences.

Unsafe spaces: burdens and microaggressions

Universities can be unsafe spaces, emotionally. They can be hostile places for people with disabilities generally (Goode 2007; Mutanga 2017), and for those with deafblindness specifically (Arndt 2010; Wolsey 2017). Goode discusses the notion of ***extra visibility*** when students have to actively campaign to have their needs met. This can be very stressful. Conversely, when needs are unmet, the student becomes invisible (Goode 2007, pp. 42–43).

Invisibility can be isolating. This was true on many occasions; for instance, when group discussions used whiteboards, technology failed, assistants were sick or unavailable, or academics declined to provide materials in an accessible format. Microaggressions abound and make tertiary institutions unpleasant environments. There aren't enough words in this chapter (and book) to document the insidious, sometimes daily, small accretive acts of aggression or discrimination a person with disabilities can face from other students. Some days, a deafblind student researcher decides which battles are worth fighting and which are not.

Goode (2007, pp. 43–44) discusses the emotional labour of being at university with disability/ies. This work is twofold:

- The work of managing your own disability and the course study loads, university life and everyday activities.
- The work of educating others as to the disability, its effects, technology use and accommodations needed.

I would add a third category; that of emotionally enduring recurrent microaggressions. Goode also elaborates:

> "Battling the system" was a very common phrase and several interviewees had come close to dropping out. In other cases, students had become "battle-hardened" and were more able to "demand" the rights to which they knew they were entitled.
>
> (Goode 2007, p. 44)

Goode (2007) describes how some students take "an 'activist' role, wanting to contribute to improved access for all students with disabilities, as well as being aware of their own rights" (Goode 2007, p. 41). For students with severe dual sensory impairment, however, being able to be an activist and advocate can only happen with support. This chapter is also a forum for this advocacy. I contend that universities must do more to render their learning spaces not only safer but inclusive. We need to be heard; for top-down embedding of disability support and inclusion, funding needs to be available for the support that is needed for each student. Inclusion should be the normal culture of the campus.

Self-care becomes a critical part of surviving the stressors of aggressions, assumptions and discrimination. Having a sensory impairment is, in itself, a major life stressor. Being a student researcher, able-bodied or not, is a major stressor. I recommend having a really good psychologist on your "team" because the going is tough. The tertiary sector is full of ableist academics and thoughtless others. In addition, if you are a student with disabilities researching your own marginalised community, support proves critical, in my professional- and life-experienced opinion. Life's possibilities and pleasures can be hard to see if you are mired in the difficulties of your comrades all the time.

Another protective factor in managing hostile environments is to make friends and engage supporters. Students with sensory impairments, however, will often need support engaging with fellow doctoral researchers, students and staff. This is yet another function performed by AAs, who take me to lunches with fellow students and brew tea for anyone who drops in for a chat. In this way, I have made friends, who now know how to better communicate with me. We offer each other support such as reading each other's work (my AAs converting draft papers for me to comment on). Mutuality of benefits is important (Shakespeare 2015). Such participation in student life has only been possible with the university funding a full-time complement of AAs.

Knowledge-building about disability

Poor academic support, non-compliant staff and the load of managing the disability are disablers to success (Goode 2007; Arndt 2010; Stoffel 2012; Wolsey 2017). Doctoral studies concern knowledge-building for specific questions within disciplines. Conversely, students with disability are also often heavily engaged in building knowledge and raising awareness in tertiary education communities (Arndt 2010, p. 1). This can result in significant emotional labour and fatigue to doctoral study loads. Deafblind people are sometimes vulnerable, Miles notes, because they lack visual and audio clues, so "persons who are deaf-blind must depend upon the good will and sensitivity of those around them to make their world safe and understandable" (2008, p. 2). Students can, therefore, be made vulnerable by the failure of institutions, academics and administration staff to provide and participate in ongoing professional development in all manner of disability-related issues. Simply put, in these terms, institutions, academics and administration staff often fail. Lack of knowledge begets lack of inclusion, especially with regard to academic teaching staff (Mutanga 2017). One student in Everson and Enos's study describes how becoming an educator to the educators was a necessary imperative to inclusion in learning:

> I found that many of the times teachers were unable to strategize with me the best way to receive and understand the course work. I felt a "we tried, but we failed" attitude. I had to come up with the lesson plans to teach me. This experience taught me that I had to be an educator too.
>
> (Everson & Enos 1995, p. 6)

My experiences mirror these. The reality is that deafblindness in student populations is rare and few of the staff will have experience or exposure to deafblind students. Universities must share in this knowledge-building to decrease the student burden. Many impairment support organisations are happy to arrange educational sessions for educators.

Methodological anxieties and tensions

There was no literature found to provide guidance on how a deafblind student might conduct qualitative interviews with deafblind participants. Consumer researchers with disabilities bring unique consumer perspectives to the research table, as well as acting as a bridge between researcher and participant. This helps to level the traditional unequal power balance between the two.

One of my pervading anxieties was the methodology. I had consulted widely among deafblind communities and impairment support organisations, and determined ethnographic interviews to be the best approach. A hard reality of being deafblind is the dependence on others for nearly all tasks. For a deafblind researcher, this means bringing to the research space a number of "others". In my case, this can mean any permutation of AA/s, voice interpreter, sighted guide and live transcriber, depending on the requirements of the situation. Initially, I felt unequal to the task of bringing an entourage to an interview with a participant and their own interpreters (for we would need two interpreters, to allow for mandated rest breaks every 15 minutes, as well as space for support workers, partners and service animals). Such a crowd, I imagined, could diminish my capacity as a researcher and person with deafblindness. More importantly, I was concerned that this plethora of people would change the narrative space, both in a physical sense as well as altering the testimonial process.

I preceded the interviews with a period of time becoming immersed in one of the impairment-support groups. This has resulted in:

- Better understanding the culturally and linguistically diverse subpopulation
- Confirming that poor hospital and healthcare experiences (my research area) were a central community concern
- Framing the research in a positive way with a solutions-focused question at the end
- Creating plain English information and consent forms because English is not the first language of many with deafblindness
- Removing Likert scales and question types that require unpacking to create a true user-friendly collaboration
- Spending time discussing research aims and questions with interpreters chosen by the participants (This delayed several interviews because there is an interpreter shortage in Australia.)
- Allowing participants to choose the space where they would like the interview to take place. This was empowering yet practical—people with deafblindness need to be safe, oriented and comfortable. No interview was conducted in a place unknown to the particular participant. Locations ranged from homes, community hubs, impairment-support organisation rooms, workplaces and virtual spaces.
- Offering to conduct interviews in whatever communication mode is preferred: a ***power to the people*** approach advocated by Alana Roy, a fellow researcher

> in deafblind studies, who created a set of better practice guidelines (2018, personal communication). This resulted in a variety of languages and technological systems being engaged, including email, National Relay Service (internet relay service with an operator as a conversation conduit) and face-to-face interaction with mixed communication: tactile, Auslan (Australian sign language), hand-over-hand, visual frame, finger spelling, spoken English and one idiosyncratic language (mix of finger spelling and individual tactile signs).

Face-to-face with everyone's entourage was the most popular mode of engagement. This (surprisingly and against my above-stated reservations) worked well. People with deafblindness are used to their social spaces being full of service animals, sighted guides, support workers, communication guides, interpreters and friends.

From a performative perspective, it became obvious early on that we needed some social haptic touch signals for the interviews. Signals for "not your turn" and "your turn now" are necessary to decrease interruptions to the flow of interpreting. Without good sight and hearing, a researcher does not follow the social cues that people are, for instance, laughing at jokes, nodding or signing an agreement, or that there is a sense that all is proceeding well. We now have a haptic for "going well"—two taps in the mid-upper arm.

Reciprocity occurs, too, some participants tell me about adaptations they have made to assistive devices, such as talking or vibrating GPS devices onto their white mobility cane. I get asked questions about my experiences as a person with deafblindness. There are experiences in common, such as being thought of as drunk, as well as discussions on how to cope with ageing. Being a consumer (student) researcher is a constant learning curve: while being in the same "tribe" confers a closer empathy, including some shared understandings of living realities, there are limits on just how much shared experience we all have.

One of the lecturers at medical school used to talk about the benefits of common experiences of illness with patients. He cautioned, however, that "if you shared all the experiences of all the patients, you will be dead pretty quickly". Despite sharing some aspects of sensory loss, I keep my eye on heterogeneity: there are numerous differences both within the communities of deafblind and between people with dual sensory impairment. Do women with sensory losses have a different experience from men? Does ageing with deafblindness bring more complexities? Does being Indigenous impact experiences? The answers are all yes, so far. I am in the midst of research, not at the end, and still learning. I have been embraced by the participants who have trust and confidence that I will take their stories, treat them well and use them to inform health policy and practice. The level of concern in the deafblind communities about my research area is high. They want changes, and working together with me, they will be agents of those changes.

A longer time is taken for arranging and coordinating these balletic exchanges and this has to be accounted for. In addition, the conversations, backfilling and debriefing needed for comprehension is fatiguing. For this reason, my supervisor mandates no more than one interview per day. A further burden that universities need to be aware of is economic. Anyone choosing to research and communicate with individuals with communication impairments will need more funds to pay for interpreters, transcription, research assistance and room hire, as well as more time. This last is so significant I made it the final step.

Vicissitudes of life

Understanding that students with disabilities do not exist as separate from ***the able*** is important. We are still subject to life's vicissitudes and impinged on by other diseases, accidents and events, in addition to the impairments we start with. Life events such as break-ups, viruses, home disasters, elderly parents, disobedient children, bereavements, financial stress and health scares may overtake any of us indiscriminately. Our universities need to acknowledge, accommodate and respect these layered complexities. Disability theorising often treats lives lived with a disability as a collective (social model) or singular (medical model) experience, rather than a motley of both collegiate (barriers and support needs) and disparate (different impairment effects and living realities) parts. Inclusion is therefore promoted by holistically gaining understandings of disabled student experiences and lives (Mutanga 2017).

Time

Time assumes elongated proportions when one is a student researcher and disabled. Goode notes:

> [Many students] faced huge obstacles in their first semester because of slowness of the bureaucratic process beyond the university and the length of time they had to wait for reasonable adjustments to be put in place. Waiting for the support they were entitled to, whether brailling, laptop, computer software, note takers or mobility related, had a huge impact on some students' ability to study effectively.
>
> (Goode 2007, p. 45)

Much of my first year was spent waiting for approvals, equipment, conversions, accessible materials, accessible formats of articles (and turnaround time for the fulfilment of these requests), assistive devices, repairs to device or hearing aids, and time also spent in hiring and training AAs, and repairs of replacement devices. More time lost. This meant increased stress as confirmation neared.

I find it is important to attempt to quantify time spent because otherwise there is much stating of "it takes longer" without any understanding of what this means. Those supporting and/or supervising student researchers also need to establish reasonable and achievable timeframes and deadlines. In an effort to delineate exactly what ***taking more time*** means, I timed a number of activities that were components of the "Twelve Weeks to Publication Course", which I undertook in 2018, based on Wendy Belcher's (2019) publication. See Table 1.2 below.

Table 1.2 Time taken for selected *Writing Your Journal Article in Twelve Weeks* activities

Activities (as specified by author Wendy Belcher)	*Estimated hours*	*Time actually taken*
Find and read a model article	90 minutes	3 hours
Draft an abstract	60 minutes	2 hours (plus more to edit)
Revise abstract according to Review	30 minutes	30 minutes (plus more to edit)
Read Chapter 3—"The Argument"	60 minutes	7 hours
Peer review each other's work	30 minutes	30 minutes (time limited as allocated by facilitator)
Draft a query letter	30 minutes	30 minutes (plus more to edit)
Read chapter	60 minutes	3 hours
Evaluate current citations	60 minutes	2 hours
Identify, find and read related literature	8 hours	36+ hours
Evaluate related literature	60+ minutes	2 hours
Week 5 activities (reading and writing)	2 hours	6 hours
Read Chapter 6	30 minutes	1 hour

Without accessibility assistance, no task was possible. Almost every task took two to seven times longer in this course. Moller (2003), in Sweden, found that people living with deafblindness lost time in almost every single activity they undertook. In addition to taking longer to read, write and participate in university life and learning, my supervisors and teachers must spend more time engaging with me. Moller concurs, writing that professionals often spend twice as long with the deafblind and book double appointment slots (Moller 2003). Universities need to accommodate those with sensory impairments with funding that will not only provide for support needs, but will also last the duration to successful completion.

Conclusion

This chapter authentically demonstrates key aspects of my disabled student researcher journey. Travelling within the doctoral research space with a significant disability is inextricably entwined with accessibility provisions and barrier removal. Without my AAs, nothing is possible. My marker of success is that I am still here on the map, despite the uneven terrain. UTS has co-created solutions and committed emphatically to funding these. My hope is that this chapter will one day be used by other student researchers with deafblindness; indeed, that this chapter provides a precedent to enable others' learning requirements as well as relating the story of what one expedition entailed. (And I wish you well on your voyage.)

Despite the teething troubles of the first months, once my university fully comprehended the needs I had, the support received has been commensurate. I have firm funding, well-trained AAs and technological assistance. There is also a mutuality of benefits for the AAs, who receive immersion in the world of a researcher-student with disabilities. They gain skills and awareness that they will take with them in their next endeavours. AAs travel with me to conferences, local, interstate and overseas. We are an interesting little microcosm, but we have the tenacity and many contacts within the deafblind-sphere: learning as we go and sharing these insights. Participating in this chapter is also about finding a sense of community because there is strength and mentorship in creating relationships with other researchers and other students with disability.

This is an account of how one can have a significant communication, access and mobility disability, and still succeed. It contains two key messages: (1) Removal of barriers and maximal support does not eliminate all consequences of my impairment; but (2) Good access can still equal success. As I stated above, the belief that removing all barriers would eliminate all disability is unrealistic (Shakespeare 2014), but providing accessibility, physical safe spaces, psychosocial wellbeing, pedagogical compliance, adequate funding and extra time fosters success for student researchers with disability. I offer this as an incomplete cartography, and also as a navigational aid for, at present, little exists to give a sense of the road ahead for disabled student researchers. As I state and restate, the research itself can only progress after access needs have been met. For some disabled student researchers, there may also be methodological conundrums and anxieties to address.

The progression of the PhD itself is too often subsumed by the access difficulties that run alongside it. Sometimes, I joke that I could finish a PhD on ***doing*** the PhD. One important consideration in all of this is the acceptance that there will be teething problems, bureaucratic delays, epic fails of technology and fatigue that delay progress. Time spent. Time lost. But not time wasted. Despite multiple difficulties and disadvantages, I am surrounded by people and technology essential to enabling activity and research. I have AAs, secure funding and deadlines I am able to meet; I have the support of my university, my faculty and my supervisors. I work in a collegial environment in which research for practical application, especially when that involves improving the experience of others, is valued. I can do this.

The overarching purpose of this chapter is to address some of the external access limitations. To shift to the architectural metaphor of the introduction, I hope to lay some foundation stonework for the next students who are constructing their own student research careers—I acknowledge that each ascent is individual. All the while, we must build knowledge about our research areas as well as about our disabilities. We must plan for accessibility assistance, support teaching and administration staff to build skills when working with deafblind students to ensure inclusion. Crucially, I want to express how capable we are and how successful we can be.

Acknowledgements

Being deafblind means a high level of dependence on the support of others to navigate an often-hostile world. Thank you to

- University of Technology, Sydney, Australia, for providing access for success
- Thank you to my "Team Annmaree" for engendering success with access
- Dr Sue Joseph, my principled principal supervisor
- Dr Sarah Wayland, and her advocacy from the very beginning
- Sophie Hopkins, Head Accessibility Assistant, who is responsible for Figure 1.1 and Table 1.1—their construction, deliverance and outcomes
- Accessibility Assistants:
  - Samantha Lejeune
  - Ly Ly Lim
  - Eloise McNally
  - Sharon Taylor
  - Ronnith Morris for corralling errant commas, positioning paragraphs and generally being the fabulous formatting fairy.
  - Hannah-Rose, Oliver and Edmund for getting Mum to Uni, properly equipped and with morale boosted.
  - Tony, the head coach and lifestyle guru for Team Annmaree.

Note

1 (The full version can be found in the appendix. https://kuurosokeat.fi/wp-content/uploads/2019/07/The-Nordic-definition-of-deafblindness.pdf)

References

Anti-Discrimination Act NSW (1977) (online) Available from: https://www.legislation.nsw.gov.au/view/html/inforce/current/act-1977-048

Arndt, K. (2011) "College Students Who Are Deaf-Blind", *National Consortium on Deaf-Blindness*, 7, 1–4.

Arndt, K. (2005) *"They Should Know they Have Usher Syndrome around Here": College Students Who Are Deafblind*, ProQuest Dissertations and Theses.

Australian Disability Services Act (1986) (online) Available from: https://www.legislation.gov.au/Details/C2018C00146

Barnes, C. and Mercer, G. (1997) "Breaking the Mould? An Introduction to Doing Disability Research", In: Barnes, C. and Mercer, G. (eds) *Doing Disability Research*. Leeds: The Disability Press, pp. 1–14.

Belcher, W.L. (2019) *Writing Your Journal Article in Twelve Weeks: A Guide to Academic Publishing Success* (2nd edn) Chicago: University of Chicago Press.

Center for Disabilities, Sanford School of Medicine (n.d.) *Transition Guide for Students Who Are Deaf-blind*. South Dakota: University of South Dakota (online) Available from: http://www.transitionplanningasia.org/sites/tpa.perkinsdev1.org/files/uploaded-files/transitionguide.pdf

Chanock, K. (2010) "'Enhancing Student Success': Meeting the Unique Needs of University Students with Deaf-blindness", *The Open Rehabilitation Journal*, 3, 9–15.

Chanock, K., Stevens, M. and Freeman, S. (2011) "A 'Visible' Woman: Learning with a Student Who Is Deaf-blind at University", *Review of Disability Studies*, 7(2), 48–58.

Chanock, K., Stevens, M. and Freeman, S. (2010) "Supporting a University Student Who Is Deaf-blind in Writing for the Disciplines", *Journal of Postsecondary Education and Disability*, 23(2), 155–8.

Clark, J.L. (2014) *Where I Stand: On the Signing Community and My Deafblind Experience*. Minneapolis: Handtype Press.

Dammeyer, J. (2014) "Deafblindness: A Review of the Literature", *Scandinavian Journal of Public Health*, 42(7), 554–562.

Dolmage, J.T. (2017) *Academic Ableism: Disability and Higher Education*. Michigan Press: University of Ann Arbor.

Dyke, P. (2013) *A Clear View: Identifying Australians Who Live with Deafblindness and Dual Sensory Loss*. Burswood: Senses Australia.

Everson, J. and Enos, J. (1995) "Postsecondary Education: Opportunities and Challenges for Students Who Are Deaf-blind", *HKNC-TAC News*, 8(1), 1–13.

Goode, J. (2007) "'Managing' Disability: Early Experiences of University Students with Disability", *Disability & Society*, 22(1), 35–48.

Jaiswal, A., Aldersley, H., Wittich, W., Mirza, M. and Finlayson, M. (2018) "Participation Experiences of People with Deafblindness or Dual Sensory Loss: A Scoping Review of Global Deafblind Literature", *PLoS ONE*, 13(9).

Lahtinen, R. and Palmer, R. (2016) "History of Social Haptic Communication" (online) Available from: https://www.deafblindinformation.org.au/wp-content/uploads/2016/01/history-of-social-haptic-communication.pdf

Larsen, F.A. and Damen, S. (2014) "Definitions of Deafblindness and Congenital Deafblindness", *Research in Developmental Disabilities*, 35(10), 2568–2576.

Luckner, J.L., Bruce, S.M. and Ferrell, K.A. (2016) "A Summary of the Communication and Literacy Evidence-Based Practices for Students Who Are Deaf or Hard of Hearing, Visually Impaired, and Deafblind", *Communication Disorders Quarterly*, 37(4), 225–241.

Mathur, P. and Yang, J. (2015) "Usher Syndrome: Hearing Loss, Retinal Degeneration and Associated Abnormalities", *Biochimica et Biophysica Acta*, 1852(3), 406–420.

Moller, C. (2003) "Deafblindness: Living with Sensory Deprivation", *The Lancet*, 362, 46–47.

Mutanga, O. (2017) "'Students with Disabilities': Experience in South African Higher Education—A Synthesis of Literature", *South African Journal of Higher Education*, 31(1), 135–154.

Nordic Centre for Welfare and Social Issues (2016) The Nordic Definition of Deafblindness" (online) Available from: https://kuurosokeat.fi/wp-content/uploads/2019/07/The-Nordic-definition-of-deafblindness.pdf

Ozdowski, S. (2002) *6th National Deafblind Conference* (online) Available from: https://www.humanrights.gov.au/news/speeches/6th-national-deafblind-conference

Restrepo, E.G.Y. and Garcia, F.G. (2016) "Noninstrusive Accessibility in Inclusive Higher Education", *Proceedings of the 7th International Conference on Software Development and Technologies for Enhancing Accessibility and Fighting Info-exclusion*, pp. 119–126.

Schneider, J., Gopinath, B. and McMahon, C. (2012) "Prevalence and 5-year Incidence of Dual Sensory Impairment in an Older Australian Population", *Annals of Epidemiology*, 22(4), 295–301.

Shakespeare, T. (2015) *Disability Research Today: International Perspectives*. Abingdon: Routledge.
Shakespeare, T. (2014) *Disability Rights and Wrongs Revisited* (2nd edn). Abingdon: Routledge.
Simcock, P. (2017) "Ageing with a Unique Impairment: A Systematically Conducted Review of Older Deafblind People's Experiences", *Ageing & Society*, 37(8), 1703–1742.
Spiers, E. and Hammett, R. (1995) *Students Who Are Deaf-blind on Campus*. Washington, DC: American Council on Education.
Stoffel, S. (2012) *Deaf-Blind Reality: Living the Life*. Washington, DC: Gallaudet University Press.
United Nations (2008) *Convention on the Rights of Persons with Disabilities* (online) Available from https://www.un.org/development/desa/disabilities/convention-on-the-rights-of-persons-with-disabilities.html
United Nations (1966) *International Covenant on Civil and Political Rights* (online) Available from https://www.ohchr.org/en/professionalinterest/pages/ccpr.aspx
United Nations (1948) *Universal Declaration of Human Rights* (online) Available from https://www.un.org/en/universal-declaration-human-rights/
Vehmas, S. and Watson, N. (2014) "Moral Wrongs, Disadvantages, and Disability: A Critique of Critical Disability Studies", *Disability & Society*, 29(4), 638–650.
Wittich, W., Southall, K., Sikora, L., Watanabe, D.H. and Gagne, J.P. (2013) "What's in a Name: Dual Sensory Impairment or Deafblindness?", *British Journal of Visual Impairment*, 31(3), 198–207.
Wolsey, J.A. (2017) "Perspectives and Experiences of Deaf Blind College Students", *The Qualitative Report*, 22(8), 2066–2089.

Chapter 2

'On the outside looking in?'

Reflections on being a disabled social and feminist geographer

Vera Chouinard

Introduction

For almost three decades now I have conducted research as a disabled social and feminist geographer. Some of that research has been autoethnographic—drawing on my lengthy struggles for fair accommodation and inclusion in an academic workplace (e.g. Chouinard, 2010). But most of my work has focused on the lives of other disabled people in Canada and, more recently, Guyana. In this chapter, I want to reflect on what it has been like to conduct and share research without enjoying the privileges of an able body and mind. And as is the case with privileges in general, they are often taken for granted until you no longer enjoy them.

The chapter begins with a discussion of the interconnections between privileges and the capacity to conduct and disseminate research. This is followed by autoethnographic reflections on some of the challenges I have encountered as a disabled researcher. These include the extra work, often invisible to one's peers, that has to be done in order to continue to make academic contributions and the need to craft research strategies that are sound but also accommodate one's needs as a non-able academic. The chapter concludes with reflections on some of the ways that not only academic workplaces but also disciplines themselves need to change in order to ensure that no one is left 'on the outside looking in'.

On power and privilege in the ableist academy

In the ableist academy, power and privilege derive from who is fortunate enough to have an able body and mind. Measures of academic 'success', usually quantitative, place a premium on who is able to get the most and largest grants, who produces the most articles and books, who receives the most awards, and so on. And these are, typically, the academics who are rewarded in terms of higher salary increments and other 'perks' such as reduced teaching loads.

Although we are not used to thinking about the academy as ableist (Mitchell, 2016; Dolmage, 2017), there are many taken for granted activities that require able bodies and/or minds. One such activity is doing research 'in the field'. This often requires the ability to travel, to have one's research funded, and always includes the ability to think in ways that make sense or seem 'rational' to others. Another related activity is attending and presenting one's work at conferences—here the ability to travel and participate in person at the conference sessions is important. So too is the ability to speak clearly and think and argue in ways that make sense to others. Although we have developed technologies that can provide 'virtual' access to conference proceedings, for example, through a mode of participation that could assist disabled researchers—at least in my experience (as I relate later on) such virtual performances still tend to be devalued and dismissed sometimes even by academics who are knowledgeable about disability issues. The latter in particular helps to highlight just how deeply ingrained ableism is in our academic environments and cultures. It is so pervasive as to impede our imaginations about doing academia differently and in less exclusionary ways. And this, in turn, perpetuates the ableism entrenched in the academy into the future.

Teaching is another realm in which research is shared and here again having an able body and/or mind confers distinct advantages and rewards. If one has a physically impaired body it will almost certainly be difficult or impossible to access classes and other spaces on campus, at least without a mobility aid. As I relate later in this chapter even if one has such an aid it will likely take longer to get to and from classes and involve the 'extra work' of being a disabled academic. Physical energy and mental acuity are also distinct advantages in the academy. Teaching is hard work at the best of times: involving a lot of preparation which takes time and energy and careful thought. If one has, as I do, a physical condition that causes chronic pain and severe mobility limitations this kind of work is going to be significantly more demanding and exhausting. If in addition, as is true in my case as well, one faces environmental barriers, such as the lack of automatic door openers to the classrooms you teach in and uncertainty about where a disabled parking spot will be available when you arrive on campus to teach, then your job is even harder to do as I discuss below. An ableist academy is also a place where more faculty and students are dealing with mental health challenges, for instance, anxiety in response to more precarious faculty positions, needs of a student to do paid work and study at the same time, and mounting burdens of student debt.

So, not only is the academy profoundly ableist, it actually, in practice, also helps to diminish the health and well-being of those working and studying within it. Ironically, then, the hyper-able neo-liberal academy helps to produce its opposite—its disabled 'other'.

This is not to argue that ableism, as a regime of power and oppression, is monolithic and gives a kind of totalized understanding of academia. Nor is it the sole lens through which our experiences of ableism in the academy and society can be understood. Rather, our experiences of ableism are also informed by other cross-cutting regimes of power, privilege and oppression. These regimes include whiteness and race, class, patriarchy and heterosexualised regimes of sexuality which are intolerant of being transgender for instance (on the latter see Doane, 2010). Depending on how we are situated at the crossroads of these regimes, groups and differences, some of these regimes are going to be more or less salient to how we experience ableism. This is the kind of feminist understanding of intersectionality and its consequences provided by Valentine (2007). In my case, as outlined below, my experiences of ableism as a disabled researcher have also been informed by patriarchy and gendered oppression, and by my whiteness and geographic location in the Global North (including academia).

I now want to share my reflections on what it has been like to be a disabled female professor of Geography and what we can learn from some of these experiences about the workings of ableism in the academy.

Looking in and looking away: autoethnographic reflections on being a disabled researcher in the ableist academy

Most of us can, if not all, relate to some degree with feelings of 'Being on the Outside Looking In' in our new jobs as researchers and academics. By this, I mean feeling like an outsider vis-a-vis more senior colleagues and someone who has to earn acceptance and respect on academia's terms.

It was not initially disability that placed me in this way although ableist forms of oppression were at work in some ways. When I started working as an assistant professor I was the only female faculty member in the entire department which was at best lonely and at worst, as I would learn, to become subject to various forms of patriarchal oppression. Moreover, the oppression I experienced had, a mere two years after joining the department, serious disabling consequences. I have recounted some of the details of these experiences elsewhere (e.g. Chouinard, 2010). I will not share a lot of those details here but will concentrate on making links between who is/becomes a disabled researcher and the workings of the ableist academy.

My first two years as a (soon to be disabled) female researcher and professor were, to put it quite mildly, extremely tough. Sexist dismissals of women and their work were extremely common in the department—one such being the notion that if women don't succeed in academia then they 'can always stay home and take care of the kids' (or so some of my male colleagues told me). I remember feeling bewildered in my first faculty meeting where we were discussing prospective new hires. All but one of the candidates were male. When it came time to discuss her case all the usual academic ways of assessing academic researchers that had been used to evaluate male candidates went out the window. Instead, the discussion degenerated into whether or not she had a male partner living outside the city and if she did would she be on campus less because of the commute. Obviously, there was more than a little wrong with this double standard and way of behaving. I also increasingly noticed mundane sexist practices that helped to place me 'on the outside looking in'. One infuriating one was when I was attending faculty meetings and contributed something to the discussion almost all of my male colleagues would continue the discussion as if I had not spoken a word—just like being the invisible woman! My junior status and lack of experience may have factored into this but my experiences suggest that the main culprit was patriarchal ways of relating to female researchers. I realise now that this is part of oppressive ways of relating to women in the academy: when privileged male colleagues 'look away' and in doing so help to silence women.

So how did I, so early on, become a disabled female researcher? The answer lies in professional harassment with an extremely heavy teaching load which made such harassment harder to deal with effectively. I have talked elsewhere about how starting out as a radical/Marxist geographer (the only one that remained in the department at the time) made me especially vulnerable to harassment. Students were told repeatedly that they should not work with me 'because I did not do real research' and that this would be problematic in terms of getting jobs. This was indirect professional harassment. There was also direct harassment by the (male) department Chair. Interestingly, this took the form of denigrating my abilities and comparing me unfavourably with more senior male colleagues. I was apparently publishing in 'wrong journals'; for example, in the flagship radical geography journal *Antipode*. These tirades always happened after he had entered my office while I was still there in the early evenings and others were no longer about. One particularly inappropriate and distressing encounter was when he ended the tirade by saying 'You are working too hard and your looks are deteriorating'. When he followed this by trying to come behind my desk, I felt unsafe and I reported the encounter to campus security.

The stress caused by professional harassment and heavy workload (I was given some of the largest undergraduate courses to teach) helped to trigger my first episode of bipolar disorder (also known as manic depression) and hospitalisation for it. This was an especially traumatic experience as my partner and I did not at the time understand what was happening. And we also were caring for two small children as well as starting our professional careers. As equality experts agreed, I was working in an extremely toxic work environment.

But the stress I had been placed under in a sexist and ableist working environment also had physical repercussions. Two years after my hospitalisation I was diagnosed with rheumatoid arthritis, an auto-immune disease in which flare-ups are triggered at least in part by stress. I have lived with this painful illness for almost all of my academic career.

So, this is the abbreviated version of how I became a disabled researcher in Geography. In our ableist academy and world becoming a disabled researcher triggers all kinds of ableist responses. One tends to be treated as 'damaged goods' inferior to able and especially able male counterparts. So not only was I told that I should leave and my career was over I was also told I would have to accept a major reduction (50%) in my salary because of a reduced (as opposed to accommodated) workload. I also had to endure many years of struggle for accommodation as a disabled researcher and for disability rights on campus so that I could do my job to the best of my ability and I would argue that in many ways I still do not have the conditions to achieve this (see Chouinard, 2010). What my experiences teach us, I think, is that sexist and ableist practices help to disable people in academic workplaces. Disability does not just happen to a researcher, but practices in the academy itself can help to produce disabled scholars. And as noted above, other regimes of power and oppression may also inform the process of disablement. In my case it was sexism and ableism but in other cases it could be whiteness or hetero or homo-normative norms about sexualities.

Of course, another reality of the ableist academy is that it often keeps disabled scholars and researchers completely on the 'outside looking in'. There are very few disabled scholars who study disability in my academic discipline. There is little understanding of or tolerance for the fact that disabled researchers will at least sometimes necessarily have different career trajectories but can still make important contributions. In rare cases where disabled researchers are hired, it is more likely to be in precarious contract positions that further diminish their opportunities to 'succeed' (Kosanic et al., 2018).

So what? Challenges of being a disabled researcher

In situations, such as mine, where the disabled researcher is forced to fight long and hard just to be able to continue their work, one, at least in retrospect, a key challenge is that this takes up enormous time and energy that ought to, at least ideally, be devoted to research, writing and teaching. Not only is this exhausting and stressful, it also means that the disabled researcher is literally, as one colleague recently put it, 'set up to fail'. In addition to doing my academic work I spent over eight years trying to convince often hostile administrators that they had a legal duty to accommodate my disability-related needs in the academic workplace. When that effort to deal with the matter internally failed, including a refusal by the then faculty association to assist even though action on accommodation issues on campus had resulted in accommodation being a term and condition of employment at the university, I was forced to hire a human rights lawyer that I could ill afford on a salary frozen at 50% of a low associate professor rate supplemented by partial disability benefits (the University used the argument that even though my performance was being assessed no salary increases were possible since the insurer would just claw back my benefits accordingly). So, while hiring an experienced human rights lawyer was helpful in many ways it also meant further work on my part. To keep costs down, he and I agreed that I would take responsibility for drafting things such as memos and letters to administrators and he would review and add legal points as needed. I learned a lot in the process but it obviously made my work even more onerous. Moreover, having to contend with frequently hostile encounters with administrators, encounters in which I was told things like I was not sufficiently 'grateful' for any accommodations made or that any of my proposals for accommodation in teaching 'would not work', further exacerbated my stress and illnesses. These are examples of some of the ways that having to perform difficult 'extra' work—work that is often not noticed by one's peers or valued in the institution—further sets up the disabled researcher to fail.

Another challenge of being a disabled researcher in the ableist academy is constantly dealing with attitudes and practices that devalue one's contributions vis-a-vis ableist norms. Academia is extremely competitive at the best of times and if you add into this mix the stigma of doing things differently because of disability then it feels even more oppressive and alienating. And this, in turn, means that one has to grapple with the psychological and emotional harms of being repeatedly constructed as inferior and lesser. This sometimes takes relatively mundane forms such as when a colleague, and one who is knowledgeable about disability issues, informed me that it was 'too bad' that I had to give a plenary talk virtually (this is because my mobility impairments mean I can no longer travel alone). If one steps outside of the ableist mindset of the academy one can imagine a very different potential response, such as, 'isn't it great that we now have alternative ways of participating in conferences and one that makes such spaces of academic life more inclusive and here's what I found interesting in your talk'. But the focus was on what I could not do rather on what I did and had to say. There are many other examples in my life of such mundane and devaluing types of interactions and they do wear you down. I have also experienced more sweeping dismissals of my work and career. I have already mentioned some that occurred early in my career. But there are recent examples as well. One was when a no doubt well-meaning colleague summed up my career in the following way: 'You are doing okay. Sort of average but nothing stellar'. Just the sort of message no academic wants to hear! And it is taken for granted that such an assessment makes sense when contributions in the academy are measured in conventional ableist and quantitative ways. What we have not yet learned to do is to begin to appreciate that groups marginalised or excluded from the academy, including disabled persons, have a great deal to contribute to making our teaching, learning, research and indeed societies not only more inclusive but also more interesting and socially relevant.

There are of course other practical challenges of being a disabled researcher in an ableist academy. I would like, for example, to secure a grant for continuing my disability research in Guyana. But I can no longer travel independently to 'the field'.

This is not an insurmountable obstacle, however, since I have had a research partnership with a women's organisation and we have been able to do some of this work through virtual means. I am also conscious of the emphasis placed by funding bodies on the dissemination of academic research and that I cannot do so at least in conventional ways such as attending conferences in person. And while I am happy to use different dissemination methods such as podcasts, I am unsure whether the funding agencies and evaluation committees will judge these to be 'not good' (read not sufficiently 'able') enough. Such worries are draining and go hand in hand with being placed by others on the 'outside looking in'.

Another challenge is being forced to expend more time and energy than my able peers to access campus facilities such as classrooms. I use a walker to walk, hopefully, a short distance (as long as unauthorized vehicles are not blocking access to disabled parking spaces) to my office where I have a scooter. Unfortunately, in recent weeks vehicles have been doing just that and, in the process, making me navigate a longer (and more painful) path to my office. And there was recently what I've dubbed 'the workday from hell'. Once again, an unauthorized vehicle was blocking access to the disabled parking spot close to the building my office is in.

Then, on the first floor, the elevator was not working and I needed to get to the third floor for a graduate class followed by a comprehensive examination. The office staff were not initially aware of the problem since no one had told them and so I ended up waiting by the elevator sitting on my walker. When a member of staff finally walked by I asked her for help. Eventually, the classroom was moved to the second floor but the only way for a non-abled-bodied person to access it was via walking around the adjacent building to reach a ramp to the second floor (which I had to do with my walker since I was not able to access the scooter). This was extremely painful and tiring for me. I did end up being able to teach a half-hour graduate class in which we talked a little about theory in Human Geography and about my ordeal on campus. When we talked about humans theorizing when there are things that happen that we do not understand, I mentioned that I had to strategically plan, often in detail, how I would access spaces on campus. One of the students wanted to know why this counted as 'theorising' and I explained that in the course of thinking strategically about how I could get to where I needed to be I frequently had to imagine why things such as vehicles blocking disabled parking spots or walkways that are not ploughed in winter, or being assigned classrooms without automatic door openers, happen on campus. To be sure this is not what is referred to as 'grand theory' but it is a form of theorising nonetheless and is part of the extra work that disabled researchers do.

I would be remiss if I did not mention that as a disabled researcher I have also experienced privileges that many do not have. As a white woman, I have not experienced the racist practices faced by many people of colour in the academy. And as a disabled woman from the Global North I have enjoyed privileges in terms of access to services such as mental health care that many in the poorer nations of the Global South do not enjoy. But, as a disabled researcher from the Global North, I have also experienced challenges associated with being a partial outsider with regard to understanding disabled people's lives in the Global South. This has been reflected, for example, in the fact that it took me considerable time to be able to gain a fuller understanding of the local and global forces shaping disabled people's lives in poorer nations of the world.

Conclusions: thinking ahead: beyond the ableist academy

As I hope the preceding autoethnographic reflections begin to illustrate, disabled researchers in the ableist academy face challenges above and beyond those encountered by their able-bodied counterparts. And with all the extra work needed to struggle to contend with these, it is clear that we are 'being set up to fail'.

I now want to shift gears a little and consider how we might work to promote academies that do not involve oppressive practices that contribute to and/or exacerbate disability and symptoms such as pain (sexism and ableism in my case for instance). But first I want to put this in a more global context to show why moving away from ableism is one of the most pressing challenges of the 21st century.

We are, unfortunately, living in times when right-wing populism is increasingly influential and where those supporting it seem focused on economic growth, the accumulation of even greater wealth by the economic elite, tighter borders and further cutting back on already meagre state assistance for those who need it. Of course, important issues get lost when one is of this mindset: the critical matter of climate change, for example, and the impairments and deaths that attend more severe weather events. Also obscured is the fact that many members of vulnerable groups such as disabled persons and the elderly are struggling desperately to survive and in many cases are losing the means to do so (witness, for example, the U.K. and opposition groups such as Black Triangle working to raise awareness of cutbacks in support of disabled people). The latter are battling what can only be understood as a form of genocide and indifference to the suffering of others.

We are also living in times and places where right-wing leaders are giving others license to arrogantly dismiss those who differ from themselves (white, male, rich and able). We have had the spectacle of Donald Trump, the U.S. president, publicly mocking a disabled reporter and bragging about sexual abuse of women, calling poorer nations of the world 'shit holes', and making such outrageous claims about the 'success' of his administration in his recent talk to the United Nations that he was openly laughed at. There are many other examples of Trump giving license to sexism, ableism and racism—an example of the latter is painting Mexican migrants to the U.S. as rapists and criminals and traumatizing and disabling practices such as separating children from their families if they cross the U.S. border.

There are similar if not as socially and spatially encompassing, developments in Canada. Ontario residents have recently elected the right-wing conservative populist Doug Ford as provincial premier on a platform of slashing social spending, cancelling green initiatives, downsizing Toronto city council and a campaign to get brewing companies to once again offer 'a buck a beer'. He has already cancelled a promising provincial pilot project that increased social assistance rates in three cities for certain recipients to a 'living wage' ($17,000 a year) and one that was reported to have made positive changes in recipients' lives such as allowing them to plan to return to University or college and to use this as a basis for employment. But the pilot was cancelled so early on that we don't know what potential it had. Ableness, work and independence from the government are so prized by Ford that the well-being of groups such as disabled Ontarians is quite simply ignored. Like Trump, he also demonstrates contempt for groups regarded as 'abnormal' and 'lesser' such as the LGBTQ community, expressed for example, in refusing to attend the annual Gay Pride parade in Toronto.

It is in this kind of context that we need to think about challenging the ableist academy. We also need to keep in mind that we live in a profoundly unequal global capitalist order which leaves disabled people and other oppressed groups such as women in especially dire straits in poorer nations. I have seen this first hand in my research in Guyana, a country that, despite government and activist efforts, still has insufficient resources to meet the needs of disabled people, women victimized by domestic violence and other marginalized groups such as LGBTQ youth. This results from limited government resources, problems such as the outmigration of health professionals in search of better jobs (professionals that have been trained at a high cost), insufficient access to mental health care services which has contributed to the country having one of the highest suicide rates in the world, and the constraints of structural adjustment programs and debt on what the government can undertake.

How in this daunting context can we fight back against the ableist academy and possibly the wider society beyond its walls? I do believe that a time will come when assessing the contributions of disabled researchers as if they were able-bodied—a kind of 'one size fits all' ableist approach to assessing academic success—will be seen as outdated, oppressive and as unacceptable as practices such as excluding women from academic disciplines such as Geography (on this see Dixon and Jones, 2006). However, the road toward such a realization will be a long and difficult one.

This is because the economic stakes are so high in continuing to perpetuate and reward ableism as well as capitalism. Many of the ultra-rich, via inheritance and/or entrepreneurial ability or both, are neither prepared to help create a more inclusive and enabling society by redistributing wealth nor even by paying their fair share of government taxes. Just as unbridled greed stands in the way of battling climate change and its disabling consequences so too does it render groups such as disabled researchers and people increasingly 'disposable'.

Challenging the ableist academy is in part about shaking up such exclusionary mindsets and practices beyond its walls. Instead of zero tolerance for people such as migrants, we need to promote zero tolerance for the oppressive practices of the global elite which fail to assume any responsibility for social justice and, in doing so, punish those who are different from and much less fortunate than themselves.

There is also, of course, much to be done within the ableist academy itself. We need to insist on the importance of having disabled researchers in academia to create a more diverse academy and act as mentors to future generations of disabled researchers. We need to recognize the importance of challenging ways of assessing disabled researchers that do not take into account facets of their work such as differing career paths, the extra work involved in being disabled in the academy and the fact that our current assessments of academic contributions boil down to rewarding those who are fortunate enough to have able bodies and/or minds. This is no more just than rewarding royal families for their ties with a monarchy or figures such as Donald Trump who display contempt for differences such as disability and gender and a blatant sense of entitlement to wealth and political power.

There is much then to be done to challenge the ableist academy and ensure that disabled researchers are not 'left on the outside looking in'. We can do it to the extent that we insist that social justice and not greed, that diversity and not exclusion and that respect and not disdain should be our guiding lights in transforming an intolerant academy and world.

References

Chouinard, V. (2010) "Like Alice through the Looking Glass II: The Struggle for Accommodation Continues", *Resources for Feminist Research*, 33(3–4), 161–177.
Dixon, D.P. and Jones, J.P. III (2006) "Feminist Geographies of Difference, Relation, and Construction", In: Aiken, S. and Valentine, G. (eds) *Approaches to Human Geography* (2nd ed.) London: Sage. pp. 49–63.
Doane, P.L. (2010) "The Tyranny of Gendered Spaces: Living Beyond the Gender Dichotomy", *Gender, Place and Culture*, 17(5), 635–654.
Dolmage, J.T. (2017) *Academic Ableism: Disability and Higher Education*. Ann Arbor: University of Michigan Press.
Kosanic, A., Hansen N., Zimmerman-Janschitz, S. and Chouinard, V. (2018) "Researchers with Disabilities in the Academic System", *Association of American Geographers Newsletter*, September 1, 2018.
Mitchell, D.T. (2016) *Disability, Diversity and Diversion: Normalization and Avoidance in Higher Education*. London: Routledge.
Valentine, G. (2007) "Theorizing and Researching Intersectionality: A Challenge for Feminist Geography", *Professional Geographer*, 59(1), 10–21.

Chapter 3

A closer look at 'wheelchair' ethnography

Ableism and the insights disabled scholars generate with – not despite – their impairments and disabilities[1]

Karen Mogendorff

Introduction

Ethnography offers unique barriers and opportunities to disabled anthropologists and sociologists. On the one hand, anthropology – the home discipline of ethnography – has the stereotypical image of toughness and daring that does not sit well with disability. Anthropologists are supposed to do research far from their home and comfort studying less well-off cultures through participant observation (Kloos, 1987; Hammersley & Atkinson, 2000). On the other hand, ethnographical ontology and epistemology offer unique opportunities to disabled anthropologists and sociologists; it recognises that scholars' positionality in research mediated through gender, age, sexual orientation, ethnicity and disability affect researchers' interests, access to the field, analyses and findings (see also Harding (1992)). Disabled people deviate from the norm and, as such, are optimally situated to expose and analyse taken-for-granted everyday ableist sociocultural practices (Mogendorff, 2010). If disabled anthropologists and sociologists engage more in reflexive ethnography – a reflection on and analysis of one's own lived experiences as a researcher in interaction with others (Davies, 1997) – insight may be increased into how knowledge is produced through lived bodies and what disabled scholars have to add to the literature (Davies, 1997; Engelsrud, 2005). Despite these benefits, relatively little is published about disabled academics' careers from an emic life course perspective (Roulstone et al., 2003; Shah, 2005) and, to my knowledge, next to nothing about disabled anthropologists' and sociologists' work lives (Kasnitz & Shuttleworth, 2001).

This contribution is about the role and function of disability in the careers of disabled anthropologists and sociologists and how they, with their lived disabled bodies, produce insights relevant to academia and beyond. Insights that may also play a role in countering ableism. Ableism is:

> a set of beliefs, processes and practices that produce - based on abilities one exhibits or values - a particular understanding of oneself, one's body and one's

> relationship with others of humanity, other species and the environment, and includes how one is judged by others.
>
> (Wolbring, 2008: 252–253)

A reason for the paucity of literature on disabled professionals from an emic perspective in general and disabled academics in particular is that disability and impairment tend to be treated as career killers in the employment and disability literature, the media and disability law and regulations (Sanders, 2006; Stone et al., 2013; Williams & Mavin, 2015). In the dominant discourse, disability is equated with unproductivity, passivity and tragedy (Haller, 2010), images that do not fit conceptualisations of the ideal worker (Foster, 2012). However, in recent years several qualitative studies – generally conducted by disabled academics – have critically addressed the barriers and opportunities disabled high-flyers face, for example, see Roulstone et al. (2003), Shah (2005), Foster and Wass (2007). Reflexive disability ethnography specifically may shed light on careers of disabled scholars who deploy their own lived experience of disability as a resource to better understand and help redirect the deeply ingrained culture of ableism.

In this chapter, I draw upon the disability career literature and on what disabled anthropologists and sociologists, myself included, have disclosed in order to explore how the lived experience of impairments and disability affect careers and what disabled anthropologists and sociologists with and through their bodies have to contribute to the literature. *Situated* disability disclosure may increase insight and appreciation of what disabled ethnographers have to add. But, as discussed later in this chapter, there are ableist processes at play in academia that make this far from easy: the disappearing disability phenomenon and the 'I am afraid you cannot take it' experience.

When it comes to other disabled anthropologists' and sociologists' experiences, I limit myself here to what they published about their lived experience of impairment and disability in relation to their work lives. There are many disabled scholars who choose NOT to publish about how impairment and disability affect their work. Disability disclosure may affect careers (e.g. see Waterfield et al., 2018), or discussing personal experiences does not fit into their ideas about 'objective' research (Harding, 1992; Hammersley & Atkinson, 2000). However, I do not need to restrict myself to already published material when it comes to my own experiences as a congenital neuromotor impaired anthropologist and non-Western sociologist.

Functions and features of reflexive disability ethnography

Most anthropologists and sociologists that do study disability are non-disabled and disabled anthropologists and sociologists tend to be marginalised within the discipline (Kasnitz & Shuttleworth, 2001; Reid-Cunningham, 2009). Disabled anthropologists and sociologists who have published about how disability informs their life and work are few, but they argue that researchers should become more open about how research is generated phenomenologically in and through lived disabled bodies by engaging in reflexive ethnography (Seymour, 2007; Howe, 2009). A complicating factor is that disability disclosure may both aid and harm disabled academics' careers: it does not help one to get a job or a promotion (Pearson et al., 2003; Sayce, 2009), but it may go a long way in:

- creating rapport and understanding with colleagues and research participants (Foster and Wass, 2007; Mogendorff, 2007, 2013);
- acquiring accommodations that allow one to participate (Mogendorff, 2002);
- creating the possibility that one is being accepted *with* one's particular difference (Roulstone et al., 2003);
- helping debunk crippling images of disability.

Advantages and disadvantages of disability disclosure depend on context, it matters greatly what is disclosed when, where, how and to whom.[2] Disabled anthropologists and sociologists, as a rule, do not draw attention to their own lived experiences of disability in their academic writing, nor in face-to-face encounters as employees of universities, it is mostly irrelevant for the business at hand. In academic texts the primary focus is on the analysis of informants' experiences, and, as employees of universities, disabled academics strive to pass as an ideal worker, as 'not really disabled', mainly because passing as normal is rewarded and accentuating difference is not (Mogendorff, 2002; Foster, 2012).

Another reason for the relative paucity of the literature on reflexive ethnography has to do with different traditions and practices in ethnographic writing and publishing. In confessional ethnographies readers gain insight into how ethnographers did come by their insights in interaction with informants, literature and colleagues. In the still popular realist ethnographies, the author is the all-knowing storyteller who presents his or her results but reflects little, if anything, on their personal role in the production of knowledge and insights (Van Maanen, 1988). This lack of reflexive writing suggests that the ethnographer's impact on the research done was negligible; what is unhelpful further is that reflexive ethnographic accounts are presumably harder to publish. It is not easy to demonstrate how personal experiences of ethnographers are of wider academic or theoretical interest (Barrett, 2014).

The reflexive disability ethnographies published by disabled anthropologists and sociologists that I collected over the years are mostly written by disabled or chronically ill, American, male and arrived sociologists born in the 1930s–1940s: Frank (2002), Karp (1996), Kimmerling (2012), Michalko (1999), Murphy (1990), Nijhof (2001), Robillard (1999) and Zola (1982). These autoethnographies are very diverse about the extent to which they show disability awareness, the level of reflection and to what extent the authors incorporate the experiences of other disabled or chronically ill people in their analyses. One may even question to what extent they are autobiographies, memoirs, reflexive ethnographies or autoethnographies, but they all tell a story, sometimes unwittingly, of how one can function as a disabled academic.[3] I did not find reflexive disability monographs written by disabled female anthropologists and sociologists, although I did find autoethnographies – broadly defined – written by female academics in other disciplines. Disabled female anthropologists and sociologists, however, have in articles reflected upon how the lived, embodied experience of impairment or disability affected relationships with research participants and enabled the generation of insights abroad and at home, for example, see Colligan (1994, 2001), Deegan (2001), Mogendorff (2007, 2013), Seymour (2007).

Reflexive ethnography is considered to be a specific form of anthropology 'at home' in that the main focus is on the ethnographers' own experiences. Traditionally, anthropology at home has a lower status within anthropology and non-Western sociology than research abroad. Immersion in another culture for an elongated time period through participant observation purportedly provides a culture shock that enables the fieldworker to critically interrogate taken-for-granted ideas and practices that shape life in the researched culture and makes it possible to examine cultural biases in one's own native culture (Hammersley & Atkinson, 2000). A culture shock that is presumed absent or less profound in anthropology at home. The culture shock is also conceptualised as a *rite de passage,* the transition that turns a student into a professional (e.g. see Kloos, 1987; Shuttleworth, 2004). By extension, anthropology at home is seen as not quite the 'real' thing, although not all anthropologists of note share this view (Shuttleworth, 2004). Moreover, Mughal (2015) has argued that anthropology at home is just as methodologically and ethically demanding as doing research abroad. Additionally, Van der Geest (2007) maintains that reflexive ethnography conducted by insiders is the most engaged form of participant observation that allows for the deepest immersion. One may only participate to the fullest in one's own life and know it totally, whereas our understanding of others' experiences remains always partial and contested.

I agree with the arguments of Van der Geest (2007) and Mughal (2015). Based on my own experience with disability ethnography at home, I would like to add that the 'home' in disability ethnography is relative. One may argue that the majority of disabled ethnographers is not totally at home in mainstream ableist society, nor are they typically born into a minority disability culture. As such, disabled anthropologists and sociologists are well-situated to research their simultaneously familiar and strange native culture.

Reflection on one's own experiences in relation to others' is not easy, it requires that one observes and analyzes oneself as an outsider, that one can alternate between involvement and detachment in order to generate insight into how one's lived experience relates to one's peers' experiences and how one is affected by culturally deeply ingrained ableism. Insights that allow disabled anthropologists and sociologists to be successful researchers through academic publishing and to act more informed in one's personal encounters with others. In keeping with this, disabled anthropologists, sociologists and disability scholars account for what they did to ensure that they were both sufficiently involved and detached from disabled informants to conduct a sound analysis (e.g. see Shah, 2006; Mogendorff, 2007; Seymour, 2007), or the authors simply perform an analysis informed by their lived experience with impairment and disability (Colligan, 1994; Deegan, 2001; Howe, 2009; Mogendorff, 2010).

From an inclusion perspective, gained awareness of how one's own and others' behaviour is affected by ableist culture is a first step in adapting's one's own behaviour in less ableist directions. For instance, doing disability research as a disabled anthropologist helped me over the years to (see also Mogendorff, 2013):

- let go of some ableist notions I had internalised in early childhood about bodies like mine;
- to acknowledge, understand and to take better care of my body's specific long-term needs;
- and to value my body as a differently abled body.

Disabled ethnographers' careers and contributions: the impact of responses to lived differently abled bodies

Disabled professionals who are gainfully employed have supposedly 'overcome' or 'conquered' their impairments; at best they may have jobs but not careers (Wilson-Kovacs et al., 2008; Williams & Mavin, 2015). A problem with 'overcoming' which disabled professionals may learn the hard way is that it generally involves doing things the able-bodied way unreflectively, even if it requires a disproportional amount of effort and discomfort. For instance, late disabled medical sociologist Irving Kenneth Zola, who walked with a brace, started using a wheelchair at airports after 20 years of travelling to and from conferences only to realise that he had previously assumed that for him pain and fatigue was a normal component of travel. He concluded that overcoming is not the same as integrating (Zola, 1996). Paying attention to how with one's differently abled body one may execute academic tasks optimally may make disabled scholars more efficient and effective. However, given that the wheelchair has become *the* symbol of severe impairment and disability, neuromotor impaired academics who can walk may opt to not use a wheelchair at airports (and other places) and accept the discomfort that goes with it, particularly when they are travelling together with an able-bodied colleague to keep up appearances of 'not really being disabled' (see also Frank [2002] on keeping up appearances in a totally different context).

Disabled professionals are inclined to (re)direct their career ambitions towards work or occupations that are objectively compatible with their impairments and in which they may follow their interests, use their talents and achieve personal and professional goals (Shah, 2005; Williams & Mavin, 2015). For instance, Wendy Seymour redirected her career towards the sociology of embodiment when her physical condition worsened and the corporeal demands of her former job as a health professional became too much (Seymour, 2007). In keeping with this, Berthoud (2008) found that educational level is a better predictor of employment success than the severity of professionals' physical impairments. Perhaps this finding may in part be explained by the idea that with higher educational level, work tends to become less physical in nature (Foster & Fosh, 2010) and problem-solving skills of employees increase, including disability management skills (Shah, 2005).[4] And, as Murphy (1990), Kimmerling (2012) and Robillard (1999) noted, severe physical impairment is compatible with the academic core business of writing and publishing. However, careers in the social sciences are increasingly defined as boundary-less and precarious, researchers achieve tenure or permanent contracts less often than before (Baruch & Hall, 2004). The latter is certainly also true for disadvantaged employee groups such as disabled scholars.

What may reinforce the marginalised position of disabled academics in ethnography is that disabled anthropologists are less likely to be encouraged to conduct fieldwork abroad. Traditionally, anthropologists are supposed to engage in fieldwork far away from home and comfort, studying less well-off cultures through participant observation. Anthropology's, admittedly, stereotypical tough and daring public image does not sit well with the hegemonic sociocultural notion of disability as inability and vulnerability; the aspirant or junior anthropologists may not seriously consider doing fieldwork abroad, simply because they or their teachers find it hard to imagine that they conduct fieldwork in 'exotic' places in a wheelchair or with some other assistive technology, particularly if they have had a sheltered upbringing (Mogendorff, 2011), or have had their competency regularly questioned by able-bodied people, teachers included. In qualitative sociology, this may be slightly different, in that doing fieldwork at home is much more common than in anthropology.

Back in 2001, as a neuromotor impaired student of anthropology, I did not have a particular interest in studying 'exotic' communities and considered with Mary Douglas (2002) studying Western cultures as relevant and worthwhile. However, I did not seriously consider doing research abroad mainly because I lacked travel experience and self-confidence in the matter and was not encouraged to try it anyway (but I have travelled to South-East Asia since then).[5]

In hindsight, I underestimated the specific opportunities developing countries for disability management offer and I underestimated my corporeal abilities due to lack of opportunity to discover and try out my physical boundaries (see also Sanders [2006] on the consequences of overprotectiveness). It certainly did not help me that the most positive remarks I received about my atypical walking style and motor abilities were: 'it is not as bad as we thought it would be' (able-bodied students with regard to the distance I walked during outings), and, 'it looks difficult' [the way you walk] (from teachers). Some disabled anthropological students have been discouraged to do fieldwork abroad for 'their own good'. If being impaired or disabled in familiar surroundings gets already classified as difficult, it is not surprising that doing fieldwork in unfamiliar less equipped surroundings may be considered a bridge too far. Often it not so much about active discouragement but lack of encouragement to do as one's able-bodied peers and conduct fieldwork abroad. Discouragement and lack of encouragement may be understood as ableist practice, particularly if judgements are not informed by careful exploration of the specific possibilities of individual disabled students.

The situation is somewhat different for disabled ethnographers with senior status; they may be considered unfit to continue doing fieldwork but found capable of supervising students (Murphy, 1990; Robillard, 1999). Also, they can, at least in part, fall back on intellectual and sociocultural capital, contacts and standing they acquired within the university before the onset of severe impairment or disability (Robillard, 1999; Kimmerling, 2012).

The disappearing disability phenomenon and 'I am afraid you cannot take it' experience

The negative impact of the disability stigma and stereotypes on careers may be somewhat mitigated by what Seymour (2007: 1193) – a disabled embodiment sociologist – coined as the disappearing disability phenomenon: 'despite clear and visible manifestations of disability, the person with a (high-status) job is seen as not really disabled'. Ruth Benedict is arguably the best example of this phenomenon in anthropology. Every anthropologist knows about Benedict's contributions to anthropology and status as a key anthropologist, but not everyone knows that she had a congenital hearing impairment (e.g. see Mead, 2005).

A problem with the disappearing disability phenomenon is that it sustains dominant-negative images of disability. If success continues to negate disability in the public eye, evidence of successful disabled professionals will, by itself, do little to weaken the strong association between disability and inability. For various reasons it is doubtful that disability really disappears and ceases to affect careers, although it may seem so at first, particularly when individual disabled anthropologists' and sociologists' achievements and professional standing equal those of their able-bodied contemporaries. Studies show that disabled professionals in senior positions face problems similar to members of other disadvantaged groups who have managed to land a senior position (Sayce, 2009); They may encounter a pay-gap, a glass ceiling – one is given less opportunity to further develop and prove oneself as one's able-bodied peers – or a glass cliff – one is given assignments with an elevated risk of failure (Wilson-Kovacs et al., 2008; Roulstone & Williams, 2014; Williams & Mavin, 2015). Moreover, the disabled anthropology and sociology professors who, according to Seymour (2007), are subject to the 'disappearing disability phenomenon' mention in their monographs instances of what I call the 'I am afraid you cannot take it' experience. Both Zola (1982) and Murphy (1990) describe how some colleagues became less critical of their work because they assumed that they had so much on their plate already with their conditions, colleagues who, when questioned about it, would say: 'I am afraid you cannot take it'.[6] It is, according to Zola (1982) – and I agree with him – one of the greatest disservices to any academic. Critical constructive feedback helps one to grow and prosper.

The 'disappearance' and subsequent reappearance of disability may have to do with sociocultural beliefs about disability in general combined with individuals' feelings of unease in the actual presence of disabled colleagues. My experience with a facility manager at a university where I was employed for several years, demonstrates this:

> A university building was several times renovated while I worked there. During renovation, disability access accommodations such as the ramp at the building's entrance were blocked. Information about temporary changes in accessibility were not included in the standard briefings about the renovation on Intranet. Every time the entrance ramp was blocked, I felt obliged to point out to the facility manager that this may pose a problem for some disabled employees, students and visitors, although I did not need to use the ramp myself. I also advised him to include accessibility information in the renovation briefings. In response, the facility manager would tell me to my face without batting an eye: 'No disabled employees work here'.
>
> I was surprised by this answer the first time I heard it. I did know for a fact that there were various students and employees who used the entrance ramp, although I did not know them personally. I also knew that the facility manager did know at least one visibly disabled employee: me! I had caught him staring on several occasions at my legs and feet – I have an in-toe walking style typical for my neuromotor condition. He had also offered me once unneeded help with some minor task, which I had politely declined.[7]
>
> I decided to change tack, after the facility manager's last statement - given that I was not a ramp user myself and asked the facility manager: 'What about disabled students and visitors who are unexpectedly confronted with a closed off ramp?'
>
> Facility manager: 'They can be carried inside, or they can call for help'.
>
> I did not think, that he really believed that it would work the way he claimed. Calling at the bottom of the stairs leading up to the entrance was not possible, there was no bell. And people who could carry wheelchair users up - and downstairs were certainly not loitering about. I concluded that the facility manager did not consider building accessibility during renovation his problem or responsibility.

From my experiences, as with Murphy's and Zola's, it may be concluded that disabilities that appear to have disappeared may pop-up unexpectedly in interactions between disabled and non-disabled employees. And that the 'disappearance' of disability is likely to reinforce ableism.

Insights from engaging with and reflecting on one's disability experiences

Ethnography is informed by standpoint ontology and epistemology, what one sees, experiences and knows partly depends on one's standpoint (Harding, 1992; Howe,

2009). Disabled anthropologists and sociologists have direct and superior access to lived experiences of disability, marginalization and normalization. Bodies are ethnographers' research instrument of choice not only in a practical functional way but also in a performative way: disabled anthropologists' and sociologists' bodies elicit responses from, among others, study participants. Responses that shed light on sociocultural beliefs and practices and the researcher-researched relationship. Or, as American anthropologist and wheelchair user Colligan (1994: 5) maintains: 'a people can "write" their own ethnography by using the ethnographer's body as text for representing themselves to outsiders'.

Colligan's body was subject to a close reading by Karaite informants that assisted her by specific activities of daily living in the context of the Jewish holiday Yom Kippur in Israel and had, as such, privileged access to an intimate knowledge of her body. The informant who provided support with certain tasks, was worried that Colligan might have her menses during the holiday, which would pose a dilemma for the informant because menstruating women are considered impure in the community where Colligan conducted her fieldwork. Due to their impurity, women are expected to spend their time in seclusion during their menses. In the context of Yom Kippur, it meant that the informant could not take care of Colligan during the festivities and Colligan could not partake in Yom Kippur, at least not in the way non-menstruating women could. Moreover, the care-providing informant used her close-reading of Colligan's body to demonstrate to her fellow Karaites that she was well-versed in and closely observed the Karaite purity rules by discussing Colligan's potential impure state during the upcoming festivities in detail with Karaite visitors.

This example shows that disabled anthropologists' and sociologists' differently abled bodies are able or capable research instruments and that disabled anthropologists do not need to confine themselves to doing fieldwork 'at home'. They also may have a less hierarchal and somewhat different relationship with their informants than able-bodied researchers that may yield interesting insights. Colligan's experience shows, and that is my experience as well, that one visibly impaired body reveals in interaction with others when and where there is room to bend social and cultural rules. Ranging from whether one should take off one's shoes, sit or stand, or whether or not one should perform tasks associated with one's gender, health status or age.

There have been issues raised within anthropology, sociology and disability research about the researcher-researched relationship. The main critique is that most disability research by social scientists reinforces existing negative disability images through, among others, (implicit) comparison with able-bodied people and the (implicit) use of the individual model of disability (Kitchin, 2000).

Mainstream ethnography is not per se focused on bringing about social change, instead, it is devoted to providing nuanced insight in the lived experience of peoples with various social and cultural backgrounds. Ethnographers are supposed to learn from their informants and to affect as little as possible the culture they are studying. In practice, however, disabled researchers and informants learn from each other. In my experience, the added value of doing disability research 'at home' lies partly in the recognition, companionship and reciprocity found in fieldwork encounters between disabled researchers and (disabled) informants.

For example, when I conducted life history research interviews with young adults with neuromotor conditions not unlike my own, informants would occasionally request extra time in between sessions because 'I made them think about their lives in ways they had not before', and they wanted 'to process things first'. Informants were curious about my lived experiences of disability. Their questions were of the type: 'Do you have that too?' And: 'How do you…?' or 'What do you think about that?' Some of these questions appeared to be a test – mostly posed by activist informants – to ascertain whether I had not internalised an ableist take on disability, but mostly they hoped to learn something from me and my research. Practical lived through acquired knowledge about how to handle mundane everyday tasks to ensure that one can live a life in agreement with one's own preferences was most valued by informants, as well as an understanding of and appreciation for the informants' own smart solutions. Research can be a mutual learning process without compromising the quality and independence of the research.

However, this still leaves the problem that research with a 'therapeutic theme' or focus on body normalisation gets more easily funded, than research on social inclusion and participation irrespective of one's health or disability status. Furthermore, most research with disabled people is mediated by or takes place in medical or care institutions informed by theoretical interests and models that have been developed with no or little input of the majority of disabled academics or citizens (Shuttleworth, 2004). The latter makes it not only important to recognise and explicate the contribution disabled academics make, but also to ensure that the funding and organization of research allow for more diversity in views and takes on disability.

Conclusion: towards an appreciation of 'wheelchair' ethnography

The focus of this chapter was on how impairment and disability not only act as a career boundary but are also resources in the work lives of disabled anthropologists and sociologists whether they engage in disability research or not, and how this is both facilitated and constrained by ethnographic ontology and epistemology. I did draw on publications of disabled anthropologists and sociologists in which they explicate the role of impairment and disability in their work lives and on my own experiences as a congenital neuromotor impaired anthropologist and non-Western sociologist to explore the disability-ethnography relationship.

In dominant discourse, disabled academics are considered unexpected workers (Stone et al., 2013), a notion that is both expressed and reinforced by the disappearing disability phenomenon (Seymour, 2007): if one has acquired a (high) status one becomes 'not really' disabled and differently abled-bodiness is ignored until it surfaces again in encounters with others who feel uncomfortable in the face of a notable difference or vulnerability. The resurfacing of disability I coined as the 'I am afraid you cannot take it' experience and should be understood as a mechanism that helps to consolidate the ableist status quo.

Disabled academics strive to pass as normal workers, and are careful about what they disclose when and where. But as I have argued, passing is not the solution to ableism. Disabled academics need to be valued for their achievements, which they accomplished not despite their differently abled bodies, but *with* and through their lived bodies. This requires disabled scholars to be reflexive and open about how negative and positive impairment and disability experiences helped to generate insight and understanding. We need what I coined 'wheelchair' ethnography – reflexive ethnography conducted by disabled anthropologists and sociologists who may or may not use a wheelchair.

Change is unlikely to be brought about by thoughtful and reflexive accounts or wheelchair ethnography alone. Addressing forms of ableism in academia such as the disappearing disability phenomenon and the 'I am afraid you cannot take it' experience, as discussed in this chapter, is necessary. Facilitating funding and organization of social research that focuses on how one may live the good life with impairments or disabilities may also help. Last but not least, extra support for disabled talent across the sciences through diversity policies and disability scholarships may increase the visibility, efficacy and appreciation of what disabled anthropologists and sociologists have to contribute with, not despite, their chronic conditions.

Notes

1 Wheelchair is put in between '' because the wheelchair is *the* sociocultural symbol of disability in the West. This contribution does NOT focus exclusively on disabled scholars who use wheelchairs.

2 Disclosure I consider equally relevant to academics with visible and invisible impairments. As I have argued elsewhere (Mogendorff, 2010), visibility of disabilities is a relative phenomenon. Invisible impairments at times become glaringly obvious – for example, in misinterpreted body language or misunderstood behaviour – and visible differences do not translate one-to-one into limitations and special needs and, as such, are subject to misinterpretation.

3 See more on the value of different forms of autoethnography in Barrett (2014), Charmaz (2006) and Davies (1997).

4 As far as I know the relationship between educational level and disability management skills as a specific form of problem-solving has not yet been researched, but it seems plausible.

5 Anthropologists who are well-regarded for their 'at home' work such as Mary Douglas generally have proven themselves first by publishing about more 'exotic' fieldwork.

6 This could be understood as a specific expression of the lowered expectations disabled citizens in general face due to negative stereotyping (Sanders, 2006).

7 Unasked and unwanted help is one of the social barriers in the social model of disability.

References

Barrett, T. (2014) "De-individualising Autobiography: A Reconsideration of the Role of Autobiographical Life Writing within Disability Studies", *Disability & Society*, *29*(10), 1569–1582.

Baruch, Y. & Hall, D.T. (2004) "The Academic Career: A Model for Future Careers in Other Sectors?", *Journal of Vocational Behavior*, *64*(2), 241–262.

Berthoud, R. (2008) "Disability Employment Penalties in Britain", *Work, Employment & Society*, *22*(1), 129–148.

Charmaz, K. (2006) "The Power of Names", *Journal of Contemporary Ethnography*, *35*(4), 396–399.

Colligan, S. (2001) "The Ethnographer's Body as Text and Context: Revisiting and Revisioning the Body through Anthropology and Disability Studies", *Disability Studies Quarterly*, *21*(3), 113–124.

Colligan, S. (1994) "The Ethnographer's Body as Text: When Disability Becomes Other-abling", *Anthropology of Work Review*, *15*(2–3), 5–9.

Davies, C.A. (1997) *Reflexive Ethnography: A Guide to Researching Selves and Others*. London: Routledge.

Deegan, J. M. (2001) "Counting Steps: The Phenomenology of Walking with Variable Mobility", *Disability Studies Quarterly*, *20*(3), 232–242.

Douglas, M. (2002, first published in 1966). *Purity and Danger*. London and New York: Routledge Classics.

Engelsrud, G. (2005) "The Lived Body as Experience and Perspective: Methodological Challenges", *Qualitative Research*, 5(3), 267–284.

Frank, A.W. (2002) *At the Will of the Body: Reflections on Illness*. Boston and New York: Houghton Mifflin Company.

Foster, D. (2012) "Disability in the Labour Market: An Exploration of Concepts of the Ideal Worker and Organisational Fit That Disadvantage Employees with Impairments", *Sociology*, *47*(4), 705–721.

Foster, D. and Fosh, P. (2010) "Negotiating 'Difference': Representing Disabled Employees in the British Workplace", *British Journal of Industrial Relations*, *48*(3), 560–582.

Foster, D. and Wass, V. (2007) "Legal Obligation or Personal Lottery? Employee Experiences of Disability and the Negotiation of Adjustments in the Public Sector Workplace", *Work, Employment & Society*, *21*(1), 67–84.

Haller, B. (2010) *Representing Disability in an Ableist World: Essays on Mass Media*. Louisville: Advocado Press.

Hammersley, M. and Atkinson, P. (2000) *Ethnography: Principles in Practice* (2nd ed.). London and New York: Routledge.

Harding, S. (1992) "Rethinking Standpoint Epistemology: What Is Strong Objectivity?", *The Centennial Review*, *36*(3), 437–470.

Howe, P.D. (2009) "Reflexive Ethnography, Impairments and the Pub", *Leisure Studies*, *28*(4), 489–496.

Karp, D.A. (1996) *Speaking of Sadness: Depression, Disconnection and the Meanings of Illness*. Oxford and New York: Oxford University Press.

Kasnitz, D. and Shuttleworth, R.P. (2001) "Introduction: Disability Studies", *Disability Studies Quarterly*, *21*(3), 2–7.

Kimmerling, B. (2012) *Marginal at the Center: The Life Story of a Public Sociologist*. New York and Oxford: Berghahn Books.

Kitchin, R. (2000) "The Researched Opinions on Research: Disabled People and Disability", *Disability & Society*, *15*(1), 25–47.
Kloos, P. (1987) *Filosofie van de antropologie*. Groningen: Noordhoff Uitgevers [Philosophy of Anthropology].
Mead, M. (2005) *Ruth Benedict: A Humanist in Anthropology*. New York: Columbia University Press.
Michalko, R. (1999) *The Two-in-One: Walking with Smokie, Walking with Blindness*. Philadelphia: Temple University Press.
Mogendorff, K.G. (2002) "Wanneer het vanzelfsprekende niet vanzelf spreekt: Geslaagd omgaan met negatieve beelden, fysieke en sociale barrières", *Medische Antropologie, 14*(-2), 303–320. [When the Taken for Granted Cannot Be Taken for Granted: Strategies to Deal with Negative Images, Physical and Social Barriers].
Mogendorff, K.G. (2007) "Looking in a Mirror: Creating Space to Explore Identities as Persons with Impairments", *Medische Antropologie*, *19*(2), 269–288.
Mogendorff, K.G. (2010) "Doing Frogs and Elephants: Or How Atypical Moving Bodies Are Affected by Predominantly Able-bodies", *Medische Antropologie*, *22*(2), 321–337.
Mogendorff, K.G. (2011) "De invloed van opvoeding op de arbeidsmarktpositie van jongeren met een beperking: Implicaties voor beleid", In: N. Blok (ed.), *Het wassende weten: Opvattingen over de toekomstige arbeidsparticipatie van jongeren met een beperking in een veranderde arbeidsmarkt vanuit verschillende disciplines*, pp. 67–72. Utrecht: Kenniscentrum Crossover. [The Impact of Parenting Style on the Labour Market Position of Young Disabled Adults: Implications for Policy].
Mogendorff, K. (2013) "The Blurring of Boundaries between Research and Everyday Life: Dilemmas of Employing One's Own Experiential Knowledge in Disability Research", *Disability Studies Quarterly*, *33*(2), *Special Topic: Self-reflection as Scholarly Praxis*. (online) Available from: http://dsq-sds.org/article/view/3713/3231
Mughal, M.A.Z. (2015) "Being and Becoming Native: A Methodological Enquiry Into Doing Anthropology at Home", *Anthropological Notebooks*, *21*(1), 121–132.
Murphy, R.F. (1990) *The Body Silent*. London: W.W. Norton.
Nijhof, G. (2001) *Ziekenwerk: Een kleine sociologie van alledaags ziekenleven*. Amsterdam: Aksant. [Translated IEnglish in 2018 as 'Sickness work: Personal reflections of a sociologist'].
Pearson, V., Ip, F., Hui, H., Yip, N. and Ho, K.K. (2003) "To Tell or Not to Tell: Disability Disclosure and Job Application Outcomes", *Journal of Rehabilitation*, *69*(4), 35–38.
Reid-Cunningham, A.R. (2009) "Anthropological Theories of Disability", *Journal of Human Behavior in the Social Environment*, *19*(1), 99–111.
Robillard, A. (1999) *Meaning of a Disability: The Lived Experience of Paralysis*. Philadelphia: Temple University Press.
Roulstone, A., Gradwell, L., Price, J. and Child, L. (2003) *Thriving and Surviving at Work: Disabled People's Employment Strategies*. Bristol: Polity Press.
Roulstone, A. and Williams, J. (2014) "Being Disabled, Being a Manager: 'Glass Partitions' and Conditional Identities in the Contemporary Workplace", *Disability & Society*, *29*(1), 16–29.
Sanders, K.Y. (2006) "Overprotection and Lowered Expectations of Persons with Disabilities: The Unforseen Consequences", *Work: A Journal of Prevention, Assessment and Rehabilitation*, *27*(2), 181–188.
Sayce, L. (2009) *Doing Seniority Differently: A Study of High Flyers Living with Ill Health, Injury or Disability*. London: Radar.

Seymour, W. (2007) "Exhuming the Body: Revisiting the Role of the Visible Body in Ethnographic Research", *Qualitative Health Research, 17*(9), 1188–1197.
Shah, S. (2005) *Career Success of Disabled High Flyers*. London: Jessica Kingsley.
Shah, S. (2006) "Sharing the World: The Researcher and Researched", *Qualitative Research*, 6(2), 207–220.
Shuttleworth, R.P. (2004) "Stigma, Community, Ethnography: Joan Ablon's Contribution to the Anthropology of Impairment-disability", *Medical Anthropology Quarterly, 18*(2), 139–161.
Stone, S.D., Crooks, V.A. and Owen, M. (2013) "Going through the Back Door: Chronically Ill Academics' Experiences as 'unexpected workers'", *Social Theory and Health, 11*(2), 151–174.
Van der Geest, S. (2007) "Is It Possible to Understand Illness and Suffering?", *Medische Antropologie, 19*(1), 9–21.
Van Maanen, J. (1988) *Tales of the Field: On Writing Ethnography*. Chicago: Chicago University Press.
Waterfield, B., Beagan, B.B. and Weinberg, M. (2018) "Disabled Academics: A Case Study in Canadian Universities", *Disability & Society, 33*(3), 327–348.
Williams, J. and Mavin, S. (2015) "Impairment Effects as a Career Boundary: A Case Study of Disabled Academics", *Studies in Higher Education, 40*(1), 123–141.
Wilson-Kovacs, D., Ryan, M., Haslam, A. and Rabinovich, M. (2008) "Just Because You Can Get a Wheelchair in the Building Doesn't Necessarily Mean That You Can Still Participate: Barriers to the Career Advancement of Disabled Professionals", *Disability & Society, 23*(7), 705–717.
Wolbring, G. (2008) "The Politics of Ableism", *Development*, 51, 252–258.
Zola, I.K. (1982) *Missing Pieces: A Chronicle of Living with a Disability*. Philadelphia: Temple University Press.
Zola, I.K. (1996) "Een moeilijk verhaal om te vertellen en te horen: Te boven komen is niet hetzelfde als integreren", In: A. Van Wijnen, Y. Koster-Dreese and A. Oderwald (eds), *Trots en treurnis: Gehandicapt in Nederland*, pp. 16–26. [Translated from: A Story Difficult to Hear and Tell: Overcoming Is Not the Same as Integrating]. Amsterdam: Bayblon-De Geus.

Chapter 4

Dilemmas of self-identification and provision of disability support

Stuart Read, Caroline Miles, and Wendy Merchant

Introduction

As disabled academics, we may need to access a range of support to assist us in our work. We therefore wish to start this chapter with a seemingly simple principle: that academics should be supported so that they are able to engage effectively in their university role. While this principle seems straightforward, and something that many people in society would endorse, it potentially becomes much more complicated and multifaceted for disabled people. In the UK, the ability for disabled academics to access support is grounded in the Equality Act 2010, which ensures that disabled people are protected from receiving less favourable treatment when compared to non-disabled individuals. One principle of the Equality Act 2010 is that all organisations, including universities, must make changes, known as 'reasonable adjustments', to ensure that disabled people do not experience disadvantage. Within academia, examples of reasonable adjustments might include modified working arrangements; accessible office spaces and teaching rooms; or access to disabled parking. However, while this legal framework is in place, disabled academics continue to describe difficulties in accessing reasonable adjustments, or being able to participate fully in the academic environment (e.g. Inckle, 2018). For example, the Equality Act 2010 potentially raises issues for identity, since protections are only in place to the extent that an employer knows, or could be 'expected to know', that an individual is disabled (S15.2). Therefore, in order to be protected under the Equality Act 2010, disabled academics may first have to go through a process of self-identification to their university.

Self-identification in reference to disability means the process that people go through in defining themselves according to their experience of disability (Darling, 2013). Disability self-identification is not a one-off or constant experience, but can instead fluidly change according to personal motivations. For example, some people, even those who acknowledge impairments, may be unwilling to self-identify as disabled (Watson, 2002). Alternatively, others may be motivated to self-identify as disabled due to a sense of disability pride or community (Nario-Redmond and Oleson, 2016), or in order to access reasonable adjustments to allow them to complete their job effectively (Stone, 2013). But deciding to self-identify is also shaped by contextual factors, including, but not limited to, whether and how support is provided by an organisation, and disabled people's identity concerns about how they will be perceived by others (e.g. Jammaers, et al., 2016; Martin, 2017; Stone, et al., 2013). Deciding to self-identify as disabled is, therefore, a complex and problematic process, with academics having to weigh up the potential benefits and costs of self-identification (Brown and Leigh, 2018). In this chapter, we are interested in sharing our thoughts as disabled academics on the process and potential challenges of self-identification in relation to accessing reasonable adjustments, and how university systems can be changed to be more inclusive of diverse needs. We wish to elucidate these points by applying theories of social practice and 'misfitting'. Using these insights allows us to explore and unpick the processes and procedures that shape how academic institutions function, for example, university procedures for providing reasonable adjustments, and, therefore, how staff both contribute to and experience these processes.

Understanding disabling social practices and 'misfitting'

Theories of social practice (e.g. Reckwitz, 2002; Shove, et al., 2012) argue that 'social practices', or the everyday activities people complete, such as going shopping, driving a car, or even attending university, shape, and are shaped by, how things get 'done' in society. Shove, et al. (2012) argue that social practices comprise three separate 'elements': competencies, materials, and meaning. Competence describes the level of knowledge or ability people build up as they carry out a particular social practice. Materials comprise the physical components that make up an individual social practice. Meaning is the understanding or social value that is placed on a social practice, for example, whether a particular behaviour is socially acceptable or unacceptable. These three elements come together to shape how social practices are enacted in society, but also give meaning to individuals about how they should feel and behave in particular situations. To provide a concrete example in relation to universities: competencies could refer to the skills and knowledge learnt at university; materials could describe university buildings or equipment; meaning could be the academic expectations of being a student or member of staff (Webb and Tarleton, 2018).

Social practice theories have great relevance within Disability Studies. We as disabled people experience our impairments, and encounter disability, in numerous and unique ways. When disabled people interact with a particular environment or situation that does not consider our needs, this can lead to a negative or disabling experience. This is what Garland-Thomson (2011) refers to as 'misfitting', or in other words, when individuals fall outside of situations that have been designed and carried out in ways that do not consider diverse needs. Using theories of social practice and misfitting can therefore help social scientists to explain how and why disabled people experience barriers caused by disabling situations (Williams, et al., 2018). Further, by understanding when and why these disabling situations occur, we have an insight into how to promote positive change. As we will argue in this chapter, academia is an environment shaped by rigid social practices that are designed in ways that exclude the contributions of disabled staff. This is true even for university environments that have been seemingly adjusted to remove some of the barriers that we may encounter. For example, Titchkosky (2008) described how accessible toilet facilities in academia may, in reality, not be designed in an accessible way at all. By exploring the social practices of academia, we are not just interested in how situations may be disabling for us as disabled academics, but also what it means for our experiences and how we feel about ourselves.

Coming back to the original principle posed in the Introduction, this chapter will address the problems of accessing academic support from a social practice perspective. We will describe how academic social practices shape disabled people's decisions to access reasonable adjustments, and the potential benefits, costs and repercussions we encounter when making these support decisions. To do this, we will draw on a substantial research project entitled 'Getting Things Changed' (2015–2018), which all the authors of this chapter were involved in. The project attempted to understand, using social practice theories, how disabled people encounter a number of different disabling environments, such as health and social care, and universities, and for disabled people to offer their perspectives on how barriers could be rectified (see Williams, et al., 2018, for more information).

For this chapter, we will focus on the university context, which incorporated collaborative narrative inquiry methodology (Trahar, 2013), centred on understanding how disabled students and staff experience academia (see Merchant, et al., 2020; Williams, et al., 2018). Focusing on disabled staff in particular, we draw on our own experiences as disabled academics, as well as the comments and experiences of other members of the research team, at least seven of whom self-identified as disabled.

We will first express our thoughts and experiences as disabled academics when accessing reasonable adjustments in academia, before moving on to describe how we construct and present our own identities when attempting to navigate the support process, as well as our awareness of the possible difficulties or dilemmas that might be encountered. The experiences that we have included in this chapter are not meant as an attack on any one university, but instead, a means of highlighting the disabling social practices within the academy as a whole. Therefore, through highlighting how processes of self-identification and provision of reasonable adjustments can be navigated, we will also describe our ideas on how disabling university practices may be changed. We will discuss how self-identification can be used to support positive change through our involvement in a university forum for disabled staff, which allows us to share our experiences and collectively challenge disabling practices as a group.

Experiences of accessing reasonable adjustments in academia

As we have discussed previously, as disabled academics we may require reasonable adjustments to allow us to address the barriers that we encounter when working at university. It is perhaps useful then to provide some context about our needs in this chapter. The three authors and their colleagues have personal experience of a number of impairments, such as physical and sensory impairments, learning disabilities, and mental health conditions, and so, reasonable adjustments we have previously requested include, but are not limited to: ensuring that our offices are wheelchair accessible and have automatic doors; provisions of suitable seating; having access to disabled parking and toilet facilities; employment of support workers. We also recognise that disability is not the only factor impacting on us as academics, and naturally, we share other characteristics with other members of staff. For instance, four of our team are women, one of whom has significant caring responsibilities, which can compound the disability-related experiences described in this chapter. Although we are predominantly from white, English backgrounds, we also recognise the compounding factors of culture, religion, and sexuality, which can create complex identity issues for many disabled academics.

While we value the support that has been provided, the process of requesting and accessing reasonable adjustments has at times been fraught with difficulty and frustration. We argue that the underlying cause of many of these issues is due in part to the many disabling social practices that prevent academia from recognising and responding effectively to the needs of disabled staff. In our experiences, we have encountered numerous examples of how understanding or actual provisions of reasonable adjustments are not embedded within the academic system. In particular, rather than universities supporting reasonable adjustments for disabled people to ensure equal and inclusive practices, adjusted support has instead been viewed as unnecessary or 'extra', and which creates a problem for universities to solve (Merchant, et al., 2020). For example, buildings or environments within universities can be inaccessible for many disabled people. We have encountered examples of buildings not being fully wheelchair accessible, or where poor attention has been given to people's sensory needs. Finding rooms or spaces that disabled academics can use safely, therefore, becomes a challenge, which has resulted in university staff having to prioritise rooms, or find alternatives. While these changes are welcomed, they are made entirely because of the requirements of individual people, which leaves disabled staff feeling exposed, and as though we are a burden, and further, creates an obligation for us to attend whichever function has been moved to an accessible venue.

This problematisation of disability and reasonable adjustments can be seen throughout the academic system. Williams, et al. (2018) demonstrated how university processes in place to support disabled students and staff may not work effectively in practice. Our own experiences as disabled academics have demonstrated how individuals within, and outside of, the university setting may not understand the processes required in providing reasonable adjustments. Previous encounters with university staff have revealed an inconsistent understanding of, a) what support is available and from where (e.g. from the university or via external agencies, such as government assistance); b) the process we will have to navigate in order to obtain this support; c) how long the process will take. Indeed, we have experienced delays in provisions of reasonable adjustments due to inconsistent communication or coordination both within the academy and between organisations.

This lack of coordination regarding provisions of reasonable adjustments presents another potential problem for disabled staff, namely, that we are expected to assume responsibility for navigating the procedures necessary to obtain the support we require. While this personal responsibility is not necessarily problematic, as this process is not experienced by non-disabled people, it exemplifies the additional pressures that disabled academics face, and the time we need to invest in obtaining needed support. This is important considering that in the UK and many countries around the world, universities are changing to focus more heavily on staff performance and measurable outcomes, which in turn may promote job requirements for university staff that are increasingly pressurised (Sang, et al., 2015). The changing climate may be particularly felt by disabled academics given the additional barriers we already encounter in terms of accessing support. For example, some disabled academics feel that the working environment of higher education may be unreasonable for their needs or work-life balance, or that they have to make personal sacrifices, such as working additional hours to justify their employment or compensate for their impairment (Brewster, et al., 2017; Wilson-Kovacs, et al., 2008). Even more concerning is that even when we invest additional time, energy, and other resources into obtaining reasonable adjustments, there is still no guarantee that this support will be provided effectively or at all (Martin, 2017).

Bringing all these experiences together, there are a number of potentially disabling social practices which act to negatively shape the extent to which we are able to access reasonable adjustments in academia. We may feel able to make requests for reasonable adjustments, but due to the exclusionary practices of the academy, we may not feel we have the material or psychological resources to take personal responsibility for navigating the support process. This is particularly true if we expect the process to be complex or challenging. The knowledge or resources that university staff and colleagues have regarding the provisions of reasonable adjustments therefore feed into our experiences. If, as our experiences have described, staff do not have the appropriate competence or materials to provide reasonable adjustments (e.g. due to a lack of funding or accessible buildings), then the process is unlikely to be smooth for disabled academics. Should universities experience problems in meeting our needs, this will have the difficult, and potentially unintended, consequence of reinforcing our sense of exclusion, and the barriers that we face.

Self-identification as a disabled academic

Provisions of reasonable adjustments have an added dimension when considering the role of what it means to 'be' a disabled academic. Our self-identities as people are complex and comprise of many different intersecting aspects, such as our gender, race, disability identity, sexual orientation, and our job role (e.g. Martin, 2017). Self-identification as disabled therefore makes up only part of our holistic self, but at the same time, has important implications for how we interact with the university environment, and how other people respond to us. Deciding to self-identify for the purposes of support therefore requires careful consideration of the potentially disabling social practices that we will likely need to navigate. These include what self-identification means for our personal sense of self, as well as our understanding of the contextual implications that may arise should we decide to self-identify.

Provisions of support are typically granted by universities or other support providers, but only after an extensive assessment process, where an individual's impairment and need for support is documented and scrutinised. Self-identification in these contexts is therefore often essential to the support process so that support providers can understand our disability and needs (Brown and Leigh, 2018). However, the process of self-identifying for the purposes of support is costly for a number of reasons. In particular, the very nature of self-identification means that we are having to share more of ourselves than would be typically expected of staff who do not identify as disabled. This can lead to difficult and uncomfortable conversations where we are sharing potentially very personal information about ourselves, and why we require support. Indeed, the process of accessing support can cause disabled people to feel that their identities are marked as 'different' to non-disabled individuals (Read, et al., 2015). Unsurprisingly then, Martin shared how disabled academics felt that the process of self-identification can be 'unhelpful, clunky, emotionally draining, dangerous and not inclusive' (2017: 17). This is particularly important to consider given that self-identification for the purposes of support access is not a singular event, but may be required even multiple times a day in the academic environment.

Yet, simply self-identifying one's need for reasonable adjustments in academia alone is rarely sufficient. Instead, self-identification becomes a complex performance, where we must decide how we self-identify, and the content that we share about ourselves, to meet the requirements of disabling university systems. The process of accessing support within academia is often deficit-focused and, therefore, assesses the difficulties we face as academics rather than how we can be best supported. The content of our self-identification, therefore, has to align with the requirements of assessments or procedures, which, in turn, may mean we are describing our needs in negative ways, and counter to how we personally see ourselves, and how we wish to be seen by others. For example, we want to be judged on our merits and the skills we bring to academia as disabled staff, not by the perceived issues our employment may cause. We want our self-expression to be authentic, and which describes our expertise and contributions as academics, but instead we have to describe ourselves in ways that highlight how we are struggling. However, at the same time, if we present ourselves in ways that describe our 'struggles' too significantly, it risks us feeling concerned about how we will be viewed by others. In other words, we have to ensure an identity expression that carefully manages our needs as disabled people, as well as the subsequent responses from others we may be exposed to as a result.

Having to explain our support needs in this way means that the process of disability self-identification raises a number of issues in terms of how disabled academics will be perceived by non-disabled individuals. In particular, disabled people may be exposed to numerous negative attitudes in the workplace (e.g. around assumed incapability for work; Louvet, 2007; Ren, et al., 2008). These attitudes also exist within universities, with Stone and colleagues (2013) reporting how disabled academics have encountered prejudicial attitudes regarding their perceived suitability for careers in academia. Stone and colleagues (2013) also described how these attitudes can interfere with how reasonable adjustments will be viewed or provided, with one of their participants describing being negatively compared with other disabled individuals who supposedly required less support. Other authors have suggested that reasonable adjustments may only be provided when the nature of the request does not interfere with the standard social practices of the academy. For example, Riddell and Weedon (2014) described how lecturers spoke of wanting to ensure that disabled students received the reasonable adjustments they required. However, at the same time, Riddell and Weedon (2014) also described how individual lecturers had potential concerns about whether the needs of certain disabled students could potentially interfere with the expected requirements of their future careers. We argue that disabled staff are held to these same assumptions regarding our ability to be academics – that is, we have to meet certain measures of academic excellence regardless of whether we access reasonable adjustments. We may therefore have to navigate our self-identification around concerns about how our requests for reasonable adjustments may be judged by our non-disabled colleagues in relation to our suitability for academia.

Concerns around identity expression are equally evident, and can take on an interesting dynamic, within the context of Disability Studies in ways that may not necessarily be evident in other academic disciplines. While Disability Studies scholars, such as the team involved in our 'Getting Things Changed' project, have generally been supportive of our self-identification as disabled staff, and in ensuring our support needs are met, at times, we still encounter issues. In particular, we still have to explain and justify our needs to others, particularly to individuals who may not self-identify as disabled. Further, raising our needs in this way does not necessarily mean that support will be provided, such as due to the wider disabling academic systems and procedures that we have previously described. We are therefore exposed to an ironic situation of both being part of a subject that supports furthering the rights and inclusion of disabled people in academia (Connor, et al., 2008) and having to fit in with a broader academic culture that may restrict our ability to participate.

Aside from these potential attitudinal and structural barriers, within the university context, should we decide to self-identify to access reasonable adjustments, there is a possibility that we will 'become' the disability label. A potential conflict in 'becoming' a disabled member of staff is that others may view us entirely through a disability lens. For example, Williams-Findlay stated how '[i]t's often assumed that by having an impairment or the label 'disabled' thrust upon you, you become part of a specific community with a distinct culture – this is far from the case' (2011: 776). This means that we might experience uncertainty over whether we are being seen in ways that reflect the academic, professional self that we wish to portray.

This 'becoming' can again have an additional relevance and meaning within Disability Studies that may not be present in other academic disciplines. For instance, Campbell (2009) described how self-identification within Disability Studies may be advantageous, as disabled academics are able to provide lived experiences to contextualise issues, as well as become activists for social change. However, at the same time, Campbell (2009) described how our disability identity becoming visible can have unintended consequences, such as increasing our sense of marginalisation, through being treated and responded to in ways that are dissimilar to our non-disabled colleagues.

Finally, as university staff will likely become more aware of a disabled person's identity following self-identification, this may place additional requirements on disabled staff which we might not have expected, and which will need to be navigated as part of our identity expression. For example, disabled academics may be asked to help educate staff on the process of requesting and accessing reasonable adjustments. Also, disabled staff may be expected to support university requests that are irrelevant or unconnected to accessing reasonable adjustments. Within the context of Disability Studies, for example, we may be asked to share personal stories for teaching and research purposes, particularly to help other non-disabled staff members; or to participate and speak on issues around supporting diversity and inclusive practices. While we welcome opportunities to influence change, all of these additional expectations again highlight how we may be required to share more of our personal self, or invest more time and energy, than would typically be expected of members of staff who do not self-identify as disabled.

In sum, what we are suggesting in this section is that social practices of the academy can actively shape how and to what extent disabled people choose to self-identify. Disability self-identification, therefore, requires a clear contextual understanding of what our needs and motivations are, as well as how we will be viewed and responded to by the academy. It is, therefore, perhaps unsurprising that disabled academics may express reluctance in self-identifying due to feelings of stigma or concerns regarding potential repercussions, such as negative attitudes from fellow academic colleagues (e.g. Brown and Leigh, 2018; Emira, et al., 2018). This is equally true for self-identifying to access reasonable adjustments, particularly if disabled people feel the process will be problematic or intrusive (e.g. Inckle, 2018; Martin, 2017; Stone, et al., 2013).

Disability dilemmas of accessing support and being an academic

Taken together, we as disabled academics have two parallel motivations when accessing reasonable adjustments. The first is ensuring that we are able to receive the right support to allow us to complete our academic roles. The second is ensuring that we are able to view and express our identities in academia in authentic ways. Ideally, both of these motivations will be realised, in that we should be able to access appropriate support, whilst also being valued by our institution and colleagues. In reality, the disabling social practices encountered by disabled staff may mean that achieving these two motivations come with costs, and potentially even contradictory implications or outcomes. Disabled academics, therefore, have to navigate difficult dilemmas in deciding whether to self-identify and/or access reasonable adjustments. For example, like all staff working in academia, as disabled academics, we want our competencies and experience to be acknowledged and supported. Therefore, we are requesting reasonable adjustments so that we can succeed in the academic environment without having to worry about potential barriers and also experience equality with other academics. However, the process of requesting reasonable adjustments is in itself a barrier, as it requires significant personal and material investment. Additional barriers may come about due to the disabling university support processes that we are having to navigate, such as by experiencing unnecessary delays or problems in accessing reasonable adjustments, due to universities or other connected organisations not being coordinated effectively. This means that disabled academics may ironically feel more disabled and excluded by going through the process of accessing reasonable adjustments, particularly if our experience is negative. Provisions of reasonable adjustments themselves, if provided, also seek to heighten differences between disabled and non-disabled people, particularly if individuals do not appreciate the meaning or importance of why this support has been provided (e.g. Read, et al., 2018).

The self-identification process itself also promotes difference in that our disability identity may become central to interactions with others, regardless of whether we would like it to be so. Our skills and competencies as academics, or other valued parts of ourselves that we wish to show to others may, therefore, become masked by our disability identity. This becomes more concerning if others do not understand our contributions, or view our contributions through a disability label – particularly as this label may be associated with negative stereotypes and assumptions (e.g. Louvet, 2007; Ren, et al., 2008). By deciding to self-identify in this way, we may be exposing ourselves to unwanted negativity or attention. This takes on additional meaning when navigating the process of accessing reasonable adjustments. We may be required to self-identify as disabled people to others, such as to colleagues or managers, which potentially privileges our disabled identity over (or at the expense of) our professional, academic, identity. We may even have to describe ourselves, and our needs, according to the barriers that we may be facing, so that the support we are requesting can be justified, which further undermines the authenticity of our identity.

What these examples highlight is that we as disabled academics have to understand the contextual demands of the social practices that are present in particular circumstances, so that we can navigate these situations effectively. Said differently, in order for disabled academics to decide to undertake the process of self-identification within the academic environment, there needs to be a meaningful reason or benefit for doing so. If we are exposed to problematic labelling from staff or organisations, this makes the process of self-identification unnecessarily challenging, and may even act as a disadvantage. Similarly, if we feel the process of requesting reasonable adjustments is too negative, complex, or resource-intensive, we may choose not to self-identify or avoid accessing the support we need to allow us to fulfil our academic roles. The possible issue to such a strategy, however, is that this may result in denying ourselves equal treatment, and may further the barriers and difficulties that we experience (e.g. Wilton, 2006). As this outcome is not ideal, we therefore potentially need to tailor our disability identity expression according to the situation we are in, so that we achieve the most optimal outcome (e.g. Stone, 2013).

Supporting change

Given the issues that we have highlighted in the previous sections regarding the dilemmas that disabled academics may encounter, an important question needs to be asked about how to better promote and ensure inclusive environments within universities. From a social practice argument, disabling encounters exist simply as a reflection of how society 'does things'. Therefore, social practices that exclude disabled people are not inherently negative, nor are they impermeable to change (Williams, et al., 2018). For social practices to be changed in ways that promote a more inclusive environment, universities must first critically reflect on how they function as organisations, and, therefore, how their conventional practices may be exclusionary. In order to understand their ways of working, universities must engage fully with disabled staff. This of course begins with universities providing disabled academics with opportunities for our voices to be heard. While this can be achieved in a number of ways, we wish to discuss the importance of disability forums. Specifically, we are part of a university disability forum which is open to, and led by, disabled staff. The purpose of this group is to provide peer support to disabled staff through listening and sharing experiences with others in similar situations and to support the academy to become more inclusive.

We have received support from the forum in helping us to manage the concerns that we encounter as staff regarding accessing reasonable adjustments, and managing our self-identification. In terms of accessing reasonable adjustments, our 'Getting Things Changed' research demonstrated how disabled staff feel isolated and alone when navigating the support process (Merchant, et al., 2020). Being part of a staff disability forum has, therefore, been influential for us by providing opportunities to receive and share information on the reasonable adjustments that are available. We have also discussed potential strategies that we could enact should we decide to request and access adjusted support. This includes support from not just within the academy, but also external providers, such as financial assistance from the government.

In terms of supporting our identities as disabled academics, the group has allowed us to network with other disabled members of staff. Seeing others 'like us' and who have similar experiences to our own, provides a sense of validation. We are able to discuss the conflicts in our identities as disabled people and academics, and how these can be potentially navigated. Raising these collective experiences and issues in a safe space has also provided us with a sense of agency and empowerment that as disabled people, we should be able to fight for equal rights and treatment.

From a social practice argument, what we are suggesting here is forums that are created and led by disabled staff can result in positive changes in challenging standard university processes. Forums can promote a sense of competence for disabled staff to advocate for our rights, but also, benefit universities through providing opportunities for sharing of disability issues and understanding the changes that are needed. For example, if universities are able to see the value in providing reasonable adjustments (i.e. meanings), this may promote a more positive experience or outcome for disabled staff. However, for disabled staff forums to work in practice, both for disabled people and for the wider academy, clarity is needed regarding how universities will support change. We advocate that sole responsibility for changing social practices should not be assigned to disabled people as this risks reinforcing the sense of misfitting that disabled staff already experience. Instead, there needs to be a meaningful and collaborative openness between the academy and its disabled staff, which requires individual universities to recognise the importance and value of its diverse workforce. To do this, universities have to move away from medical model approaches to disability, where disabled people are seen as problems and burdens (much like the experiences described in this chapter), to a social model (Oliver, 2013). By taking a social model stance to disability, universities will be able to take a critical look at how disabling social practices with their organisations have become embedded, and, therefore, how these can be changed to become more inclusive (Merchant, et al., 2020). In many cases, the disabling nature of existing social practices may not be immediately obvious, particularly for members of staff who do not identify as disabled. This is why it is important for universities to take all opportunities to effectively and thoroughly engage with disabled staff forums. Moreover, taking a social model stance to disability shows disabled staff that we are being listened to and that we are valuable assets to our institution.

A social model perspective in academia is important when considering the dilemmas that we as disabled people encounter when deciding to self-identify to access reasonable adjustments. If universities decide to advocate for and emphasise the positive contributions that disabled staff can make, this can potentially have powerful implications for how we choose to express our identities. In terms of accessing reasonable adjustments, rather than this process being viewed as unnecessary and a disability 'problem', universities can instead shape a narrative (i.e. meaning) where all staff are encouraged to access support (regardless of whether they self-identify as disabled or not). Universities can then meet this culture shift through, a) ensuring that the right support is provided for all members of staff;

b) the support process is authentic to staff members' individual needs; c) that all of its workforces recognise and are respectful to the fact that disabled people may require additional support. Universities can further demonstrate this commitment by providing as standard, reasonable adjustments which many disabled people commonly require (e.g. ensuring that all of their buildings are wheelchair accessible). In terms of what it means to be a disabled academic, if universities recognise the skills and qualities that disabled people bring to the academy, this may encourage staff to feel confident about self-identifying, as well as feeling that we have control over how we express ourselves. This can be reinforced further by universities educating their staff on the importance of diversity and inclusivity. In sum, what we are suggesting is that the dilemmas around support and identity that we experience as disabled staff may be reduced, or even removed, if the social practices of universities were redesigned in ways that supported, rather than excluded, disabled people's needs.

Concluding comments

In this chapter we sought to explain through our personal thoughts and experiences as disabled academics, the dilemmas we face in both accessing reasonable adjustments to ensure that we are able to participate equally with our non-disabled colleagues, and also ensuring the integrity of our professional identity. While the Equality Act 2010 is in place to support disabled academics, our problems in accessing reasonable adjustments highlight that universities may not be implementing this policy effectively. From a social practice argument, such problems arise when practices are created and shaped without awareness of disabled people's needs. Questions such as what reasonable adjustments 'look like' for disabled people and why they are important, and what it means to 'be' a disabled academic, may not typically be discussed in universities. The lack of thought around such questions exemplifies the exclusionary practices that we as disabled academics encounter, and why change is needed. Therefore, thinking about reasonable adjustments and self-identification using theories of social practices can help the academy understand how it supports the inclusion of its disabled staff, and what this means for disabled people's sense of self. What we are proposing is that in order to address the dilemmas that disabled academics encounter, the social practices that encourage and reinforce exclusion need to be redesigned in ways that include and understand the positive contributions of disabled people.

Acknowledgements

This chapter was supported by a grant from the Economic and Social Research Council entitled 'Tackling Disabling Practices: Co-production and Change'; grant number: ES/M008339/1. We would like to thank other members of the 'Getting Things Changed' team who shared their experiences with us that we drew upon in this chapter.

References

Brown, N. and Leigh, J. (2018) "Ableism in academia: Where are the disabled and ill academics?", *Disability & Society*, *33*(6), 985–989.
Brewster, S., Duncan, N., Emira, M. and Clifford, A. (2017) "Personal sacrifice and corporate cultures: Career progression for disabled staff in higher education", *Disability & Society*, *32*(7), 1027–1042.
Campbell, F. K. (2009) "Having a career in disability studies without even becoming disabled! The strains of the disabled teaching body", *International Journal of Inclusive Education*, 13(7), 713–725.
Connor, D. J., Gabel, S. L., Gallagher, D. J. and Morton, M. (2008) "Disability studies and inclusive education – implications for theory, research, and practice", *International Journal of Inclusive Education*, *12*(5–6), 441–457.
Darling, R. B. (2013). *Disability and identity: Negotiating self in a changing society*. Boulder, CO: Lynne Rienner Publishers.
Emira, M., Brewster, S., Duncan, N. and Clifford, A. (2018) "What disability? I am a leader! Understanding leadership in HE from a disability perspective", *Educational Management Administration & Leadership*, *46*(3), 457–473.
Equality Act (2010) London: The Stationery Office.
Garland-Thomson, R. (2011) "Misfits: A feminist materialist disability concept", *Hypatia*, *26*(3), 591–609.
Inckle, K. (2018) "Unreasonable adjustments: The additional unpaid labour of academics with disabilities", *Disability & Society*, *33*(8), 1372–1376.
Jammaers, E., Zanoni, P. and Hardonk, S. (2016) "Constructing positive identities in ableist workplaces: Disabled employees' discursive practices engaging with the discourse of lower productivity", *Human Relations*, 69(6), 1365–1386.
Louvet, E. (2007) "Social judgment toward job applicants with disabilities: Perception of personal qualities and competences", *Rehabilitation Psychology*, 52(3), 297–303.
Martin, N. (2017) *Encouraging disabled leaders in higher education: Recognising hidden talents*. London: Leadership Foundation for Higher Education.
Merchant, W., Read, S., D'Evelyn, S., Miles, C., and Williams, V. (2020) "The insider view: Tackling disabling practices in higher education institutions", Higher Education, 80(2), 273–287.
Nario-Redmond, M. R., and Oleson, K. C. (2016) "Disability group identification and disability-rights advocacy: Contingencies among emerging and other adults", *Emerging Adulthood*, 4(3), 207–218.
Oliver, M. (2013) "The social model of disability: Thirty years on", *Disability & Society*, *28*(7), 1024–1026.
Read, S. A., Morton, T. A. and Ryan, M. K. (2015) "Negotiating identity: A qualitative analysis of stigma and support seeking for individuals with cerebral palsy", *Disability and Rehabilitation*, *37*(13), 1162–1169.
Read, S., Williams, V., Heslop, P., Mason-Angelow, V. and Miles, C. (2018) "Being a disabled patient: Negotiating the social practices of hospitals in England", *Social Inclusion*, 6(2), 74–82.
Reckwitz, A. (2002) "Toward a theory of social practices: A development in culturalist theorizing", *European Journal of Social Theory*, 5(2), 243–263.
Ren, L. R., Paetzold, R. L. and Colella, A. J. (2008) "A Meta-analysis of experimental studies on the effects of disability on human resource judgments", *Human Resource Management Review*, *18*(3), 191–203.

Riddell, S. and Weedon, E. (2014) "Disabled students in higher education: Discourses of disability and the negotiation of identity", *International Journal of Educational Research*, 63, 38–46.

Sang, K., Powell, A., Finkel, R. and Richards, J. (2015) "Being an academic is not a 9–5 Job: Long working hours and the 'ideal worker' in UK academia", *Labour & Industry*, *25*(3), 235–249.

Shove, E., Pantzar, M. and Watson, M. (2012) *The dynamics of social practice: Everyday life and how it changes*. London: Sage Publications.

Stone, S. D. (2013) "The situated nature of disability", In: Cutchin, M.P. and Dickie, V.A. (eds.) *Transactional perspectives on occupation*. New York: Springer. pp. 95–106.

Stone, S. D., Crooks, V. A. and Owen, M. (2013) "Going through the back door: Chronically ill academics' experiences as 'unexpected workers'", *Social Theory & Health*, *11*(2), 151–174.

Titchkosky, T. (2008) "'To pee or not to pee?' Ordinary talk about extraordinary exclusions in a university environment", *Canadian Journal of Sociology*, *33*(1), 37–60.

Trahar, S. (2013) *Contextualising narrative inquiry: Developing methodological approaches for local contexts*. Oxford: Routledge.

Watson, N. (2002) "Well, I know this is going to sound very strange to you, but I don't see myself as a disabled person: Identity and disability", *Disability & Society*, *17*(5), 509–527.

Webb, J. and Tarleton, B. (2018) *Getting things changed: Social practices booklet*. Bristol: University of Bristol.

Williams, V., Tarleton, B., Heslop, P., Porter, S., Sass, B., Blue, S., Merchant, W. and Mason-Angelow, V. (2018) "Understanding disabling barriers: A fruitful partnership between disability studies and social practices?", *Disability & Society*, *33*(2), 157–174.

Williams-Findlay, R. (2011) "Lifting the lid on disabled people against cuts", *Disability & Society*, *26*(6), 773–778.

Wilson-Kovacs, D., Ryan, M. K., Haslam, S. A. and Rabinovich, A. (2008) "'Just because you can get a wheelchair in the building doesn't necessarily mean that you can still participate': Barriers to the career advancement of disabled professionals", *Disability & Society*, *23*(7), 705–717.

Wilton, R. (2006) "Disability disclosure in the workplace", *Just Labour: A Canadian Journal of Work and Society*, 8(Spring), 24–39.

Part 2

Conducting research 'in the field'

Chapter 5

The continuing adventures of a four-legged female academic researcher

Nancy Hansen

Introduction

There is a certain social comfort level acquired by engaging in traditional practices, (whatever they may be) in a manner accepted by those in power. The world of academic research is no exception. I am a four-legged academic researcher (using crutches for mobility). The presence of non-conformist physicality (in whatever form) often disrupts established research practices of the academy. Similarly, the *effort* required simply to undertake research is usually unrecognised. My speed, space, time and energy realities can be different from my-non-disabled counterparts which may necessitate organising my daily life and research activities in different ways. The traditional research dynamic is slow within and outside the academy. The places and spaces of knowledge-production and in particular 'valued' knowledge are changing. Academic research, approach, subject and methodology are adapting. Areas are examined that until recently have had limited (if any) analysis. Long-established fixed physical and attitudinal boundaries are slowly becoming more fluid in part, owing largely to the presence of disabled researchers. This chapter documents and celebrates the creativity needed to navigate these unexpected places and spaces through the front line experiences of a disabled researcher.

Laying the groundwork

Where does the researcher's body *fit* in academic research? (Dolmage, 2017). In traditional research it is as if the body of the researcher is a non-entity (Brown and Boardman, 2011). It would seem there is a level of bodily arrogance at work here in that there is the assumption that all researcher's bodies are the same and do not factor into the research equation (Dolmage, 2017). Although researchers have discussed and studied bodies of difference, (racialised, Indigenous, gender, LGBTQ, and to a certain extent disability and/or impairment) (Kobayashi, 1994), until comparatively recently, there has been a level of silence concerning the space and place of the body in research (Hansen and Philo, 2007). There has been, which can best be described as a 'colonial' 'corrective' approach to the disabled body as defective and in need of 'adjustment' and 'tutoring' in the ways of non-disability (Hansen, 2009). With the growth of the social model (examining physical and social barriers as opposed to 'defects' related to what is traditionally attributed to disability and the disabled body), the relationship between disabled people and researchers has evolved somewhat in that research partnerships are more common (Oliver, 1990; Stone and Priestley, 1996). However, the academy has yet to develop a comfort level with the presence of disabled researchers (Titchkosky, 2011; Dolmage, 2017).

Disabled researchers have always been present in the Academy. However, our acceptance remains tentative (Hansen, 2018). It is as if our presence somehow compromises the elite perception of the institution (Dolmage, 2017). The academic research establishment tends to view research involving marginalised bodies or population groups, particularly disabled people, as somewhat exceptional and on the margins of legitimate academic research (Kobayashi, 1994; Sibley, 1995; Chouinard and Grant, 1997). To some degree, it can be argued that this type of research has been marginalised in much the same fashion (Zarb, 1992; Stone and Priestley, 1996). Disabled researchers are slowly shifting research space. The work of Reg Golledge, a human geographer with a vision impairment, is an early example and his efforts put disability in geography and academic 'space (Golledge, 1993; Hansen, 2002). Similarly, Gerald Gold, an anthropologist and wheelchair user changed the location and nature of the 'field' itself, in that his desktop computer provided access to the 'field' and the 'field' itself is virtual enabling much greater ease of access for both the disabled researcher and participants (Gold, 2003).

Building new roads finding new paths

I have a mobility disability and I have proudly used crutches my entire life. However, despite my disability pride, I had never written myself into the research script until I began writing my PhD (Hansen, 2002). I had never allowed the realities of my own disability to enter into the research process itself. I do not associate disability with 'fault' and, yet, I did view it as solely my responsibility to 'manage'. If I had ever discussed coordination or fine motor skills even though I was never ashamed of my coordination differences, there remained an unspoken fear that my provisional status as an academic researcher would suddenly be withdrawn. A strange form of dissonance indeed. Therefore, an inability to 'independently manage' my disability might somehow be perceived as a lack of 'professionalism' on my part. Consequently, I had internalised the belief that, as a disabled researcher studying disability, I dared not get too close to the subject matter so as not to lose my objectivity.

The explicit, written acknowledgement of my disability was a milestone for me. I do not wish to dismiss the very real physical mobility, access and restriction in motor (writing/typing) speed realities that are present with my disability. I did not wish to be constrained by the physical processing requirements of the field research that I could not manage without physical and administrative assistance. I had finally figured out that obtaining assistance typing my field interviews was not an admission of lack of ability or 'coping' skills. Using crutches and having impacted fine motor coordination, time is a genuine concern for me as the nature of my disability (cerebral palsy) is such that any physical activity takes significantly more time and effort than it would for a non-disabled researcher. To that end, I began a process that I had never undergone before, exploring my own human geography as a disabled researcher undertaking field research (Hansen, 2002). Perhaps because I did not want to appear too *close* to the subject matter and thereby compromise my 'professionalism'. Thankfully when I began my fieldwork my thinking on the subject had evolved considerably. Coming out of the disability research *closet* if you will, was profoundly liberating, (it should be noted that disabled researchers do not necessarily study disability). Being able to explore in a substantive manner the realities of having a disability or impairment in the field brings an added realism and engagement with the subject matter. As a disabled researcher, I take great pleasure in documenting and dissecting elements of research space at a micro-level highlighting the various environmental complexities that I and my research partner-participants encounter. In a very real sense, I am in effect 'living' my research. I am an 'outsider' and an 'insider' at the same time. For disabled researchers, reflexivity is not an abstract theoretical concept, we are often a part of or experience that which we study (Hansen, 2002). I do believe that my experience as a disabled woman enables me to establish a level of credibility and trustworthiness with the people I interview (Moss, 1999). I am not engaging in 'disability tourism' or studying disability as a type of voyeurism or because of some type of funding availability (Hansen and Philo, 2007). We share many of the day-to-day realities of having a disability in Western society. Also, my knowledge of disability issues and involvement with the disability rights movement gives further integrity to the valorisation of and commitment to an understanding of the subject matter (McFarlane and Hansen, 2007).

I readily admit that my background has given me more opportunities and options than many. I am white, straight, I come from an upper-middle-class family and my mobility impairment (use of crutches) is such that I can *fit* into these research spaces to a certain degree. However, this 'fitness' comes with a strict caveat that I am 'allowed' such options insofar as the perimeters established by the non-disabled majority (Hansen, 2002). I have had a few disabled research mentors in my academic research career. Indeed, for many years the writings of bell hooks, the African American, feminist academic and disabled feminists Rosemary Garland-Thomson, Susan Wendell and Vera Chouinard provided comfort, a familiarity in the 'voice' of similar experiences (hooks, 1982; Wendell, 1996; Chouinard, 1997; Garland-Thomson, 1997). Much of what I have read over the years relating to research methodology is alarming. Phrases such as 'going native' or the characterisation of participant behaviours as 'bazaar' is illustrative of xenophobic, ableist, colonial understandings that frequently imbue traditional research practices (Burgess, 1993).

A disabled person's interaction with the mainstream world is often fraught with 'adventure' as we move through everyday spaces, not of our making (Hansen, 2008). Seemingly mundane aspects of daily life such as riding an elevator/ lift or going through airport security have morphed into interesting research opportunities although this was not the original intention (Hansen and Driedger, 2010). Hence, I almost always have a small notebook at hand.

I am always profoundly aware of my own 'positionality', and take great pains to keep it in check so as not to impose on or influence unduly the individuals that I interview. However, perhaps this was a result of the process of the interview itself, providing an 'understanding space' of mental and emotional 'safety and awareness' in which to express themselves and just as importantly be 'understood'. Owing to my life experience interviewees do not have to set the 'information stage' to the same extent as a non-disabled researcher might require. Although writing one's self into one's work is a long-established tradition amongst feminist writers, I approach this element with some degree of reservation (Moss, 1999; Thomas, 1999). After all, if I am interviewing disabled people about their experience of disability and impairment, it is only reasonable that I am upfront about my own. Realistically, when I arrive using wooden crutches, I have identifiable 'hardware' that provide the established cultural markers of disability. However, I have no desire to cross the line between including relevant biographical elements and descending into the depths of the personal confessional (Moss, 1999).

I understand that there are different embodiments of disability and impairment but only insofar as the participants themselves wish to discuss them. I am happy to perplex the reader by not knowing myself what the participant's impairment is. In my view, it serves no purpose, other than to engage in some form of socially primitive voyeurism further 'othering' in the process. For this reason, impairment is not dealt with in any diagnostic detail.

Before I begin any field research, I must quite literally work out the micro mechanics of the various field elements of the information gathering process. Discussing my access requirements with my research partners, disabled and non-disabled alike, is made possible only because of a high level of trust and excellent rapport. Without this substantive support, my own silence on the micro-details of timing and spacing would have been maintained; these crucial factors engendered the confidence in me to discuss fieldwork research issues.

As a disabled woman studying disability issues, I became acutely aware that most research on the subject of disability is de-gendered, referring almost solely to disabled people with few, if any, references to distinctions between disabled men or women, let alone any other factors. More disturbing, however, is the fixation on the personal mechanics of disability, that is, focusing on the individualised mental or physical difference which is almost dehumanising. The hegemonic 'knowledge' of functional capacity and representations of disability are often framed in the 'discomfort zone' of the non-disabled; this approach contributes to the 'remoteness' and othering often experienced by disabled people in traditional academic research (Oliver and Barnes, 1997).

I find fieldwork demanding. Travelling to 'the field' was not always easy for me, climbing on and off aeroplanes, trains and in and out of taxis leave their mark, quite literally in the form of muscle pulls and bruised shins. Furthermore, the speed of research is changing as the nature of research becomes increasingly bureaucratic and business-oriented, focused on throughput (Berg and Seeber, 2016). Added to that is my ever-present concern of being 'on time' for the participants I interview which highlighted my own issues with pace of movement and getting around areas with which I may be unfamiliar. Some days I am able to complete multiple interviews, while at other times I complete far fewer. I regularly find the pace quite hectic and despite having enjoyed the actual interviews, I am often physically and mentally exhausted just organising myself. Fieldwork is an exciting prospect, however, but the ableist tenets of the process (a standard of non-disability) itself assume the indulgence of ease of access that is often remote to many researchers with physical disabilities (Tregaskis, 2004). Researchers in Disability Studies have noted that speed and timing take on much greater significance when disability enters the picture and that is rarely understood by funding agencies focused on the end result (Stone and Priestley, 1996).

Places for interviews vary according to the preferences of the people I interview, which could be workplaces, homes, restaurants and coffee shops. At times, I have had to find a location that meets both of our access requirements. Many participants I interview are not used to having the option of deciding where, when and how interviews are done (Hansen, 2009). As a point of interest, where funding is provided, added costs of accessibility are largely not covered by funding agencies, and I regularly cover costs out of my own pocket (Stone and Priestley, 1996). I want these participants to know that I value their time and input and that I genuinely want to hear what they have to say. It substantively illustrates respect at a fundamental level. I buy a beverage, a snack or a meal. The participant's time and knowledge have value. Financial remuneration is rarely possible owing to lack of funding.

For me, the fieldwork is enjoyable, if at times physically and emotionally taxing, forcing me to engage with, develop further and refine my own organisational skills, again underscoring at a micro-level the idiosyncrasies of my non-conformist body. Transportation and physical accessibility requirements dictate that I need to be acutely aware of my surroundings even though I may be in unfamiliar spaces. The presence of non-conformist physicality often disrupts established comfortable practices simply by being there (Brown and Boardman, 2011).

Disability issues are rarely at the centre of funding agencies research agendas. Online funding applications are usually massive requiring hours of typing, and they frequently 'time-out' with no 'saving' option (not being able to save typed work) and limited possibility of uptake. Consequently, my research work though published is rarely funded. I develop research projects drawn from observations and experiences in the spaces and places where disabled people find themselves or where disability is found (Oliver and Barnes, 1997). We work along the margins and in the residual spaces and places that mainstream academia is largely unaware of or has overlooked (Hansen and Philo, 2007) Many of my research projects do not start out as such but rather evolve in that direction looking at the social-political impact of a pair of fashion-forward red and black crutches that were originally envisioned as a simple wardrobe accessory (Hansen and Driedger, 2010). Furthermore, smaller research projects enable me to have more control over the research process space and use my energy, speed, space and time parameters to the best advantage (Hansen and Driedger, 2010).

Adventures in fieldwork

Often, there are subtle and at times not so subtle normative cues that dictate who belongs and is expected in research space. Venturing out into the field is often akin to being a stranger in a strange land (Hansen and Philo, 2007). Disabled researchers work together in order to support and facilitate each other adapting and to some extent revamping as we go (Hansen, 2018). Indeed, there are times when funders have specifically sought out disabled researchers for their insight, knowledge base or skill set (Driedger and Hansen. 2014). At other times, working with my non-disabled colleagues, their physicality has been instrumental in enabling me to access inaccessible field interview locations (Byrne, Mizzi and Hansen, 2017). What follows as examples are personal reflections of my adventures from 'the field'. I relate these experiences not to engender pity, sympathy, visions of struggle, bravery or pluckiness, rather, to illustrate some of the ableist expectations built into the research process itself and the many ways in which we as disabled researchers must continually adapt, rethink and reconstruct the research landscape in which we find ourselves (Brown and Boardman, 2011).

A trip to an archives building is a case in point. Built in 2011, this is a modern building. However, the wheelchair access ramp is at the side of the building. There are no windows to the inside and the ramp itself is largely removed from public view. The ramp itself is massive and lengthy. One has a full workout even before entering the building. High-gloss tiles are located just beyond the sliding front doors which are very slippery when dry and even more so when wet. It seems an odd choice given the rainy climate of the place where the building is located.

There are no seats in the lobby save the one where researcher identification photos are taken. Archive protocol specified that all my belongings had to be stored in a locker (again there are no chairs in this area but a security guard was able to find one for me). I am allowed to carry my notebook in a clear plastic bag provided to all visitors. The security guard carries the bag for me and we take the elevator (lift), up from the ground to the first floor. It is important to note that all public toilets are located on the ground floor. The toilet is also covered with slippery tiles.

Archival document searches are carried out on the first floor at one end of the building and retrievals take place at the other. The security guard asked an archive librarian if I can do both in one place and he is told this is not possible. We walk to the opposite end of the building. To open the door, I must press a small green button wave my ID and walk to the other end of the hallway to the lift elevator. I must wave my ID at a certain angle for the doors to open, not a straightforward task while using crutches. I felt rather like a gymnast. The archive computers are located at the opposite end of the room. I must type in the ID code that is printed on the lanyard around my neck into the computer every 15 minutes or I will lose my research. I enquire about taking a printout, but I am told this is not usually done and they make an exception for me from a printer that is located away from public view. I make note of other references and decide to leave as I do not want to get stuck or caught short making my way to the toilet. I get up to leave with my locker keys and notebook, and it is very awkward. Although I was able to obtain the information required, I felt *handicapped* by the whole process. There appears to be very little flexibility in this process and no concept of diversity of researchers and the lack of creativity is frustrating. It is clear that non-conformist bodies are not expected in this space.

A research visit to an historic site presented another set of interesting situations. I arrive in the car with my research partner, (another Professor with no visible disabilities). We are met with a huge circular staircase at the front entrance which is completely inaccessible to me. Laughing and thinking quickly I said, 'Drive around to where they take the garbage out. There is usually a ramp there'. There was indeed a ramp and we entered through the kitchen. Greeted by the site manager, our research interview was punctuated by repeated queries as to whether I would like a wheelchair which I politely declined. The ground floor space once inside was quite accessible and a wheelchair was unnecessary in any case.

During the interview itself, my questions were largely ignored whereas when my colleague asked similar questions they were answered without hesitation. After the interview in our customary debriefing session, my colleague also noted this discrepancy. We postulated that he (the site manager) had little exposure to disability and consequently was unfamiliar with disabled people in a researcher position.

Finally, most recently, I was involved in an information-gathering field trip in a post-conflict region. We – my non-disabled colleagues and I – brought important information to the fieldwork process. However, I could not have accessed the majority of interview locations had it not been for the assistance of my non-disabled research partners. They repeatedly assisted me without hesitation, up and down stairs without railings, pushing door buzzers located well-above my head and opening fire doors. The lack of access in this situation was interesting given that many of these organisations assist injured and disabled individuals.

The way forward

In order to reconfigure the research landscape and be inclusive of disabled academic researchers. a full and forthright discussion and serious reflection must take place. We must move beyond semantics and platitudes factoring the body (in all its forms and locations), into academic research (Tregaskis, 2004; Hansen and Philo, 2007). Furthermore, we must examine the nature of academic research itself and move in a truly inclusive direction removing 'in-built ableisms' of traditional research (Stone and Priestley, 1996). The adoption of a modernised business model of the speed and time to completion has significantly changed the nature of research in the academy (Berg and Seeber, 2016). In doing so disabled researchers remain for the most part chronic outsiders. Flexibility with speed, time and funding factors need to reflect the changing nature of both academic research and the researcher. Recognising that disabled researchers are present and enabling accommodation from the outset will go a long way to substantively demonstrate that disabled researchers truly belong.

References

Berg, K. and Seeber B. (2016) *The Slow Professor: Challenging the Culture of Speed in the Academy*. Toronto: University of Toronto Press.

Brown, L. and Boardman (2011) "Accessing the field: Disability and the research process", *Social Science & Medicine*, *72*(1), 23–30.

Burgess, R. (1993) *In the Field: An Introduction to Field Research*. London: Routledge.

Byrne, S., Mizzi, R.C. and Hansen, N. (2017) "Living in a liminal peace: Where is the social justice for LGBTQ and disability communities residing in post peace accord Northern Ireland?", *Journal for Peace and Justice Studies*, *27*(1), 24–51.

Chouinard, V. (1997) "Making space for disabling differences: Challenging ableist geographies", *Environment and Planning D: Society and Space*, *15*(4), 379–386.

Chouinard, V. and Grant, A. (1997) "On not being anywhere near the project: Revolutionary ways of putting ourselves in the picture", In: L. McDowell and J. Sharp (eds) *Space, Gender and Knowledge: Feminist Readings*. London: Arnold, pp. 147–170.

Dolmage, J. (2017) *Academic Ableism: Disability and Higher Education*. Ann Arbor: University of Michigan Press.

Driedger, D. and Hansen, N. (2014) "Work literacy and disability: A study in transformation", *Professional Development: The International Journal in Social*, 17(2), 43–51.

Garland-Thomson, R. (1997) *Extraordinary Bodies: Figuring Physical Disability in American Culture and Literature*. New York: Columbia University Press.

Gold, G. (2003) "Rediscovering place: Experiences of a quadriplegic anthropologist", *Canadian Geographer*, 47(4), 467–479.

Golledge, R. (1993) "Geography and the disabled: A survey with special reference to vision impaired and blind populations", *Transactions of the Institute of British Geographers*, 18(1), 63–85.

Hansen, N. (2002) *Passing Through Other People's Spaces: Disabled Women Geography and Work*. PhD Thesis.

Hansen, N. (2008) "A delicate balance chronic conditions in workspace", In: Driedger, D. and Owen, M. (eds.) *Dissonant Disabilities: Women with Chronic Illnesses Explore Their Lives*. Toronto: Canadian Scholars' Press. pp. 131–145.

Hansen, N. (2009) "Remapping the medical terrain on our terms", *Aporia*, 1(3), 28–34.

Hansen, N. (2018), *Researchers with Disabilities, and the Obstacles They Face in Academia*. New Orleans: Panel AAG.

Hansen, N. and Driedger, D. (2010) "Art, sticks and politics", In: Driedger, D. (ed.) *Living the Edges a Disabled Women's Reader*. Toronto: Inanna Publications and Education, pp. 195–203.

Hansen, N. and Philo, C. (2007) "The normality of doing things differently: Further thoughts on Bodies, Spaces and Disability Geography", *Tijdschrift voor Economische en Sociale Geografie*, 98(4), 493–506.

hooks, b. (1982) *Ain't I a Woman: Black Women and Feminism*. London: Pluto Press.

Kobayashi, A. (1994) "Colouring the field: Gender, race and the politics of field work", *The Professional Geographer*, 46(1), 73–80.

McFarlane, H. and Hansen, N. (2007) "Including people with disabilities in participatory action research in Scotland and Canada", In: Kindon, S., Pain, R. and Kesby, M. (eds) *Participatory Action Research Approaches and Methods: Connecting People, Participation and Place*. London: Routledge, pp. 88–94.

Moss, P. (1999) "Autobiographical notes on chronic illness", In: Butler, R. and Parr, H. (eds) *Mind and Body Spaces: Geographies of Illness, Impairment and Disability*. London: Routledge, pp. 155–166.

Oliver, M. (1990) *The Politics of Disablement*. London: Macmillan.

Oliver, M. and Barnes, C. (1997) "Current issues: All we are saying is give disabled researchers a chance", *Disability & Society*, 12(8), 811–813.

Sibley, D. (1995) *Geographies of Exclusion Society and Difference in the West*. London: Routledge.

Stone, E. and Priestley, M. (1996) Parasites, pawns and partners: Disability research and the role of non-disabled researchers", *The British Journal of Sociology*, 47(4), 699–716.

Thomas, C. (1999) "Narrative Identity and the Disabled Self", In: Corker, M. and French, S. (eds.) *Disability Discourse*. Buckingham: Oxford University Press, pp. 47–55.

Titchkosky, T. (2011) *The Question of Access: Disability, Space, Meaning*. Toronto: University of Toronto Press.

Tregaskis, C. (2004) "Identity, positionality and power: Issues for disabled researcher: A response paper to Broun & Heshusius", *Disability Studies Quarterly*, 24(2), https://dsq-sds.org/article/view/492/669.

Wendell, S. (1996) *The Rejected Body: Feminist Philosophical Reflections on Disability*. New York: Routledge.

Zarb, G. (1992) "On the road to Damascus: First steps towards changing the relations of disability research production", *Disability, Handicap and Society*, 7(2), 125–138.

Chapter 6

Ten affects of hidden, mental dis/abilities and the act of disclosure

Anita Z Goldschmied

an affect: the capacity to affect and be affected
an effect: a change, a result of an influence

Introduction

I am a PhD candidate who lives with similar dis/abilities as those participants I collaborate with. I was diagnosed only a few years ago with autism (Asperger Syndrome) when in my late 30's. I grew up in a multicultural, multi-religious, white and well-educated family. Whilst the signs have always been there, a late diagnosis for my generation is not uncommon regardless of the background. I only started to recognise something was different when I moved to the UK and whilst learning how to say something in English only to notice how much social context impacted on what was expressed. I now realise that being Hungarian-born British, my accent helped me to mask my different communication style and gave me an opportunity. I became interested in how we are often overlooked and deserve more research attention. In particular, to be in a position as an adult to naturally (re)learn things. I believe it made a difference that people were generally more tolerant with me, presumably, as they attributed my unpolished utterances to the fact that English is my second language.

My research performance takes such observations into account and is primarily one of "noticing". The notion of visibility and materiality is theoretically relevant because the panoramic spectrum of hidden, mental dis/abilities such as autism, intellectual disability and other mental health problems can typically show no symptoms and so fail to remind us that seeing can be considered a dualist state of presence/absence. In addition to discussing how researchers negotiate their hidden dis/abilities throughout the various stages of research, my aim in this chapter is to explore the challenges and dilemmas I, as a dis/abled researcher face, when conducting research focusing on the questions of disclosure. First, I will clarify some definitions, the particularities of hidden dis/abilities and the consequences for disclosure. Second, drawing on my personal experiences, explore the opportunities and dilemmas of being a researcher with a hidden dis/ability. Third, I will elaborate on the researcher's role and how disclosure might influence the research process looking at mainly the question of neutrality, partnership and reflexivity. Fourth, I offer some pragmatic discussions about the emergence of the 10 affects of the act of disclosure (as noted in the quote above, affect is a capacity to change) in the various stages of research practice.

Definition and terminology

To begin, it seems the lack of agreed terminology is well known in dis/ability research. Therefore, it remains important to explain the approach we have taken (McBrien 2003; United Nations 2005; Bradley 2009; Shakespeare 2014). The notion of visibility and materiality has a central role in the life of people living with various mental and cognitive conditions as first, our difficulties are often not apparent to the observers, and second, these conditions cannot be readily described by an evident underlying physical anomaly or represented by materials. Brown and Broadman (2011) argue that the visible presence of a wheelchair or an assistance dog are generally accepted signals of a dis/ability and as such provide grounds for negotiating barriers. Disclosure *per se* is rarely a decision to be made when visibility is present. On the other hand, by virtue of the materiality and the visibility of autism, the various mental health conditions or intellectual disability being beyond our reach everything is permitted as anything can be demonstrated (Latour 1993). Many probably would ask at this point the question: is depression or autism a dis/ability at all?

The preferred term by the diagnostic manuals (ICD, World Health Organisation 2016; DSM, American Psychology Association 2013) and various legislation such as the Mental Health Act (Department of Health 1983) is "disorder". Disability is the terminology used by the Equality Act (Government Equalities Office 2010) for a person who has a physical or mental impairment that impacts a person's ability to carry out normal day-to-day activities. Whilst studies like Mcclimens (2007), Kittelsaa (2013) and Kenny *et al.* (2016) emphasise most dis/abled people probably would prefer to leave behind such differentiation altogether. I use the term dis/ability to signal that the notion of "ability" and "disability" as a binary concept is potentially outmoded and a mistaken view of human differences and their complex representations (Latour 1993, p. 32; Baudrillard 1994, p. 133). For example, depression is different from intellectual disability, schizophrenia or autism. However, people who live with various mental and cognitive conditions also share certain adventures. One of those is the invisible and often misunderstood nature of their performances. And, of course, the ambivalent act of disclosure.

The act of disclosure

What does a diagnosis of a dis/ability perform? Disclosure of a dis/ability has the capacity to affect and mediate how others will act. And those actions then affect not only how you feel about yourself but also your research (Latour 2005). The research arena demands many decisions related to disclosure and the everyday performances of dis/ability. You constantly need to make decisions about whether you disclose it to your boss, colleagues, friends and the people you encounter in your daily life. The feelings of awkwardness, the how to and when to talk about it, and to whom are just some of the accompanying difficulties of disclosure. The fear and insecurity of what will happen next? I often say disclosure is like talking dirty, letting out some deeply buried family secrets. And the receiver of disclosure often reinforces this notion: "Thank you for disclosing it, I promise I won't tell anybody". Why not? What is wrong with being autistic? Intellectually disabled? Or depressed?

Most of us in our dis/ability journey will hope for open disclosure, where you can just say something like, "look, I am Autistic, sorry if I say something silly, or my humour bites, or I zone out. I do my best, and you can support me. A dash of humour would be a good start". But we quickly learn, it rarely works like this. What I have found that most of the time, people have no, or limited or very rigid ideas of what Asperger syndrome means and how it might affect you. Talking to participants about the experiences of disclosure and cross-member checking typifies the unpredictable nature of disclosure as a shared event between people who have autism, depression, obsessive-compulsive disorder, intellectual disability or bipolar disorder. As I will go on to consider, our hidden dis/ability itself is a condition of possibilities. The journey is not a stable, fixed and ordered state. Dis/ability is constantly perFormed, disSolved and reProduced by diverse actors interacting in complex webs of relations. Networks temporarily stabilise. The labels play a key role in this and help create the impression that hidden, mental dis/abilities are objective, definite and permanent conditions (Goldschmied 2017).

An actor-network-theory appreciation of dis/ability and the act of disclosure as personal and connected rather than objective and distant

Five actions of Actor-Network-Theory (ANT) and the act of disclosure:

1 *Disclosure is more than a say-out-loud ethical or political consideration.*
2 *Disclosure has the capacity to affect and be affected.*
3 *Disclosure should act so as to reframe change, not bias.*
4 *Disclosure is action aiming to enable noticing.*
5 *Disclosure recognises its capacity to disrupt conventional research thinking.*

When disclosure is not personal, it can appear straightforward and uncomplicated. Yet, the sterility of distance when researchers have attempted to remain objectively removed from their data collection has been and is, ironically distant from my ANT approach. To date, in my research practice, I have had many disclosure experiences, some subtle and others more intentional and direct where I have just stated: "I am autistic", and more often than not it has had an observable effect. Sometimes the unpredictability of affects so often anticipated by traditional approaches, so as to encourage distance pushes its way into the frame as informants do any number of things such as terminate all contact, become embarrassed, attempt to hide their lack of faith in my abilities or their relief and admiration in what I am trying to do. Others start considering how often I have tantrums and meltdowns. Some ask questions, others don't say a word. They consider scenarios that might have never occurred to them otherwise. "Are you a vulnerable adult?", "Do you have the capacity to consent to sex?", "But you are not dribbling, how come?" just to offer a few. So, if disclosure has an affect of labelling, then with the label comes the support (Ventegodt 2005; Craddock et al. 2008; Reed 2010) and also the launch of a roller-coaster ride (Galasiński 2008; Livingston and Boyd 2010; Frigerio, Montali and Fine 2013). I attended a seminar about research methodology where the established researcher, a reader in health studies, quickly settled the concern of objectivity and reflexivity in research with a statement of "I always state at the beginning of my fieldwork that I'm a nurse so bias could not be a question in my project". I believe she is missing the point.

Disclosure framed as an ethical issue, bias or objectivity in terms of having a distance from your research and the participants might prevent us from exploring the associations it forms and as such study the notion of dis/ability itself. In other words, dis/ability and disclosure offer much more prospects than a one-off announcement at the beginning of research and one or two sentence reflexive statement at the end of a written account. Examining dis/ability and the act of disclosure through ANT, a semiotic-material approach (e.g. concerned with signs), disclosure is not a question of bias or objectivity but an actor that enters the research process with the capacity to affect and be affected. In ANT, an actor is always a network of elements, and a network is fully defined by its actors (Law 2004; Latour et al. 2012). In other words, everything is relational including the human actors, such as the researcher and the participants, as well as the non-human actors such as dis/ability and disclosure. There is no overall social, natural or conceptual framework within which dis/ability and the act of disclosure exist as nothing is arranged in advance. Dis/ability itself is an effect of temporally formed associations (Latour 2005). Dis/ability, as well as disclosure, has a "voice". Disclosure is an actor with the potential to affect other actors and their actions in the associations they form. With the disclosure of a dis/ability researcher and participant, dis and ability, expert discourse and personal stories become entangled providing us with opportunities to reveal the processes that compose dis/ability and how according to Latour and Woolgar (1986) such composition should be "discussed, evaluated and negotiated".

The task of the researcher is then to explore the actions, and their effects such as disclosure perform in the stories they encounter. Dis/ability can enter research through disclosure not as an essence but as an uncertain actor that has the capacity to affect, to change and make a difference. In other words, the act of disclosure shifts the focus from immobile frames to the processes by which the visibility of a hidden dis/ability might be obtained. Disclosure is no longer a concern about objectivity and contamination but rather can make dis/ability observable, more dimensional and active amongst signs to reveal its connections and its role as a connector (Latour 2013; Bilodeau and Potvin 2016). Something hidden and obscure can become detectable and, thus, enhance the interest in how dis/ability is composed and noticed. On the other hand, the danger of disclosure is of course that with visibility, perceived stability and predictability we are risking exchanging a movement for a static position. That is, the shifting nature of dis/ability with apparently fixed, independent and permanent attributes. Every time we disclose, we make some part of us visible but, we also hide, anchor and stabilise whilst subsequently destabilising and highlighting what Law and Urry (2004) suggest are opportunities to make visible different associations and effects in research leading to a particular way of composing knowledge and the concept of dis/ability.

Disclosure blurs the line between the personal and the professional roles

My personal experiences of disclosure showed me that the act of disclosure makes actors do surprising things: they oppose, they separate, they unify. Can we and should we utilise our personal experiences in research? Disclosure appears to blur the line between the personal and the professional roles as it provides a material, semiotic and discursive continuum between the various situations within which I perform. In other words, my role as an ANT researcher is not to assume an *a priori* controlled, ordered and predictable dis/ability independent of us to be discovered by the act of disclosure. On the contrary, as we are learning, the researcher's dis/ability and the act of disclosure does not shy away from the affects it has on other actors. When those affects produce an effect, a change that we can notice and thus record we can treat it as potential data shaping our understanding of phenomena, and specifically the notion of dis/ability. The act of disclosure then becomes indispensable from other actors' performance of dis/ability in the various stages of research (Latour 1998; Galis 2011). So, having discussed how disclosure is an integral move in engaging, sustaining and promoting data through the affective dynamics of disruption, inseparability and connectivity I will now introduce and discuss 10 potential theoretics of disclosure. The development of the 10 affects was inspired by the works and philosophy of Jean Baudrillard (1993, 1994; Pawlett 2007) and Bruno Latour (1993, 2005). Table 6.1 below summarises the 10 potential affects of the act of disclosure. They operate in specific ways leading to various effects and as such composition of dis/abilities.

10 potential affects of hidden, mental dis/abilities and the act of disclosure

Table 6.1 10 potential affects of hidden, mental dis/abilities and the act of disclosure

Separation	*Disclosure may bring about the binary oppositions of disabled and non-disabled.*	*Simulation*	*Disclosure can offer reference of one label to another composing dis/abilities.*
Apparent objectivity	*Disclosure can present dis/ability as an existing thing in its own right.*	*Uncertainty*	*Disclosure of a dis/ability enters research as an additional unstable actor.*
Fragmentation	*Disclosure may promote the individual labels offering an identity and a sense of self.*	*Composition*	*Disclosure may reveal that dis/ability is not a given, it is assembled.*
Enactment	*Disclosure does not only narrate dis/ability but also performs it.*	*Agency*	*Both disclosure and dis/ability can be the effect of other actors' actions.*
Multiplicity	*Disclosure can show how dis/ability presents differently in various relations.*	*Relationality*	*Disclosure can make a dis/ability visible revealing its connections and its role as a connector.*

Separation

You are dis/abled, I am not. Some people express relief when you disclose a dis/ability. You are different from me. Me and You, your "disability" and my "ability" are now in binary oppositions. Some people obtain self-confidence and power as an effect of disclosure. The structure of differences based on binary oppositions such as neurotypical and atypical is a powerful tool to achieve senses of control. Paradoxically, whilst these people separate your disability from their normality, they seem to be unable to distinguish your skills from your difficulties.

Apparent objectivity

People who have set assumptions and fixed ideas about dis/ability finally find a reason, a cause and perceived objectification of the existence of dis/abilities. It is often accompanied by effects of pity like "it must be terrible living with autism" as if dis/ability was a permanent and justified thing. Their reality has been confirmed by your disclosure as your label helps build an external reality of dis/abilities.

Disclosure, the voice of dis/ability makes it possible to describe and manipulate this reality that seems to exist in its own right.

Fragmentation

One of my participants with ADHD expressed she was not dis/abled as her peer from college who has autism needs more support. The proliferation of the labels with the corresponding disciplines, policies and organisations led to a fragmental world. Some people including both dis/abled and non-dis/abled persons will perform such effects as individual labels can offer them an identity at the expense of other labels. It follows, disclosing a dis/ability does not mean automatic access to and acceptance by other dis/abled people, their significant others and other participants.

Enactment

You disclose dis/ability to someone who does not want to know about your dis/ability. "Why did you have to tell me? Now I have to do something. I wish you had never told me". And they make you feel as you have just ruined their day. The effects of disclosure are never straightforward as disclosure does not only narrate dis/ability but also performs it. What happens next depends on the complex relations of all the actors that bring about different performances of dis/ability for each person in various situations.

Multiplicity

Effects of disclosure like "you do not have it", "it may go away", "we are all on the spectrum" or "but you can maintain eye contact" can show that disability is not settled, a fact or a question of perspective but dis/ability itself is multiple. Dis/ability is not merely an "ability" from one view and a "disability" from another, rather, dis/ability is actor-network dependent and performs differently in various relations. Disclosure might reveal that multiplicity is the attribute of dis/ability as well as the actors that compose them, not a question of interpretation.

Simulation

People with all sorts of labels and problems can be subject to simulation (a substitution of real for signs) which, theoretically at least, has an effect of becoming your best friend and worst enemy because in ANT research there is still a pressure to produce viable aims and results, define theory and present pragmatic outcomes. This can be difficult when arguing for the significance of simulated experiences. So, it is important to note here as expressed by one of my participants that Asperger is neither a mental health condition nor autism or an intellectual disability in the real sense. Reference of one label to another can compose dis/abilities and accept them as factual. Stereotyped labels refer to other labels in the system, not to an external reality lapsing into simulation.

Uncertainty

People who struggle to manage your disclosure may not know what to say or how to behave because they either have no experience or lack the skills to handle such acts, but in my experience, they tend to be genuinely concerned and worried that they might say something inappropriate. Research is uncertainty, awkward and, therefore, rich for disruption. Dis/ability and the act of disclosure bring these additional uncertain factors to the process, whilst also offering opportunities for collaboration and negotiation to compose together the notion of dis/ability as well as the research, even if both remain temporary and unstable.

Composition

Some people openly acknowledge that the label is just one of your attributes and as an effect aim to learn who you are, what you do and not what the label represents. Whilst in many cases it is possible to reach this seemingly ideal state with your participants, it is rare that the act of disclosure will take you here instantly in research. It is these effects though that reinforce dis/ability is not a given, a permanent impairment but an assemblage. It has to be performed and noticed each and every time.

Agency

Dis/ability is constantly formed and performed, solved and dissolved, produced and reproduced by the complex associations of actors. We, dis/abled researchers are not the only one with an agency. Other actors performing in the research can have agency. They also have the capacity to affect, to mediate and to change. Disclosure and the making of your hidden dis/ability visible can be the effect of other actors' actions. Our behaviour, an unintentional comment or our relationship with objects can lead to the noticing of dis/ability without your act of disclosure.

Relationality

Human actors in research such as researchers and participants are connected through other actors like objects, ideas and experiences. Some of my participants knew I was dis/abled. I know they knew it without ever disclosing it or saying the word autistic. One of my participants had a diagnosis, but he rejected it. In these cases, there is no disclosure, open or otherwise, in the traditional sense but rather, it performs through its relations to other actors. Non-disclosure can affect the research and compose dis/ability the same way as an open disclosure leaves it untouched.

Research as an association of actors, noticing and the act of disclosure at the various stages

The 10 affects show us that disclosure promotes an approach to research which has the potential to generate unexpected effects. It is an uncertain event with the prospect to generate controversies about what we mean by a dis/ability. Following on Latour's account (2005, p. 39) the uncertainty of disclosure is the capacity of the actors. In other words, disclosure has the capacity to either transform my label, that is to say, modify and change the understanding of dis/ability or merely transport it, namely, mirror what I have expected to see without observable effects. The affects of disclosure can only be noticed and thus recorded if it is performed, makes a difference and produces change leaving a visible effect behind. Our concern is to notice those effects and the associations they form at the various stages of research. Noticing is the key activity researchers do. As it is then when a dis/ability and the act of disclosure can become data and an integral part of the research (Latour 1996). We should appreciate this as now we do not have to choose between objectivity and subjectivity, between fact and myth any longer. On the contrary, we can show how disclosure has performed on our research, how my dis/ability has affected and was affected by other actors leading to alternative understandings of how the enactment of associations lead to particular outcomes (Latour 2004; Law and Mol 2011; Holyoake 2013). It reminds us that nothing is permanent and fixed, that both research as a process and dis/ability as a concept is a temporary state and depends on the webs of relations.

In my personal life, I could experiment with disclosure, taking small risks, considering the effects and learning from the experience. In research, we do not necessarily have this freedom. With certain approaches, such as biographical, longitudinal or ethnography research, it is common to meet the respondent on more than one occasion. However, the majority of designs using, for example, questionnaires, focus-group or a single measure data collection will not provide the researcher with such opportunities. We do not meet with our participant a second time, if at all, or build close relationships with them and, therefore, flexibly change our approach if it did not go so well. In sum, we have no overall control over how our dis/ability and disclosure might affect others and the research project. I disclose my diagnosis of Autism throughout the research at various stages, however, the mode and time of disclosure depend on various factors. We, researchers, can make certain decisions about disclosure considering the particular association of actors our methodology advances. On the one hand, dis/ability and disclosure always have the potential to influence research, and as such the knowledge we bring to light. On the other hand, every methodology, design and method represent a more or less set arrangement of actors and potential relations (Fox and Alldred 2015). In the next section, I will offer some pragmatic considerations how disclosure might then impact in the various stages of research (see also Figure 6.1).

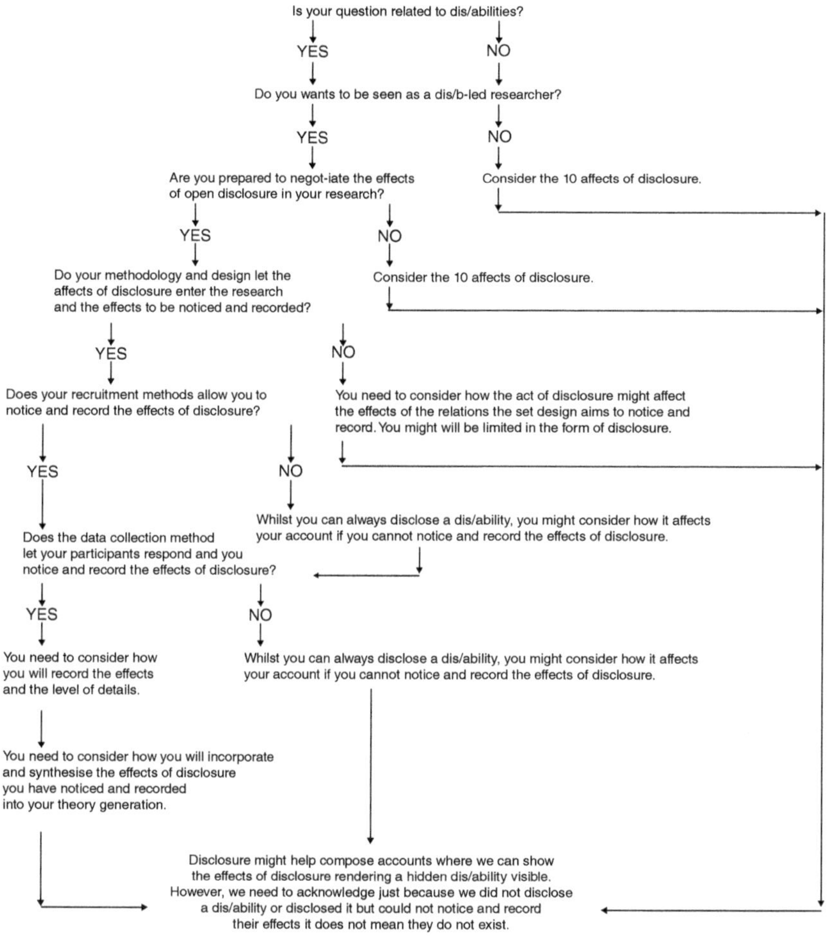

Figure 6.1 Research as an association of actors and the act of disclosure at the various stages.

The research question, aim and design

The five ANT contributions are:

1 *Control is also an affect with a capacity to be disrupted*
2 *Researching the social is always relational and involves disclosure*
3 *Disclosure is a composition made up of capacity and noticed arrangement*
4 *Disclosure enables flexibility through modes of relationality*
5 *The flow of disclosure is rarely linear (consider your aims and design as ongoing)*

Every research project is a particular arrangement of specific approaches and tools for the exploration of events. It will establish set ways to select, order and notice particular actors, their relations and the effects they perform. The modes of selecting and ordering specify conditions of possibility for noticing, making some associations easier and others difficult or impossible, more or less stable and durable. It is the configuration of the actor-networks of the particular methodology that produces relative stability, durability and a particular outcome (Law 2007). Considering disclosure than in such activities as selecting, ordering and noticing becomes our main concern as once we make certain decisions, we set limits to the conditions of possibility of disclosure and the effects we can notice (ibid. 2007). When we establish our research question, the design and the underlying assumptions we need to explore is how they intend to manage the various actors, their capacity to affect and be affected and the kind of knowledge it aims to create. Every methodology focuses on aspects of events whilst sacrifices something else in order to reduce complexity into workable knowledge of phenomena.

In a randomised controlled trial or pretest/post-test design, for example, it is a key consideration to keep actors under as much control as possible throughout the research. It follows, we need to consider how the 10 potential affects of disclosure might interact with the set limiters if we disclose our disability to the control group only or after the pretest but before the post-test. In other words, designs are very specific about the expected *relationality* of the actors and the effects they wish to observe. On the other hand, in ethnography that aims to explore phenomena in the naturalistic environment, disclosure can be an additional *uncertainty* to the recording of events as they happen, giving more flexibility to the researcher. In between the rigidity of a fixed randomised controlled trial and the flexible possibilities of an ethnography, we find other approaches with varying degrees and number of limiters. Some questionnaires that only allow set responses have already filtered the events they aim to explore and, thus, the effects we can record, so once again we might have limited opportunities to notice any effects of disclosure. Phenomenology, on the other hand, might provide disclosure with more opportunities for the researcher to privilege the emotive connectivity, both intra- and interpersonal.

We are not concerned by designs *per se* but focus on the understanding of its limiters, the room they allow for the actors to affect and the researcher to notice those effects. In other words, most of the time we can disclose a dis/ability be it ethical, moral or political importance for us. This could add to our understanding of the *enactment* of dis/ability but only if we can notice and thus record the effects. In ANT, if no observable mark is left behind, no visible thus recordable effects have been produced, disclosure offers no information for the researcher, thus, we cannot explore its potential role in our research (Latour 2005 p. 53). Moreover, the flow of affects is not entirely flexible, linear and logical either, even if the design permits variations of disclosure. First, once we start the selecting and ordering, disclosure also begins to stabilise effecting the future decisions and performances of research. Second, although designs aim for control, disclosure can have agency.

Disclosure can happen as a result of other actors' action. I had participants who had known I was autistic before I could consider disclosing it. Then it became more complex when I attended an event to observe and someone disclosed my autism to the rest of the group. Such actions might enhance our noticing of events and the various ways people negotiate, compose and influence their world.

> In summary, at the early stage of research, our initial strategy of dis/ability and the 10 potential affects of disclosure needs to be considered with the design overall strategy. Credibility, validity and objectivity are then the results of revealing how we attempted to select and order the actors and how we could notice or not the effects of the act disclosure.

Collaboration, sampling, data collection and data analysis

The five ANT contributions are:

1 *Disclosure promotes collaboration and alliance*
2 *Disclosure means creative methods for contact, engagement and learning*
3 *Disclosure offers opportunities to notice and record effects*
4 *Disclosure allows responses to reveal values, ideologies, practices*
5 *Disclosure can make visible the connections*

Once we have unpacked our particular design, we need to consider how dis/ability and the act of disclosure might enact in the stages of recruitment, data collection and analysis. As with designs, the various sampling techniques will have set limiters for exclusion, and inclusion and disclosure should be considered with their specific approach (Fox and Alldred 2017). Then, we need to think about our communication method with the gatekeepers and potential participants. Are you going to meet with them or send a letter? What is your relationship with them? The question is for ANT what opportunities your sampling strategy, recruitment and data collection method offer for noticing. The decision of disclosure should not be governed by the notion that it will create order, simplify complexity or end controversies. The 10 potential affects remind us that it is unlikely disclosure will deliver such aspirations. On the contrary, disclosure can add a new, dynamic and uncertain actor to all the other actors in the process revealing the multiplicity of dis/ability (Latour 2005, pp. 30, 45). When our sampling, recruitment and data collection method allow the effects of disclosure to be noticed, it reveals values, ideologies, and performances of dis/abilities, participants and researchers. From all the stages of research, it is data collection that can show best the *multiplicity* of disability, how it is composed differently in relations when we have direct interaction with our participants.

We might consider how likely it is that your participants will meet and talk to each other, how many times they will meet with you or whether they can have any information about your dis/ability. What can make a difference between accounts at this stage is the level of details and analysis we intend to explore. Actors are constantly positioning themselves and are positioned by other actors, establishing relations to others and things, forming and rejecting connections. How much we wish to explore the effects of disclosure and all the actors' action in a given situation: legislation, personal experiences, cultural expectations or a movie our participant watched the day before. Disclosure of a dis/ability to participants encourages the researcher to observe the effects, how they compose and make visible the connections and disclosure as a connector. On one occasion we were talking about the age of diagnosis. One of my participants in the group had a late diagnosis like me and he was like me, but older. I disclosed my diagnosis, and something changed. There were observable effects. He did not engage with me for the rest of the day. It took me a few occasions to interact with him again. I had been fragmented! Fragmentation was an affect of my disclosure since our similarity had at least two dimensions as alluded to by Pawlett (2013, p. 132) which was not only an advantage but dangerous; whilst others in the group have continued to talk about the diagnosis as the most natural thing. Ask yourself: will your data collection method permit such noticing?

The 10 potential affects of disclosure showed us that the researcher is not the only actor with possible agency in research as dis/ability performs in relation to others and things. For example, when I was interviewing about ideal employment, I spontaneously responded: "yes, being a lecturer is good for autistic people too, when I mark and research I don't have to interact with others". Her laughter and the comments that followed made it apparent that my response transformed the situation. When you do research with people who are either autistic themselves, have some other hidden, mental dis/abilities, care for or work with them, you have to be ready they have the skills and experience to detect the smallest signs of differences without such obvious comments. This is often confirmed immediately or later on. Participants either ask you, "are you autistic"? or when you disclose it they will respond, "yes, I know it from the moment we met".

> In summary, controversies arise as a result of disclosure as the examples illustrate and drawing on such tensions are essential if we to better understand dis/ability and how many ways it can be composed and performed. It opens up opportunities to collaborate and learn from each other. It reminds us of the uncertain and temperamental nature of research.

Theory and discussion generation

The five ANT contributions are:

1 *Disclosure provides opportunities to explore the participants' world-making activities*
2 *Shared experiences can help notice what might otherwise go unnoticed*
3 *Disclosure supports reflexive accounts*

4 *The uncertainty of disclosure offers diverse translations of experiences*
5 *The more the performances, the more visible it becomes how dis/ability is composed*

In the previous paragraphs, we have considered whether we will introduce ourselves as a dis/abled researcher or a researcher? Does the topic have a direct reference to dis/ability? We have explored how the design might affect whether we can notice the effects of disclosure through set arrangements only or somewhat flexibly (see also Figure 6.2). We have discussed that a one-off purposeful disclosure built into the design might appear as an act of keeping the research assemblage under our control to achieve neutrality and objectivity. The 10 affects showed us, it probably will not and should not deliver such aspirations. Instead, we should embrace the uncertainty and potential mediating effect of disclosure in research, thus appreciating the opportunities to compose different translation of experiences in our theory generation. One way to synthesise our dis/ability and the act of disclosure into our research is to follow the actions of the actors and notice when and how they mediate if they do at all. This way we can analyse more openly what might have influenced and composed our findings. Research seen as a habitual, normative and a set way of doing things might not allow such discussions. And this is the mistaken view our researcher has taken at the beginning of the chapter, that reflexivity and in this case, disclosure is an unconnected, independent event that can somehow be resolved not for a moment but all along the research process.

1. List the ways disclosure noticeably impacts upon your methodology and design.
2. How open are you about your dis/ability and what effects are you prepared to negotiate? Disclosure or non-disclosure?
3. What kind of limiters are built in the sampling for disclosure to affect and the noticing of such effects?
4. How does the recruitment and data collection method allow your participants to respond? Can you notice, observe and discuss the effects of disclosure?
5. How often will you meet with your participants ? Do you have more opportunities for disclosure and/or to follow the effects? Will your participants meet?
6. How does the data analysis method allow for the effects of disclosure to be entered, coded and analysed as data?
7. How do you intend to notice and record the effects of disclosure and how much details are you prepared to record?
8. How will the noticing, recording and analysing of effects of disclosure advance your topic and contribution?
9. How will the effects of disclosure be synthesised and transformed in your discussion?
10. How might the effects of disclosure affect your audience, discipline and the sharing of knowledge? Can you and will you notice and record the effects?

Figure 6.2 10 questions to notice the potential effects of the act of disclosure in research.

Disclosure is a continuously unfolding story rather than a one-off announcement. All researchers regardless of the presence or absence of dis/ability will select, order and notice specific actions whilst let slip others. The question for ANT is not which account reflects the notion of dis/ability best. Different approaches allow us to explore the various enactments of dis/abilities that might overlap at certain parts and will be different at others. And then we can ask the question of how we negotiate the diverse outcomes? To negotiate, I argue the more performances we explore, the more visible it becomes how dis/ability has been composed, the better the chance we have to find temporally closure and solution (Latour and Weibel 2002). This can be particularly significant in dis/ability studies where the shared experiences can help notice what might otherwise go unnoticed. However, instead of looking at dis/abled researchers and disclosure as distinctive actors from all the other personal attributes researchers possess that in fact may accentuate stigma (McClimens 2003; Gernsbacher 2017) we can use the opportunities to reveal different accounts.

Equality, inclusivity, social justice to mention a few aims disabled as well as non-dis/abled people wish for is not a pre-existing state we can simply demand. We, researchers and participants, with and without a dis/ability have to compose it together. Reflexivity then means our participants are allowed to express their world-making activities (Serres and Latour 1995, p. 173). Research in most textbooks demands for rigour, control and predictability just to mention a few key attributes. Paradoxically, giving a voice to dis/ability, disclosure, an unstable and dubious actor will make the network, and as such the research process, not only more transparent and reflexive but better managed and inclusive. Partnership now is not just a symbolic act expected in contemporary research but becomes an active, dynamic and expressive association. Disclosure is a way of connecting as there is always something between a researcher and a participant. When we apply ANT in the spirit of Law (1999) and Latour (1999) we recognise that in the act of disclosure, "dis" and "ability", expert discourse and personal experience become entangled to potentially increase our understanding of phenomena to be discussed, evaluated and negotiated.

> We aim to compose accounts where the effects of hidden, mental dis/abilities and disclosure are visible. However, we need to acknowledge just because we did not disclose our dis/ability or disclosed it but could not notice and record their effects it does not mean they do not exist. Eventually, we need to reduce both complexity and uncertainty if we aim to compose pragmatic messages but doing it at a too early stage of research might miss opportunities to more subtle explorations.

Summary

In summary, disclosure of a dis/ability offers the potential to enrich our research culture and enhance collaboration. First, disclosure might compose entangled accounts and help reveal and notice actions and their effects that a non-disabled researcher might not envisage. Second, disclosure does not act alone. Disclosure adds to the complexity of living with a dis/ability as it interacts with other actors providing us with opportunities for a more profound understanding of accounts. Third, not giving voice to our dis/ability does not automatically lead to non-effect. Other actors can make our dis/ability enact and perform without our disclosure. Fourth, being a dis/abled researcher and disclosing a dis/ability to dis/abled and non-disabled participants will not result in a more faithful reflection of reality. It does, however, compose a different account to advance our understanding of phenomena, values and expectations. Fifth, disclosure and the enactment of dis/ability connects the researcher contextually to the participants as well as other actors. Research itself should arise from these enacted practices of fieldwork.

Conclusion

As opposed to conventional views, dis/ability is not a fixed condition, and disclosure is not a single act of achieving neutrality. Disclosure has the capacity to affect but the effects of disclosure are not a concern of perspective. It impacts on other actors and their actions by performing differently in various relations. It might evoke unity or resistance, rejection or support. It affects other enacted actors. Disclosure becomes indispensable from other actors in the performance of dis/ability in research. Researchers regardless of their chosen design and methodology should consider the potential affects of their dis/ability and other identity signifiers be it ethnicity, gender or accent as these all have the capacity to affect and be affected. A hidden dis/ability can be given a voice through disclosure making it visible and, thus, detectable offering opportunities to negotiate our values, ideals and expectations of dis/abilities. My research as a dis/abled person is no more or no less objective, no more or no less justified to make a dis/abled world visible. It is a different way of composing our concerns. The more accounts we reveal, by disabled and non-disabled researchers, about dis/ability the better position we might be in to discuss the complex and ethically charged question of what sort of society we live in.

References

American Psychiatric Association (2013) *Diagnostic and Statistical Manual of Mental Disorders: DSM-5* (5th ed.) Washington, DC: American Psychiatric Publishing.

Baudrillard, J. (1993) *Symbolic Exchange and Death*. London: Sage.

Baudrillard, J. (1994) *Simulacra and Simulation*. Ann Arbor: University of Michigan Press.

Bilodeau, A. and Potvin, L. (2016) "Unpacking complexity in public health interventions with the actor-network theory", *Health Promotion International*, *33*(1), 173–181.

Bradley, Lord (2009) *The Bradley Report: Lord Bradley's Review of People with Mental Health Problems or Learning Disabilities in the Criminal Justice System*. London: Department of Health.

Brown, L. and Boardman, F. (2011) "Accessing the field: Disability and the research process", *Social Science and Medicine*, *72*(1), 23–30.

Craddock, N., Antebi, D., Attenburrow, M., Bailey, A., Carson, A., Cowen, P., Craddock, B., *et al.* (2008) "Wake-up call for British psychiatry", *The British Journal of Psychiatry: The Journal of Mental Science, 193*(1), 6–9.

Department of Health (1983) *Mental Health Act 1983*. London: HMSO.

Fox, N. and Alldred, P. (2015) "New materialist social inquiry: Designs, methods and the research-assemblage", *International Journal of Social Research Methodology, 18*(4), 399–414.

Fox, N. and Alldred, P. (2017) *Sociology and the New Materialism: Theory, Research, Action*. London: SAGE Publications Ltd.

Frigerio, A., Montali, L. and Fine, M. (2013) "Attention deficit/hyperactivity disorder blame game: A study on the positioning of professionals, teachers and parents", *Health, 17*(6), 584–604.

Galasiński, D. (2008) *Men's Discourses of Depression*. London: Palgrave Macmillan.

Galis, V. (2011) "Enacting disability: How can science and technology studies inform disability studies?", *Disability & Society, 26*(7), 825–838.

Gernsbacher, M.A. (2017) "Editorial perspective: The use of person-first language in scholarly writing may accentuate stigma", *Journal of Child Psychology and Psychiatry, 58*(7), 859–861.

Goldschmied, A.Z. (2017) *Rendering the invisible visible*. British Sociological Association: Medical-Sociology Conference, York September 13–15, 2017, York.

Government Equalities Office (2010) *Equality Act 2010*. London: HMSO.

Holyoake, D.D. (2013) "I spy with my little eye something beginning with O: Looking at what the myth of 'doing the observations' means in mental health nursing culture", *Journal of Psychiatric and Mental Health Nursing, 20*(9), 840–850.

Kenny, L., Hattersley, C., Molins, B., Buckley, C., Povey, C. and Pellicano, E. (2016) "Which terms should be used to describe autism? Perspectives from the UK autism community", *Autism, 20*(4), 442–462.

Kittelsaa, A. (2013) "Self-Presentations and Intellectual Disability", *Scandinavian Journal of Disability Research, 16*(1), 29–44.

Law, J. (1999) "After ANT: Complexity, naming and topology", *Sociological Review, 47*(1), 1–14.

Law, J. (2004) *After Method: Mess in Social Science Research*. London: Routledge.

Law, J. (2007) *Actor Network Theory and Material Semiotics*. (online) Available from: http://www.heterogeneities.net/publications/Law2007ANTandMaterialSemiotics.pdf

Law, J. and Mol, A. (2011) "Veterinary Realities: What is Foot and Mouth Disease? (Report)", *Sociologia Ruralis, 51*(1), 1–16.

Law, J. and Urry, J. (2004) "Enacting the Social", *Economy and Society, 33*(3), 390–410.

Latour, B. (1993) *We Have Never Been Modern*. Cambridge: Harvard University Press.

Latour, B. (1996) "On actor-network theory: A few clarifications plus more than a few complications", *Soziale Welt, 47*(4), 369–381.

Latour, B. (1998) "From the world of science to the world of research?", *Science, 280*(5361), 208–209.

Latour, B. (1999) "On recalling ANT", *Sociological Review, 47*(1), 15–25.

Latour, B (2004) *Politics of Nature: How to bring the sciences into democracy*. Cambridge: Harvard University Press.

Latour, B (2005) *Reassembling the Social: An Introduction to Actor-network-theory*. Oxford: Oxford University Press.

Latour, B. (2013) "Is there an ANT at the beginning of ANThropology?: A few responses to the subject matter of the collection", *Social Anthropology*, *21*(4), 560–563.

Latour, B., Jensen, P., Venturini, T., Grauwin, S. and Boullier, D. (2012) "'The Whole is Always Smaller Than its Parts' – A digital test of Gabriel Tardes' monads", *The British Journal of Sociology*, *63*(4), 590–615.

Latour, B. and Weibel, P. (2002) *Iconoclash: [Beyond the Image Wars in Science, Religion, and Art]*. Karlsruhe: ZKM.

Latour, B. and Woolgar S. (1986) *Laboratory Life: The Construction of Scientific Facts*. Princeton: Princeton University Press.

Livingston, J. and Boyd, J. (2010) "Correlates and consequences of internalized stigma for people living with mental illness: A systematic review and meta-analysis", *Social Science and Medicine*, *71*(12), 2150–2161.

McBrien J., (2003) "The intellectually disabled offender: Methodological problems in identification", *Journal of Applied Research in Intellectual Disabilities*, *16*(2), 95–105.

McClimens, A. (2003) "Beyond a joke: Is disability a fit subject for laughs? Alex McClimens ponders comic taboos", *Nursing Standard*, *18*(9), 22.

McClimens, A. (2007) "Language, labels and diagnosis: An idiot's guide to learning disability", *Journal of Intellectual Disabilities*, *11*(3), 257–266.

Pawlett W. (2007) *Jean Baudrillard: Against Banality*. London: Routledge.

Pawlett W. (2013) *Violence, Society and Radical Theory: Bataille, Baudrillard and Contemporary Society*. Aldershot: Ashgate Publishing Group.

Reed, G.M. (2010) "Toward ICD-11: Improving the Clinical Utility of WHO's International Classification of Mental Disorders", *Professional Psychology: Research and Practice*, *41*, 457–464.

Serres, M. and Latour, B. (1995) *Conversations on Science, Culture and Time*. Cambridge: University of Michigan Press.

Shakespeare, T. (2014) *Disability Rights and Wrongs Revisited* (2nd ed.). New York: Routledge.

United Nations, Economic and Social Council, Commission on Human Rights (2005) *Report of the Special Rapporteur on the Right of Everyone to the Enjoyment of the Highest Attainable Standard of Physical and Mental Health, Paul Hunt*, E/CN.4/2005/51 UN, EU. (online) Available from: https://digitallibrary.un.org/record/517605/files/E_CN-4_2004_49_Add-1-EN.pdf

Ventegodt, S., Andersen, N., Neikrug, S., Kandel, I. and Merrick, J. (2005) "Clinical holistic medicine: Holistic treatment of mental disorders", *The Scientific World Journal*, *5*, 427–445.

World Health Organisation (2016) *International Statistical Classification of Diseases and Related Health Problems 10th Revision*. (online) Available from: http://apps.who.int/classifications/icd10/browse/2016/en

Chapter 7

Lived experience researchers

Opportunities and challenges in mental health

Helena Roennfeldt and Louise Byrne

Structured as an informal conversation in the first person between two experienced researchers, the quotes were collected through a process of recorded semi-structured interviews between the authors and supplemented with written reflections. Opinion and dialogue are supported by summaries of relevant research. This approach provides personal experience, anecdote and deep reflection, as well as grounding opinion in traditional forms of evidence.

The disjunction between definitions of disability and contemporary concepts of mental health are discussed, with emphasis on contradictions between disability, chronicity, deficits focus and the underpinning ideas of the contemporary 'Recovery approach' in mental health.

Issues regarding the emotional and personal cost of facing both actual and anticipated prejudicial attitudes, the impact of discrimination, and emerging credibility of the roles are considered. The Catch 22 of needing to be exposed to potential discrimination in order to ultimately shift prejudicial attitudes is raised. Appearing to be as 'mainstream' (i.e.: not mentally unwell) as possible to increase credibility and avoid discrimination is explored as a flawed but effective means of gaining acceptance. The limitations of this as a strategy are considered and questions are raised about the validity of representation as a means of providing a unique perspective.

A persistent barrier to lived experience work is reflected upon: the idea that 'everyone has a lived experience' and whether designated lived experience mental health roles are necessary. This is connected to the need to frequently explain what the relevant 'lived experience' is referring to; namely the shared experiences of marginalisation, oppression, loss of personhood, citizenship, status etc. rather than simply an individual experience of diagnosis or illness.

The researchers discuss feeling vulnerable when deeply personal and usually private life experiences are made public and managing the expectations of others regarding sharing these experiences. The need for open and honest discussion with non-lived experience colleagues and the ability to set appropriate boundaries is explained as a means of managing expectations.

The researchers additionally reflect on being a minority voice in the workplace and the consequential lack of understanding of the roles, feelings of isolation and

Note on terminology

Lived Experience: Terminology is contested within lived experience work in mental health. Whilst recognising that there are international and intranational differences in labelling, the term 'lived experience' is used to refer to people who have been variously labelled as having a mental illness or mental health challenge (Deegan, 1988). Other terms that are also commonly used are service user, consumer or peer.

Mental Health Challenge: As people who have experienced recovery, we prefer the term, 'mental health challenge' to terms like 'mental illness'. Phrasing a period of mental un-wellness as a 'difficulty' or 'challenge' describes it as a short-term situation that will be overcome (Slade, 2010). It also clearly differentiates me, as a person, from the challenge I am facing. Further, it separates the experience of the mental health difficulty from the rest of my life, making it clear it is only an aspect of my life and not the defining characteristic.

'othering'. The need for meaningful co-production – professional relationships of equality with colleagues in traditional roles, is explored as an existing and evolving means of addressing this issue.

Introduction

> "You must learn to use your life experience in your intellectual work: continually to examine it and interpret it. In this sense craftsmanship is the center of yourself and you are personally involved in every intellectual product upon which you may work."
>
> (C. Wright Mills 1959: 196)

Often our lives take us on unexpected paths and our careers turn out differently than we anticipated. For both Louise and I, our lives were interrupted by experiences of mental health diagnosis and extended admissions in psychiatric facilities. This formative experience shaped not only our lives but also our future careers.

The stirring force of our work as lived experience (LE) researchers is the desire for knowledge and for change. We consciously choose to draw from our lived experience of extreme distress, receiving support and the subsequent journey of healing to challenge perceptions and hopefully contribute to positive change within our mental health systems. By using our lived experience and putting both story and knowledge into the public sphere, we hope to make a difference to how mental health challenges are seen and treated. Our work is personal, professional and political. We understand the concept of 'mental illness' as a form of

> **Recovery and mental health**
>
> Personal Recovery refers to the individual's capacity to live a meaningful and personally rewarding life regardless of the experience of mental health symptoms (Anthony, 1993). Moreover, personal Recovery applies to living a self-defined 'good life' as distinct from clinical recovery, meaning the absence of symptoms and a return to the state of pre-illness (Deegan, 2002). Both personal Recovery and self-righting describe a natural and individual ability to heal and overcome.
>
> > I know that I am resilient. I have overcome some incredibly traumatic life experiences. I don't really see myself as recovered or even in Recovery. What I do connect with is living a life that is vibrant and self-directed- a life where I choose and have control over what is right for me- Helena

meaning-making; a profound longing expressed though our emotions and bodies to make sense of often very difficult experiences. This is contrasted by the dominant model where systems impose external knowledge and power over people's choices and options for healing.

This lived experience gives a certain sensitivity to the research questions we consider, with our research focus frequently linked to painful and subjective experience. Often, it brings additional challenges in dealing with research methodology and ethics in a way that acknowledges power imbalances within.

This chapter deals with our longing for shared power and bringing collective knowledge to the foreground in influencing change. Structured as an informal conversation in the first person, the quotes were collected through a process of semi-structured interviews between the authors and supplemented with written reflections. Opinion and dialogue are supported by summaries of relevant research. This approach provides personal experience, anecdote and deep reflection, as well as grounding opinion in traditional forms of evidence.

Although the authorship here is ours, our work and research are never wholly just ours, since our work embraces the knowledge of many other people who have experienced mental health challenges. This chapter therefore also explores the role of collective knowledge and co-production in research.

History of LE roles in MH – why identify LE roles?

LE work gained prominence through the consumer movement of the 1960s (Frese & Davis, 1997). This heralded a new wave of mental health service delivery, marked by appealing to a system to restore agency and promote opportunities for community inclusion. Institutionalisation was replaced with a pervasive medical discourse that is credited with making it possible for individuals to live in the community yet is still at odds with contemporary approaches of personal Recovery. The medical model underlines the role of the expert as the authority of treatment, with an inherent disregard for 'lived experience' (Byrne, Happell & Reid-Searl, 2015). In response, it is argued that designated LE roles are required to counter the marginalisation and loss of power of those diagnosed and subjected to ongoing stigma and discrimination (Perkins & Repper, 2014.

Conceptualising the role of the LE researcher

As LE researchers, we are identified through our experience. Yet, a persistent barrier to LE work is the idea that 'everyone has a lived experience'. This manifests in a need to frequently justify the relevance of knowledge and expertise gained through our experience of mental distress and system use. Lived experience within identified LE roles refers to the shared experiences of marginalisation, oppression, loss of personhood, citizenship, status etc. that accompany experiences of mental health challenges, rather than simply an individual experience of diagnosis or illness (Daniels et al., 2017). We agree with those who argue that lived experience exists on a continuum of shared experience, however we contend, and research supports there is a unique point of difference for people who have experienced diagnosis and system use (Daniels et al, 2017).

As professionals identified through lived experience, there is also a liminality of our role and status. We are in an in-between state (Warner & Gabe, 2004). Not seen as a service user but also not really perceived or given equal status as an academic/researcher.

> I sometimes struggle with being defined through one aspect of my life. My experiences within the mental health system were formative in my concept

Stigma

Experiences of stigma among people with mental illness are common. Those experiencing mental illness are more likely to be stigmatised than individuals with a learning or physical disability and individuals suffering from a health condition (Kaushik et al., 2016). Moreover, sigma surrounding mental illness is wide-reaching as many parts of the world exhibit some form of prejudice or discrimination towards individuals with mental illness (Seeman et al., 2016).

> My work still isn't seen as essential. Unless I fit in with their social mores, their ways of doing I won't be allowed to their meetings anymore- Louise

> of self, however I am shaped by many life experiences and sometimes I resist the label and all that it carries. At times, I desire to discover credibility for my work and knowledge where my lived experience of diagnosis and service use is not foregrounded. Personally, I carry my own self-stigma that continues to shape who I am and continues to impact people around me. Yet, every time I hear of human rights violations and cruelty within the system I feel compelled to act and use every means possible to bring change- including wearing my experience- Helena
>
> ... the term 'lived experience researcher' describes the knowledge I've gained from experience. My experience of mental health challenges, service use and periods of healing. Some of the other terminology I find alien, I don't respond to it emotionally and I don't feel like it tells my story. Whereas the term LE researcher tells something about the unique knowledge I have that informs my work- Louise

Part of the role of LE researcher is the relationship between lived experience and the research it informs; between theory and life experience.

> I have taken my lived experience of mental distress as intertwined with the language and focus of my work, as greatly influenced by the meaning of personal experience. I see our perceptions as malleable through language and experience. I describe the process of Recovery or transformation as a reciprocal one in which meaning arises from the experience of people within relationship, as each is changed by the language we use and the value and meanings we ascribe- Helena

Representativeness of experience

Often, the research questions that originally sparked our interest were entwined with personal experience, but then other perspectives and stories suggested further problems and new solutions.

> I was working in a lived experience role and even though this organisation espoused they were coming from a Recovery perspective, I still felt there was poor understanding of my role and there were on-going difficulties getting people to collaborate with me. I wondered if doing research about this and seeing if other people had experienced this difficulty may be a valuable contribution. Basically, it was frustrating. There was a problem and I wanted to be part of the solution- Louise

The struggle to be recognised and valued for our roles and contribution has led to a focus on research into supporting LE work. Louise's PhD work on 'A grounded theory study of lived experience mental health practitioners within the wider workforce', conferred in 2014, was significant in bringing these issues to light and delving further into ways to uphold the value and further expand LE roles.

> An interest in narratives, creativity and identity politics, along with a generous dose of curiosity has led to an interest in subjective experience and meaning making. Knowing other's experiences has reinforced and at times changed the way I interpret and tell my own story. The similarities and differences have created new lines of enquiry- Helena

Each of our experiences makes up and comes from a broader story of experiences of mental health challenges and transformation that we all share. Since our experiences of mental health challenges are also shaped by the society in which we live, our experiences also reflect and need to be examined within our broader social context.

> I am open about my particular story to make clear the difference between myself and others and avoid projecting it unexamined onto other narratives- Helena

Research ethics

Ethical research involves the daily practice of research as well as ensuring the dignity of those participating in the research (Fouka & Mantzorou, 2011). When LE researchers engage in research, they manage complex value systems of individuals, system change and society. As LE researchers, we attempt to challenge the traditional power relations that are involved when people in expert positions conduct research on those who are oppressed through systems. Within LE philosophy, values of self-determination and self-expertise are prioritised and inform how we work with participants.

Often the process of obtaining ethics is fraught with assumptions of vulnerability and incapacity. Questions of determining the capacity of participants who have experiences of mental health challenges are often opposed to values of self-determination, autonomy and a belief in Recovery. Capacity through a LE lens is viewed as complex, fluctuating and not assumed on the basis on diagnosis (Eastman & Starling, 2006). More recently, questions of capacity have been reframed based on themes of personal Recovery in ensuring the rights and citizenship of service users (McSherry, 2015).

As researchers, we acknowledge the personal and often political motivation in our work. We endeavour to be transparent in our agenda and driven by a longing not to objectify people's experiences of personal distress or appropriate people's stories. At the centre of our work is the desire for collective and inclusive practice, where the researcher and the participants together drive the research agenda. As people with an acknowledged lived experience, our interactions with service users are determined more by our commonality and our peer status than our position as 'researchers'. We challenge the assumption of the researcher as the 'healed expert' and the participants as 'vulnerable', and ask, can the researcher, themselves, be vulnerable? Participants involved in LE research recognise the significance of engaging with LE researchers, in giving accounts of their experiences and the feelings of trust and respect (Ning et al., 2010).

Political implications

One of the aims of LE research is to create a counter-discourse to the dominant psychiatric stories about mental illness, through accounts of personal Recovery and transformation. Given the pervasiveness of myths about mental health challenges, the need for alternate models of mental distress and 'illness' is significant. The more available alternate discourses are in the public sphere, the less negative beliefs and prognosis of doom and chronicity will dominate public perceptions.

> I want to provide credible alternatives and stronger narratives of transformation and possibility- for individuals and communities. We are confronted with images of mental 'illness' as pervasive and biological. We are still not hearing the overwhelming evidence of the links to trauma or the healing impacts of dialogue and compassion- Helena

Mental unwellness and its counterpart 'recovery' are both personal and social phenomena, impacted by societal structures and social determinants of health.

> I think Mental Health is everyone's issue. I think the fact that we went down the path of viewing mental health treatment within the domain of services – unwittingly disempowering families and communities was a massive mistake. I can understand why it happened, but Mental Health is not an individual issue, it's a community and societal issue. Particularly in this digital age, it is an 'insane' time to live, we are so disconnected from the natural world. So many people are just trying to cope and the continued pretence that they are the only ones struggling is not helping. We need to collectively make change, a collective movement towards change and there are natural leaders who can contribute to that change. LE perspectives and leadership could transform the way we as a society engage around mental health and the way we view mental health- Louise
>
> Through the stories and experiences of people, I have reached the conclusion that mental health challenges and Recovery are experienced as personal but depend on the understandings reached through a variety of sociological discourses- Helena

These alternate understandings of experience are present, though sometimes in the form of 'less clinical' ideas and practice that create tension for contemporary biological ideas of 'illness'. There is mounting evidence on the effectiveness of alternate viewpoints in approaches such as the Hearing Voices Network (Ruddle et al., 2011; Corstens et al., 2014), peer support (Davidson et al., 1999; Sledge et al., 2011) and Open Dialogue (Seikkula et al., 2011; Lakeman, 2014). The philosophy and practice of 'Intentional Peer Support' are significant as an alternative framework for understanding the value of lived experience not only in practice but also within research (Mead, 2003). These alternative discourses not only redefine dominant perceptions of individual 'illness', they also challenge our knowledge of the mind, emotions and the role of community in contributing to healing (Mead & Hilton, 2003). These perceptions are present in personal stories of Recovery, which is why researching these stories are so important.

Straddling two worlds – disability and health

There are disjunctions between definitions of disability and contemporary concepts of mental health challenges. The lived experience of mental distress and extreme states often does not fit comfortably either within an illness or a disability framework. The current Recovery focus in mental health recognises a personally meaningful and hopeful life with or without the presence of symptoms (Anthony, 1993). This does not discount the reality of clinical recovery but encompasses diversity in meanings and approaches to treatments and healing. Whereas, the experiences of mental health challenges within disability are equally challenging, with many people describing their experiences as episodic or time-limited.

Liminality of role

LE roles are described as a liminal occupation. Warner and Gabe (2004, p. 388) define liminality as a state of being 'in-between' two otherwise distinct identities. In the case of lived experience, liminality arises from the fact that LE workers identify as those who have and can still be receiving services and a paid provider of services. They are often located within the system and, at the same time, share in the stigma associated with being service users.

The liminality in LE research leads to a tension that is experienced in relation to the questions of value, competency and risk (Warner & Gabe, 2004). LE researchers are drawn in different directions. They are pulled towards adopting mainstream methods and practices by wider risk discourses, including scepticism of LE work. At the same time, they are drawn towards the recognition of their own experiences of resilience and the LE philosophies.

At times in my life I have been diagnosed as having a disability. It is a difficult one. The definition of disability as being permanent and chronic is so at odds with the philosophy of Recovery. I am choosing to see mental health challenge as part of a whole life but not defining my life. With a Recovery focus we are looking at a life that is chosen and has meaning and whether it is accurate or not it feels like the term disability clashes with that definition. Certainly, being on a Disability Support Pension[1] did damage my view of myself. I found it hard and transitioned out of that for a couple of years by only working the number of hours I was allowed to and still retain the pension. I was terrified that if I took the plunge and went into fulltime work I wouldn't cope. I was afraid I wasn't capable of fulltime work and frankly even now, I wouldn't be capable of some things. I have a work- life structure that is flexible, I work from home and I don't have to interact with people a whole lot and I get to choose my hours, but I still get a fulltime wage. It was certainly lodged in my brain – that idea of self that was partially constructed through a concept of disability. It hurt me, and it hurt my view of my potential. It created roadblocks. It stopped me from taking risks or rather opportunities in life- Louise

I had a similar experience of being on a DSP [Disability Support Pension] and it gave me a story of myself that I didn't have before. I had a new narrative of who I was and what I was capable of. It felt permanent and it added to my experience of shame and confusion- Helena

Areas of research

Clinical accounts of illness and evidence of treatment is written primarily by and for clinicians and are widely available in journal articles. As 'expert and scientific', they typically carry more weight in the discourse on mental health challenges and Recovery than any lived experience and phenomenological evidence available. LE research remains mysterious to many in mainstream research, largely because of the historic and continued 'low expectations' of people with mental health challenges. This is also reflected in the largely unchanged power disparity between clinicians and service users. Studies by LE researchers have an inherent desire to allow people with lived experience to have a voice. We believe the LE research provides richer accounts of all perspectives. Louise has focused on workforce development and supporting the voice and experience of the LE workforce.

We don't receive recognition or representation. There is no union. We don't have base rates. We often don't have proper position descriptions. The rest of the industry doesn't, by and large value or agree with us being there. You can have the best product in the world but if the rest of the people in your team do not understand, value or want to engage with the product then its impact is limited. The work that I do and am passionate about is how do we get the rest of the sector to understand, acknowledge and engage with LE work so that it doesn't end up ignored, co-opted or fading away...Louise

Methodology

As LE researchers, the relationship between the researcher and researched is of special interest. We have a personal investment in the research and an identification with participants with lived experience. As LE researchers, there is benefit in the insider perspective. Yet, it can be a double-edged sword with criticisms of a lack of objectivity (Garrett, 1998). However, complete objectivity within research we argue is not possible nor desirable (Scott & Garner, 2013). Like many LE workers, our experience of diagnosis and negative experiences of service use are strong drivers for mental health reform and shape areas of research interest (Davidson et al., 2012). Although we have initially chosen to research areas that are sparked by personal experience, we have often branched into the unknown, such as the impact of managers perspectives on the LE workforce.

The philosophy and values of LE work inform our 'way of working' as researchers. The relationship is always at the centre of our work and we gravitate to practices that aim to reduce power imbalances, honour individual voices and methodology that enhances social justice. Chosen methodologies have included Grounded Theory (Strauss & Corbin, 1997); Interpretive Phenomenological Analysis (Smith, 2004); Participatory Action Research (Kemmis & McTaggart, 2005). Here, objectivity and accountability are maximised by using participatory and phenomenological approaches – letting the participants' experience drive the research. We have also used memos to question bias and chosen to work collaboratively with other LE researchers or collegially with researchers from other disciplines.

Collaborative work

As LE researchers, working together has certainly been poetic, since the work brings to life the interconnections and shared experiences which are richly part of our personal and professional lives. This connectedness is also part of bracing against the ruggedness of fitting in as a marginalised worker and brings a type of healing that is apparent in peer relationships.

> I have learnt so much from Louise. She is a mountain of knowledge with a unique presence that helps me to unravel the complexity of research. She has a dogged determination, and a compulsion to live and work authentically that connects with my own 'why' and fuels my desire to contribute meaningfully to this work- Helena
>
> A lot of what is so hard to deal with is not intended, it's a consequence of being poorly understood and having limited credibility in a system that has historically oppressed people like us. It's a consequence of half-hearted

> attempts at reform that ultimately leave power where it has always resided. For me, without Helena particularly and a handful of other peer researchers, this work would be impossible. Helena is the person I can turn to for confirmation of my perspectives and reality. She's the person who lets me know I'm not wandering the wilderness alone and the touchstone that keeps me going when I frequently want to give up- Louise

Collegial work

Collaborating with people who don't have a lived experience can provide relationships which break down the isolation of our work and restore a sense of worth, repairing some of the stigma we often feel exposed to. Working with disciplines as varied as nursing, pharmacy, social work, psychology and business opens up transformative possibilities and mutual learning, especially when power is shared. Unfortunately, power imbalances can be present in many guises, from tokenism to not being invited onto publications.

> I am often on the outside, where I am invited onto multi-disciplinary research teams to be the 'consumer' voice but am excluded from communications and the expectation is that I will come in and share the lived experience perspective and then walk out. There is not the same value in being a part of the research team from start to finish- Helena

Minority voice in the workplace, the lack of understanding of the roles, feelings of isolation and 'Othering'

Different role expectations for LE researchers may result in disparate opportunities to mainstream roles. As LE researchers, we often find ourselves with little job stability and restricted access to career advancement. Socially excluded groups, such as those with mental health challenges are excluded from participating in ways that others take for granted, such as social opportunities (Goffman, 2009). Experiences of marginalisation are complex and diverse, but the interplay of factors that influence exclusion are often played out in the use of language that denotes negative meanings and devalued status in society (Wolfensberger, 2011).

> One of the first things people ask is 'what do you do'? So I tell them, and I have to briefly summarise what that means because most people haven't heard of lived experience work. 99 times out of 100 they will go 'oh, that make total sense, obviously we need people with lived experience in those roles'. The people who seem to have the most difficulty are those who are trained in traditional mental health roles. They don't see it as a common-sense thing, they don't grasp onto it and they often get defensive and push it/us away. People who respond positively, typically have a world view that is able to receive

these kinds of ideas and even conservative people I meet see the sense in experiential learning, practical learning. I don't think it is a left wing/right wing thing. The biggest divide I think is between people in traditional mental health roles and the rest of the population- Louise

For me marginalisation has been the precursor and impetus to show people that I am capable and can 'pass' as someone who has not experienced mental health challenges. This means working harder and proving my worth. Self-censoring is sometimes a necessity. I have learnt that changing people's perceptions is slow and deliberate. To fit in and 'pass' as someone who is not mentally unwell, some experiences are better not shared in the lunchroom- Helena

Compromise and challenge in research

There is an inherent need for LE work and research to work as change agents and to understand the requirements for societal and systems change. The reality of opportunities for practice as LE workers and researchers does not always align with the evidence for best practice. Recent research supports the need for LE workers to occupy roles in all levels of service delivery, including executive governance, within mental health services as instrumental to systems change (Byrne et al., 2018).

The overarching intention for me has always been to challenge stereotypes and unacceptable experiences, human rights violations that deny people access to social goods and opportunities. Our experiences mark us as different or 'other' enough to be treated in ways that would be completely unacceptable if we didn't have the label of 'mentally ill'. I want to bring these horrible injustices to the forefront…but who wants to invest in that? I am also conscious of not opening up people's lives to a voyeuristic gaze- Helena

Some of my papers are much more controversial than I would be in person because I find it's essential to get along with people and not rock the boat too hard and keep that door open and communication happening. That can be a bitter pill to swallow but, at the same time that's adult diplomacy. If I want to sit at the adult table then there is a sense that is what I have to do. On the other hand I have seen psychiatrists and mental health nurses walk into meetings and really vent – uncensored, and nobody questions their professionalism. There is one rule for people in traditional roles and one rule for people in lived experience roles- Louise

A key challenge to LE research is a lack of funding. There is no designated LE research funding and limited opportunities within the wider funding pools which limits the scale and scope of studies. Similarly, a lack of LE researchers, particularly with the track record and experience to lead projects and attract funding, limits the impact of LE perspectives on the research design.

Overcoming challenges

Our experiences of continued discrimination and low expectations have required personal grit and determination. This battle has also been fuelled by hope and a fire for change. Strategies, such as meaning-making and self-compassion, gained through our experiences of personal Recovery have been invaluable in confronting our experiences of both external and internalised stigma. Likewise, training in Intentional Peer Support has also supported our work and provided a frame to effectively explore change (Mead & MacNeil, 2005).

In Australia, there are few LE research roles. Typically, only one LE researcher/role will be located within traditional health disciplines. This can be isolating and lonely. Fostering connections with other peers provides a strong foundation, both personally and professionally.

> It's good to have strong networks outside of your place of research, as you're probably going to be quite isolated. There may be a lack of collaboration and feel like you're not properly included. That is tough, and you need an LE network. Not necessarily researchers but people who understand what it is like to be on the outside looking in. It also helps to stay connected to a sense of deeper purpose- Louise

Current National agendas upholding the role of lived experience have given value to LE knowledge (Commonwealth of Australia, 2013; Department of Health, 2017) however there has also been a need to creatively and boldly promote LE research so it is not subsumed within a more dominant discipline.

> Sometimes, being the lone voice that stands up for lived experience in a room filled with 'real' academics isn't easy, but it isn't a choice- it is a necessity- Helena

For longevity of the roles, it is important to find support within the workplace as well as financial backing. Allies are invaluable because they often have more power and can champion on behalf of lived experience. Enabling greater impact of LE perspectives within research will require open and honest discussion with non-LE colleagues and the ability to set appropriate boundaries as a means of managing other's expectations.

> We must find courage to influence and respectfully challenge and to be eye to eye- Helena

Ultimately, what will create the greatest opportunity for the future of LE research is recognition and a place for LE research that allow for greater autonomy and control.

> We need our own centres of power and to not always speak other people's language. Spaces where there is not one of us sitting in the school

or college, we could start to have more influence, start to shift priorities. Having collective lived experience spaces and not have to fight to gain credibility- Louise

Conclusions and future

This chapter sought to bring together the threads of the complex role and consequent challenges of LE research. Our personal reflections as researchers echo many of the wider systemic challenges facing the LE workforce in mental health. Our reflections have focused on challenges relating to identity, experiences of marginalisation and finding a platform for the credibility of LE knowledge. What follows are the key messages we have learnt while finding our own place within our work.

First, there is a need for meaningful cross-disciplinary partnerships – relationships of equality with colleagues in traditional roles, as an evolving means of addressing the issue of imbalance and inequality. Respect is needed on both sides to value different ways of knowing.

Second, LE researchers are slowly being accepted and the roles recognised, yet, LE researchers feel they must conform to traditional approaches and ways of expressing that may be inauthentic and stigmatising. More work is needed to embrace and embed LE knowledge within its own discipline.

Last, speaking from experiences of distress and marginalisation is personally challenging. Confronting that sinking feeling in your stomach because of your desire for change may be inevitable but is made considerably more bearable through openness and acceptance.

In writing this chapter, we have sought to share our alternate voice to the more dominant clinical approaches in mental health research, and to offer not a step-by-step guide to LE research but a narrative approach that allows the reader to 'walk our hallways' for a moment. We argue that counter-narratives are needed to allow the perspectives of people with lived experience to be heard. Historically, too many voices have been silenced or hidden creating a narrow and uncontested 'mental illness' script. Instead, there is a need for diverse representations within mental health discourse. We argue that LE researchers, in adopting peer and participatory methodologies, are uniquely placed in revealing the presence of human rights violations and the negative impacts of shame and stigma that continue to pervade mental health service delivery. In closing, we would like to acknowledge those who have boldly and compassionately used their lived experience to inform, challenge and give hope.

Note

1 Disability Support Pension (DSP) is an Australian Government subsidy for persons deemed to have a permanent intellectual, physical or psychiatric disability that prevents them from working https://www.humanservices.gov.au/individuals/services/centrelink/disability-support-pension

References

Anthony, W. A. (1993) "Recovery from mental illness: The guiding vision of the mental health service system in the 1990s", *Psychosocial Rehabilitation Journal*, *16*(4), 11–23.

Byrne, L., Happell, B. and Reid-Searl, K. (2015) "Lived experience practitioners and the medical model: World's colliding?", *Journal of Mental Health*, *25*(3), 217–223.

Byrne, L., Roennfeldt, H., O'Shea, P. and Macdonald, F. (2018) "Taking a gamble for high rewards? Management perspectives on the value of mental health peer workers", *International Journal of Environmental Research and Public Health*, *15*(4), 746.

Commonwealth of Australia (2013) *A National Framework for Recovery-oriented Mental Health Services: Policy and Theory*. (online) Available from: http://www.mhima.org.au/pdfs/Recovery%20Framework%202013_Policy_theory.pdf

Corstens, D., Longden, E., McCarthy-Jones, S., Waddingham, R. and Thomas, N. (2014) "Emerging perspectives from the hearing voices movement: Implications for research and practice. *Schizophrenia Bulletin*, *40*(4), 285–294.

Daniels, A. S., Bergeson, S. and Myrick, K. J. (2017) "Defining peer roles and status among community health workers and peer support specialists in integrated systems of care" *Psychiatric Services*, 68(12), 1296–1298.

Davidson, L., Bellamy, C., Guy, K. and Miller, R. (2012) "Peer support among persons with severe mental illnesses: A review of evidence and experience", *World Psychiatry*, *11*(2), 123–128.

Davidson, L., Chinman, M., Kloos, B., Weingarten, R., Stayner, D. and Tebes, J. K. (1999) "Peer support among individuals with severe mental illness: A review of the Evidence", *Clinical Psychology: Science and Practice*, 6(2), 165–187.

Deegan, P. E. (1988) "Recovery: The lived experience of rehabilitation", *Psychosocial Rehabilitation Journal*, *11*(4), 11.

Deegan, P. (2002) "Recovery as a self-directed process of healing and transformation", *Occupational Therapy in Mental Health*, *17*(3–4), 5–21.

Department of Health (2017) *The fifth national mental health and suicide prevention plan*. (online) Available from: https://www.health.gov.au/internet/main/publishing.nsf/content/mental-fifth-national-mental-health-plan

Eastman, N. and Starling, B. (2006) "Mental disorder ethics: Theory and empirical Investigation", *Journal of Medical Ethics*, *32*(2), 94–99.

Fouka, G. and Mantzorou, M. (2011) "What are the major ethical issues in conducting research? Is there a conflict between the research ethics and the nature of nursing?", *Health Science Journal*, 5(1), 3–14.

Frese, F. J. and Davis, W. W. (1997) "The consumer–survivor movement, recovery, and consumer professionals", *Professional Psychology: Research and Practice*, 28(3), 243.

Garrett, C. (1998) *Beyond Anorexia: Narrative, Spirituality and Recovery*. Cambridge: Cambridge University Press.

Goffman, E. (2009) *Stigma: Notes on the Management of Spoiled Identity*. New Jersey: Simon and Schuster.

Kaushik, A., Kostaki, E. and Kyriakopoulos, M. (2016) "The stigma of mental illness in children and adolescents: A systematic review", *Psychiatry Research*, *243*, 469–494.

Kemmis, S. and McTaggart, R. (2005) *Participatory Action Research: Communicative Action and the Public Sphere*. Thousand Oaks: Sage Publications Ltd.

Lakeman, R. (2014) "The Finnish open dialogue approach to crisis intervention in psychosis: A review", *Psychotherapy in Australia*, 20(3), 28.

McSherry, B. (2015) "Decision-making, legal capacity and neuroscience: Implications for mental health laws", *Laws*, 4(2), 125–138.
Mead, S. (2003) "Defining peer support. Intentional peer support: An alternative approach. (online) Available from: http://www.intentionalpeersupport.org
Mead, S. and Hilton, D. (2003) "Crisis and connection", *Psychiatric Rehabilitation Journal*, *27*(1), 87.
Mead, S. and MacNeil, C. (2005) "Peer support: A systemic approach", *Family Therapy Magazine*, *4*(5), 28–31.
Mills, C.W. (2000) *The Sociological Imagination*. New York: Oxford University Press.
Ning, L., Weavell, W. and Woodhouse, S. (2010) "Consumer participation in research", *New Paradigm: The Australian Journal on Psychosocial Rehabilitation* (autumn edition).
Perkins, R. and Repper, J. (2014) "Challenging discrimination within mental health services: The importance of using lived experience in the work place", *Mental Health and Social Inclusion*. (online) Available from: https://doi.org/10.1108/MHSI-07-2014-0023
Ruddle, A., Mason, O. and Wykes, T. (2011) "A review of hearing voices groups: Evidence and mechanisms of change", *Clinical Psychology Review*, *31*(5), 757–766.
Scott, G. and Garner, R. (2013) *Doing Qualitative Research: Designs, Methods, and Techniques*. Upper Saddle River: Pearson.
Seeman, N., Tang, S., Brown, A. D. and Ing, A. (2016) "World survey of mental illness stigma", *Journal of Affective Disorders*, *190*, 115–121.
Seikkula, J., Alakare, B. and Aaltonen, J. (2011) "The comprehensive open-dialogue approach in Western Lapland: Long-term stability of acute psychosis outcomes in advanced community care", *Psychosis*, *3*(3), 192–204.
Slade, M. (2010) "Mental illness and well-being: The central importance of positive psychology and recovery approaches", *BMC Health Services Research*, *10*(1), 26.
Sledge, W. H., Lawless, M., Sells, D., Wieland, M., O'Connell, M. J. and Davidson, L. (2011) "Effectiveness of peer support in reducing readmissions of persons with multiple psychiatric hospitalizations", *Psychiatric Services*, *62*(5), 541–544.
Smith, J. A. (2004) "Reflecting on the development of interpretative phenomenological analysis and its contribution to qualitative research in psychology", *Qualitative Research in Psychology*, *1*(1), 39–54.
Strauss, A. and Corbin, J. M. (1997) *Grounded Theory in Practice*. Thousand Oaks: Sage.
Warner, J. and Gabe, J. (2004) "Risk and liminality in mental health social work", *Health, Risk & Society*, 6(4), 387–399.
Wolfensberger, W. (2011) "Social role valorization: A proposed new term for the principle of normalization", *Intellectual and Developmental Disabilities*, *49*(6), 435–440.

Part 3

Shifting methodologies

Chapter 8

Unsettling ableism in research traditions

Toward establishing blind methodologies

Cynthia Bruce

Introduction

Disability and research have long been entangled in an objectifying and dehumanizing relationship that has been substantially demarcated by the disciplines of medicine and psychology. Disability is ubiquitously situated as a condition to be studied and theorized within objective research frameworks so that valid and reliable measures of ability can inform the development of treatment, intervention, and cure (Linton, 1998b). This tenacious entanglement relies on a limited and limiting understanding of disability as a deficit or lack (Oliver, 2009), and it has contributed powerfully to the privileging of non-disabled researchers and practitioners as the unquestioned 'experts' on all things disabled.

The growth of disability studies as an academic discipline has led to an important increase in scholarship generated by disabled researchers. Yet despite this growth, ableism pervades the academy in myriad ways, and scholars are continually working to uncover and articulate the intractable nature of institutional preferences for 'normal' ways of knowing and doing (Bolt, 2004; Bruce, 2016, 2017; Dolmage, 2017; Hayman, 2010; Hutcheon & Wolbring, 2012). It can often be difficult to define what specific practices and processes constitute ableism, but it generally relies on the maintenance of the ability/disability binary and the certain belief that ability is disability's desirable and even essential other. This epistemic conviction insidiously entrenches ableism in our everyday thoughts and actions, often rendering us largely unaware of its force in our lives. We breathe its logic, are shaped by its politics, and are unknowingly complicit in nurturing its power (Campbell, 2008b, 2009, 2012). Ability and disability work to sustain one another by perpetuating a clear distinction through the assignment of discrete meanings to each. Ability is good and empowering, but disability is bad, disabling, and clearly unwanted (Titchkosky, 2007, Chapter 6, Section 7, para. 4). Consequently, academic settings tend to privilege normative modes of performance and marginalize or exclude those who fail to emulate normal as a sign of success (Bruce, 2016; Campbell, 2008a; Dolmage, 2017).

This chapter synthesizes and extends aspects of my doctoral dissertation to delve into one relatively unexamined manifestation of ableism in academia. I aim to expose the extent to which qualitative data analysis traditions construct sighted individuals as natural and, therefore, legitimate producers and purveyors of knowledge. It is a realization of ableist normativity that exposes the social positioning of blind academics as unanticipated producers of disability-related knowledge. We are not expected in the academy as either competent or prolific researchers, so the tools of analysis are fundamentally incompatible with our auditory ways of working and knowing. This is a reality that forces a kind of analytic innovation that brings focus to the potential inherent in assistive technology and in specific process representation choices to support the assertion of blind methodological frameworks as a valid research practice.

As a blind doctoral candidate, there was no small irony in encountering substantial unanticipated thesis completion barriers within conventional data analysis procedures in a study that aimed to consider the experiences of disabled university students by drawing on an ableist analytic framework. My problem-solving process involved substantive reference to the aims of the study itself and the specific disciplinary orientation of the research. It is, therefore, appropriate to provide a brief account of the doctoral project that led to the conundrum I was forced to resolve when I entered the analysis phase of my dissertation. Interestingly, I was exploring student/faculty relationships to gain a better understanding of their influence on disability experiences in university learning when I unexpectedly encountered multiple barriers to establishing a meaningful and workable relationship with my interview data. Researching within the discipline of disability studies supported the work of forming this relationship and of asserting blind methodologies as rigorous and legitimate. So, I will also provide an overview of the field as a way of framing the discussion of my methodological process. Delineating the field supports the claim that the academy must value what blindness tells us about the exclusionary nature of existing procedures. It similarly highlights the importance of attending to possibilities uncovered by centring blindness – an approach that necessarily expands understandings of what constitutes valid and reliable research process.

Research context

As I began to formulate a doctoral dissertation proposal, I grappled with the privilege and marginalization I was experiencing as a white disabled woman returning to graduate studies in her early 40s. I was a blind student and a university instructor who interacted frequently with disabled students and disability services, and all of these intersecting experiences generated deep interest in conducting research that would elucidate how post-secondary disability support structures in Nova Scotia, Canada, shape the relationships that develop between disabled students and their university professors. Deep engagement with the literature revealed the potential for emergent thinking about the relational nature of post-secondary disability support structures to offer new avenues to probe the links between specific disability accommodation practices and the student/faculty relationships they produce. Studies in this area had not substantively considered disability as a reality that is lived and produced within student/faculty relationships, and they had rarely investigated how these connections might help to structure pedagogical methods that anticipate student diversity. Inspired by the work of Tanya Titchkosky (2011), my research called attention to the importance of the relational elements embedded within accommodation procedures by exploring how socio-political conventions and perceptions contributed to post-secondary constructions of participation and belonging.

As students work to make academic arrangements in Canadian universities, formal procedures require multiple interpersonal exchanges with faculty and disability services staff. These obligatory interactions often draw students into conversations where they encounter varying perspectives on disability and academic support. As a result, they are exposed to numerous viewpoints related to disability in academic settings, and those perspectives can shape their sense of themselves as either valued or marginalized members of their learning communities.

The myriad views to which students are exposed through these dialogues can intersect in difficult ways with the significant individual responsibility they are expected to assume when making academic support arrangements. Disabled students are usually taught that they must develop the knowledge and skill to discuss their disabilities and to assert their learning-specific needs and rights in order to achieve academic success (Shaw, Madaus, & Dukes, 2010; Test, Fowler, Wood, Brewer, & Eddy, 2005; Walker& Test, 2011). Asserting their rights requires students to expend substantial effort to participate in a process that can, according to many disabled students, produce ongoing fears of rejection (Madaus, 2008). This system also constitutes a highly individualized practise that is lived only by students not served through typical teaching and assessment procedures, and it reinforces faculty/student power inequities that often surface when students request individual support (Erten, 2011; Mullins & Preyde, 2013; Warick, 2004).

Teaching disabled students that they must develop skills related to self-identifying as disabled and communicating with faculty about their disability-related needs in order to achieve university success privileges deficit-focused methods and potentially imposes hierarchical and mutually anxiety-provoking student-faculty relationships (Claiborne, Cornforth, Gibson, & Smith, 2011). Continually focusing on individual students allows institutions to minimize their responsibility for diverse course pathways, and it places the burden of ensuring inclusive university learning on the disabled students themselves (Aspis, 1997; Dowse, 2001). Accordingly, my study explored how disability accommodation processes and self-advocacy were understood, constructed, and experienced by disabled students and university faculty. Through a critical qualitative methodology, I worked to generate lived knowledge that would disrupt dominant deficit-driven perceptions of disabled students, position faculty as viable resources for the facilitation of learning, and expand thinking about student-faculty relations beyond discussions of the barriers they potentially embody.

Disability studies

The decision to situate this inquiry in the activist academic discipline of disability studies was unambiguously political. Extensive experience as a disabled student and university instructor led me to a research topic and approach that might work against epistemological and methodological assumptions that promote and sustain deficit-oriented and remedial responses to disability (Tremain, 2005). Disability studies scholars do the vital work of exploring disability as a sociocultural phenomenon, and they work to establish its legitimacy as a form of lived knowledge. In educational settings, the aim is to foster social, political, and educational transformation by increasing understandings of disability in sociopolitical contexts. Academic writing aims to reveal and redress the erasure of disability from our histories and cultures, to situate disabled students as capable learners deserving of meaningful access to the general curriculum, and to expose harmful manifestations of neoliberal ableist commitments to independence and autonomy (Ashby, 2010; Connor, Gabel, Gallagher, & Morton, 2008; Goodley, 2014). Rather than simply promoting another normative framework within which disability in education can be understood, disability studies in education researchers urge all educators to reject deficit constructions of disability perpetuated by medical and psychological discourses and to engage with the lived knowledge that disabled people bring to a more socio-politically informed perspective.

As an established academic discipline, disability studies is rooted in political and theoretical formulations that grew out of the disabled people's movement in the late 1960s and early 1970s (Roulstone, Thomas, & Watson, 2012). Crucial to its epistemological grounding is the construction of disability as a social issue, an orientation that firmly situates disabled people as disadvantaged and a group of people who can legitimately lay claim to minority status (Shakespeare & Watson, 2001). Simi Linton (1998b) has argued that 'disability studies' must be delineated from 'not disability studies' in order to establish its importance as a response to traditional medicalized approaches to disability. 'In a sense, the development of disability studies is a remedial endeavour, redressing the sins of omission and commission in the canon' (p. 525). It is, as Linton explains, the socio-political-cultural model of disability incarnate.

Disability studies is, therefore, a way of challenging or unsettling conventional forms of knowledge and knowledge generation through an interdisciplinary approach that draws from multiple genres in the social sciences and humanities to re-form established understandings of disability across histories and cultures (Ware, 2005). Integral to this work is a commitment to expand disability-related research beyond the confines of exploring and classifying variations inherent in human embodiment. It allows researchers to take up methodologies that promote critical engagement with the meaning we make of those variations (Baglieri & Knopf, 2004; Linton, 1998a), and with the multiple ways that those meanings shape interpretations of human difference and diversity (Peters, Johnstone, & Ferguson, 2005).

Deficit interpretations of disability are an ever-present reality in my daily experiences in the academy. As a university researcher and instructor, I generally experience blindness interpreted by others as lack – as a sensory impairment or an embodied variation that naturally prevents access to conventional research tools and processes. The presumption of sightedness becomes increasingly clear with every step I endeavour to complete, and it exposes a normatively oriented academy that does not expect researchers whose way of doing things is incompatible with established analysis methods. The problem this reality presents is layered and complex. It creates a precarious access space (Bruce, 2017; Titchkosky, 2011) where relationships with people and process must usefully come together in the construction of a solution. It requires significant skill related to data analysis software packages and to how they will interact with specific assistive technology programs. It necessitates a great deal of consultation with respect to technological function and capacity alongside discussions about acceptable research procedures. Finally, it adds significant labour to an already burdensome accommodation-related workload (Bruce, 2017; Denhart, 2008; Dowrick, Anderson, Heyer, & Acosta, 2005; Goode, 2007; Kioko & Makoelle, 2014; Mullins & Preyde, 2013; Ross, 2008) to generate accessible analysis procedures that will be recognized and accepted as rigorous and valid. Consequently, drawing on a disability studies framework to confront and disrupt the dominance of these sighted conventions offers a way of making space for blindness as methodology; and it challenges scholars and institutions to reconsider narrowly defined conceptions of research validity and analytic rigor.

In the final sections of this chapter, I detail the blind methodological processes I developed to work through all aspects of data analysis. I begin with the dilemma created when I was confronted with the requirements and restrictions of traditional methods and tools. The utility and process of transcription creation are considered with specific reference to how each was resolved. With a particular focus on remaining deeply connected to my participant conversations, I then discuss the helpful process of writing, and I conclude with specific commentary on how all of the aforementioned pieces supported decisions related to representation. My research findings are minimally addressed for the purpose of detailing the methodological framework, but a more complete dissemination of my study is anticipated in coming publications.

Confronting the conventions

Entering the analysis phase of my doctoral dissertation meant confronting established and arguably ableist standards for determining analytic rigor in qualitative data analysis. As a blind researcher, it was not immediately apparent that my way of working and knowing would be compatible with accepted norms. For example, convention prescribes that audio recordings will be transcribed and then analysed as textual data (Markle, West, & Rich, 2011). Yet analysing that textual data is generally a highly visual task. While it is true that I can work with the text using a screen reader, it seemed that doing so would be less productive, and perhaps even less efficient, than working directly with my recorded conversations. My life and work orient generally around the auditory relationships I construct with people and environments, and I knew I had already connected strongly with my data through the voices of my participants.

I did, however, understand that there might be some pragmatic benefits to engaging with my data through the process of creating transcripts. It could be an important interpretive act that would simultaneously be informed by my theoretical orientation and help to keep me rooted in that stance (Lapadat & Lindsay, 1998; 1999). Attending to the authentic conveyance of my participants' words and the important contextual details of our conversations could be of significance in privileging their voices, not simply in establishing trustworthiness and demonstrating rigor (Poland, 1995, 2003). The difficulty then was to preserve these elements while developing and committing to a fully accessible process that centred disability, or my disabled way of doing (Price & Kerschbaum, 2016).

The next challenge arose when I began to consider how I would code or sort the data, and I often seemed to encounter more questions than readily available answers. While my process clearly needed to be thorough and defensible, it also needed to be manageable. How was I going to make sense of and then make accessible a large corpus of data that included 46 interviews ranging from 30 to 90 minutes in length? Basit (2003) asserts that answers to such questions depend largely on the size of the project, the availability of time and funding, and the inclination and expertise of the researcher. My project was large, and the time and/or financial resources required to transcribe and code were substantial; but electronic coding was simply not an option. Computer-assisted qualitative data analysis programs are not accessible. That is, they are not compatible with screen reader technology. They also rely heavily on visual interaction with the data to sort and analyse.

I began to look at this technology when I was still conducting interviews because of the potential such programs offered to work directly with recordings rather than primarily with text. However, it became evident that, in addition to screen-reader incompatibility, the extensive use of colour-coding and other visual cues and devices was going to render electronic coding impossible. With the removal of this option, I returned to the original intent of my research in order to ask myself what process, beginning with transcription, would support my commitment to privileging the voices of my participants (Bird, 2005). I also took up what I hoped was a methodologically disruptive question and began to wonder how I might work to assert the legitimacy and rigor of my auditory way of working and knowing.

These vital decisions were critical in the development of my approach to analysis, and they laid 'the question of access' (Titchkosky, 2011) before me in ways I had never considered. Suddenly, my conundrum was no longer limited to the problem of how I would access and work with my data. That was certainly a pragmatic concern that was going to require a workable solution. However, my current reality was exposing the unquestioned assumptions that have constituted and naturalized sighted academics as the legitimate producers and purveyors of knowledge. Such researchers are people who can read transcripts with their eyes, can recognize colour-coded passages of text, and can make visually mediated decisions about what their data are saying. They are scholars who can recognize visually displayed patterns and organize and reorganize using visual markers. They are not primarily auditory knowers, analysts, or co-creators of knowledge.

This was a powerful revelation, but it did not resolve the challenges that such visually oriented analytic paradigms were presenting. At this point, I was working closely with Dr Cornelia Schneider from the Faculty of Education at Mount Saint Vincent University in Halifax, Nova Scotia. She was one of my dissertation committee members, and she supported the analysis phase of my dissertation in helpful ways. As we discussed my options, it became clear that I needed to remain closely connected to the interview recordings as I moved through my analysis. I had worked as an active interviewer (Holstein and Gubrium, 1995) to establish a relationship with my participants, and it made cognitive and interpretive sense to extend that relationship by remaining rooted in our conversations. What follows is a detailed description of my method, articulated as a way of offering transparency. It is intended to serve as an entry point into the cognitive processes that informed my analytic decisions and to demonstrate that auditory analytic processes yield a deep and meaningful understanding of categories and themes.

Grappling with transcription

The purpose of the transcript, as noted above, was to provide a textual representation of a social interaction to support careful and detailed analysis of the data. However, the purpose of such a product was much less clear for me because, regardless of presentation, I was going to interact with my data in an auditory manner. It seemed counter-intuitive to listen to a transcript read by a computerized screen-reader voice because it felt like it would distance me from those vital conversations. While sighted researchers may also work to maintain this sort of connection, listening to a computerized voice adds a layer of distance that makes the maintenance of that connection through the memory of particular voices virtually impossible. Therefore, it made sense for me to work directly and extensively with the recordings, and to transcribe in a way that would grant me timely and efficient access to relevant passages in the recordings when necessary. This would keep me immersed in the data while addressing the pragmatic need to have a text I could reference for the purposes of coding and writing (Bird, 2005).

I began the process by listening, by living with my participants and their stories without pausing to transcribe. During the interview process, I had kept a researcher journal in order to document immediate impressions and questions that surfaced during each conversation, and I referred to and expanded upon this journal as I listened. I sat down each day and listened to three or four interviews, depending on their length. I knew I risked becoming distracted and consequently distanced from the conversations if I tried to attend to more in any given day. After listening carefully to each of the conversations, I moved into a process of partial transcription.

As I mentioned previously, I originally researched qualitative data analysis software because of the potential it offered to work directly with recordings. Although none was accessible, I did discover that Kurzweil 1000, the screen-reading package I use to read and annotate many of my texts, would allow me to use the bookmarking feature to write text that would link directly to specific places in the recording. It is important to note that this option was not evident as a feature of the technology. It required trial and error and discussion with helpful technical support staff to uncover this most useful option.

Discovering this previously unidentified Kurzweil 1000 possibility was vital to the development of a methodological framework that would build on my blind ways of working as a strength rather than expecting me to devise a way of simulating sightedness in order to work around it. The technology was made for me; it was not made for visually oriented users and then retrofitted to accommodate disabled individuals. It expected me to be using it for multiple tasks, so it centred intuitively my blind/auditory ways of doing.

Kurzweil allowed me to bookmark a passage in the recording, transcribe the passage within the bookmark, and then select the bookmark to return to the specific passage at any time. So, I was able to listen to each recording again and transcribe within the recording to ensure efficient access to the raw data. I transcribed some passages verbatim while others were truncated or summarized. Nothing was completely omitted, and all transcribing was designed and carried out to guarantee all topics of discussion were easily accessible in their original form. I had intended to (and did) return frequently to the recordings throughout the entire analytic process.

Interview profiles

Writing became a key creative process that supported the next stage of sensemaking for me. Immersion in the conversations had been critically important because it had facilitated deep engagement with individual stories. However, I needed to approach the data from another perspective to see what it might be telling me about what was being said and done more broadly in the name of disability access on campus (Titchkosky, 2011, Preface, para.2). Writing individual participant profiles facilitated the crystallization of my thinking, a process that brought to light different patterns, perspectives, and details than listening and transcribing had done (Richardson & St. Pierre, 2005).

I drew on recordings, transcripts and journal notes in order to construct the profiles. They varied in length from one to four pages. This was once again dependent on the relative length of the interview itself. Each profile contained the demographic data, a short summary of the participant's overall experience, and a sequential profile of the interview conversation. Similar to the creation of transcripts, writing these profiles involved interpretation of both the audio-recording and the transcriptions themselves. They represented a construction of my participants' experiences that provided me with a deeply situated textual account from which I could proceed with coding and categorizing.

Coding

As I read through the profiles, I began to develop a set of initial codes in order to organize the data into common themes and salient discussion topics (Saldana, 2009). This was yet another way of approaching the data, and it allowed me to see what participants were saying and how they were contextualizing and framing their comments. I kept the codes intentionally broad to maintain the context in which discussions occurred and to make space for tensions among differing perspectives and experiences to emerge. Initial codes included accommodations, belonging, intersectionality, negotiation, networks of support, pedagogy, perspectives on process, reciprocity, resistance, and self-advocacy.

This process was enormously important because it gave me a rich sense of what my participants were talking about, of what was important to them in the teaching and learning context, and of their sources of support and frustration. However, it also limited my understanding of the broader context in which post-secondary disability access was being lived. It was reducing what was emerging as an incredibly complex discourse to a set of individualized or discrete learning and participation barriers and success strategies. While this was certainly important information, it was constraining my capacity to gain a rich understanding of the broader context of post-secondary disability access and of what lived experience of access processes had to say about the place of disability in the university milieu.

Relational categories

Working to cultivate a critical understanding of how disability-specific difference was being interpreted in my participants' university environments led me back to the journal notes, interview recordings, transcripts, and profiles; a process that caused me to re-sort data under three relational categories. I came to consider my data from this relational perspective as I reflected on Titchkosky's (2011) discussion of access as perception, as talk and conduct, and as a form of consciousness that leads us to ask how access can be an interpretive move that puts people into different kinds of relations with their surroundings (p. 13). What I had learned from working with the data to this point and from immersing myself in it from numerous perspectives, was that the formal process of organizing accommodations had placed disabled students and faculty into relations that could be characterized in one of three ways. The most common relations revolved around compliance. Relations of compliance captured a spectrum of interactions and encounters that centred on ensuring student and faculty adherence to the formal requirements of the accommodation process. Providing documentation of disability, approaching faculty, signing forms, returning forms to disability services, and following procedures to book exam accommodations, academic coaches, and tutors were all activities associated with this particular category.

There were also relations that were largely characterized by resistance. Within this category, students experienced difficulty with faculty who either refused their accommodations outright, or they had to engage in significant periods of negotiation, a process that one student described as a tug of war, in order to have their approved accommodations implemented. This category also included data from faculty members who were aware of colleagues who resisted, questioned, or simply refused accommodation requests.

Finally, there were some relations that elucidated potential for transgression, and for pushing the boundaries that bureaucratic structures had imposed around post-secondary disability access. Data in this category included both faculty and students who had developed strong learning relationships that were characterized as flexible, supportive, and reciprocal. Reciprocity seemed particularly important and was representative of an environment where mutual learning was desirable, and even promoted. Potential for transgression also emerged when pedagogy was seen as a central focus for faculty, and when the development of strong learning relationships was part of their pedagogical commitment. Importantly, it was in this category that the significance of shared experience emerged. Faculty who had lived experience of disability and who were open to sharing that experience with students were particularly committed to supporting a diverse range of students. Yet personal experience with academic struggle or with disability in one's family also emerged as an influential dynamic in this category.

Representation of the data

The emergence of these relational categories was a significant analytic development for me, and it represented a reorientation to my data that invited a re-reading of the phenomenon of self-advocacy. Although self-advocacy was discussed by participants in terms of the vital role it had played in organizing post-secondary disability support, it became evident that an exploration of self-advocacy might also reveal its social and institutional construction as a phenomenon that was simultaneously sustaining and being sustained by the individualized and medicalized perspectives from which disability support services emanate. It was also the daily phenomenon through which disabled students and faculty were being placed into the previously discussed relational categories. This reframing of self-advocacy as the entry point into the daily relations that make visible the place of disability on campus presented an opportunity to scrutinize how self-advocacy is so often situated as the unquestioned and necessary route to effective post-secondary disability support. It offered a different understanding of self-advocacy, at least as it is deployed in the post-secondary milieu, as the point through which students are introduced to a very complex and even uncertain world.

This uncertainty became central as I began exploring how I would represent the experiences of my participants in written form. As I began to write, it seemed logical to devote a single chapter to each of my three relational categories. Yet working through the drafts brought the reductive nature of that approach into focus for me once again. Experiences within and across categories continued to lead me into discussions of individual barriers and solutions, and I truly began to see that the complexity of the environment would be more richly represented if I could dwell in the lived realities of access as that space between what is and what ought to be (Titchkosky, 2011, p. 23).

Living in that space and considering what the data were saying, led me to three important representational decisions. Self-advocacy had been elucidated as the phenomenon facilitating entry to formal structures of disability support – it was all about getting in. Disabled students were expected to be and supported to become self-advocates, and the activities they described as self-advocacy brought them into relation with their professors who were primarily responsible for granting and facilitating individual accommodations. Negotiation emerged as an ongoing, often daily, requirement as students and faculty interacted through formal support mechanisms, and it inextricably linked self-advocacy and accommodations through its daily relational and interactional necessities. Therefore, I chose to explicate constructions of self-advocacy grounded by the necessities of gaining entry into the formal system of academic accommodations. I then took up accommodation and considered what students are actually gaining entry to when self-advocating in order to organize individual learning adjustments. Finally, I chose to weave negotiation throughout the entire discussion because it emerged as the ground on which student/faculty access relations are generated and the space in which uncertainty is produced when students encounter variable responses to accommodation requests.

Concluding thoughts

Disrupting ableist notions of who is and who is not a competent and prolific researcher and of what constitutes legitimately rigorous research methodology is a daunting undertaking. Universities have become so entrenched in the idea that inclusion is a mission to be achieved through the development of individual skill and the provision of individual accommodation that the transformation of long-standing academic tradition is rarely if ever considered. Disabled students, and by extension disabled faculty, are in need of enhancement because of a disability that impairs their full inclusion in the academy (Titchkosky, 2011). It is not the university itself that requires fundamental systemic reform. This was the marginalizing construction of disability as an individual problem in need of an individual solution (Titchkosky & Michalko, 2012) that naturalized the failure of research traditions to anticipate and plan for my blindness as a valid and natural way of working.

In this chapter, I have endeavoured to make evident the rigor of those ways of doing to work against the dominance of sighted conventions and to establish blind methodologies as legitimate within an ever-expanding body of methodological choices. Ableism has a strong hold within academic traditions and it frequently manifests in the pervasive preference for and privileging of normalcy and normative ways of doing. "Battling academic ableism will be as difficult, ongoing, messy, bottom-up, and unpredictable as retrofitting is limited, bordered, constrained, top-down, and rubber-stamped" (Dolmage, 2017, p. 94). This intractability, therefore, calls on disabled researchers to contribute to the battle by asserting the utility, legitimacy, and rigor of a wide array of disabled methodologies across multiple academic disciplines, and it compels us to disseminate assertions of legitimacy as frequently and broadly as we can.

References

Ashby, C. (2010). The trouble with normal: The struggle for meaningful access for middle school students with developmental disability labels. *Disability & Society, 25*(3), 345–358. doi: 10.1080/09687591003701249

Aspis, S. (1997). Self-advocacy for people with learning difficulties: Does it have a future? *Disability & Society, 12*(4), 647–654.

Baglieri, S., & Knopf, J. H. (2004). Normalizing difference in inclusive teaching. *Journal of Learn Disabilities, 37*(6), 525–529.

Basit, T. (2003). Manual or electronic? The role of coding in qualitative data analysis. *Educational research, 45*(2), 143–154.

Bird, C. M. (2005). How I stopped dreading and learned to love transcription. *Qualitative Inquiry, 11*(2), 226–248.

Bolt, D. (2004). Disability and the rhetoric of inclusive higher education. *Journal of Further and Higher Education, 28*(4), 353–358. doi: 10.1080/0309877042000298849

Bruce, C. A. (2016). Divergent encounters with normal: Are they really so different after all? *Canadian Journal of Disability Studies, 5*(1), 133–157.

Bruce, C. A. (2017). *Precarious Possibilities: Disability, Self-Advocacy, and University Learning.* (Unpublished Doctoral Dissertation), Acadia University, Wolfville, NS.

Campbell, F. K. (2008a). Exploring internalized ableism using critical race theory. *Disability & Society, 23*(2), 151–162. doi: 10.1080/09687590701841190

Campbell, F. K. (2008b). Refusing able(ness): A preliminary conversation about ableism. *M/C Journal, 11*(3). http://journal.media-culture.org.au/index.php/mcjournal/article/view/46

Campbell, F. K. (2009). *Contours of Ableism: The Production of Disability and Abledness.* London: Palgrave Macmillan.

Campbell, F. K. (2012). Stocking ableism: Using disability to expose 'abled' narcissism. In D. Goodley, B. Hughes & L. Davis (Eds.), *Disability and Social Theory: New Developments and Directions* (pp. 212–230). London: Palgrave Macmillan.

Claiborne, L. B., Cornforth, S., Gibson, A., & Smith, A. (2011). Supporting students with impairments in higher education: Social inclusion of cold comfort? *International Journal of Inclusive Education, 15*(5), 513–527.

Connor, D. J., Gabel, S. L., Gallagher, D. J., & Morton, M. (2008). Disability studies and inclusive education—implications for theory, research, and practice. *International Journal of Inclusive Education, 12*(5–6), 441–457. doi: 10.1080/13603110802377482

Denhart, H. (2008). Deconstructing barriers perceptions of students labeled with learning disabilities in higher education. *Journal of Learning Disabilities, 41*(6), 483–497.

Dolmage, J. T. (2017). *Academic Ableism: Disability and Higher Education (Kindle version)*. Ann Arbor: University of Michigan Press.
Dowrick, P. W., Anderson, J., Heyer, K., & Acosta, J. (2005). Postsecondary education across the USA: Experiences of adults with disabilities. *Journal of Vocational Rehabilitation, 22*, 41–47.
Dowse, L. (2001). Contesting practices, challenging codes: Self-advocacy, disability politics and the social model. *Disability & Society, 16*(1), 123–141.
Erten, O. (2011). Facing challenges: Experiences of young women with disabilities attending a canadian university. *Journal of Postsecondary Education and Disability, 24*(2), 101–114.
Goode, J. (2007). 'Managing' disability: Early experiences of university students with disabilities. *Disability & Society, 22*(1), 35–48.
Goodley, D. (2014). *Dis/ability Studies: Theorizing Disableism and Ableism* (iBooks version). New York: Routledge.
Hayman, E. (2010). Re-thinking disability in public: The making of theUTS AccessAbility website project. *Discourse: Studies in the Cultural Politics of Education, 31*(4), 453–467. doi: 10.1080/01596306.2010.504362
Holstein, J. A., & Gubrium, J. F. (1995). The active interview. In J. A. Holstein & J. F. Gubrium (Eds.), *The Active Interview* (pp. 1–32). Thousand Oaks: Sage.
Hutcheon, E. J., & Wolbring, G. (2012). Voices of "disabled" Post secondary Students: Examining higher education "disability" policy using an ableism lens. *Journal of Diversity in Higher Education, 5*(1), 39–49. doi: 10.1037/a0027002
Kioko, V. K., & Makoelle, T. M. (2014). Inclusion in higher education: Learning experiences of disabled students at Winchester University. *International Education Studies, 7*(6), 106–116.
Lapadat, J. C., & Lindsay, A. C. (1998). *Examining Transcription: A Theory-Laden Methodology*. Paper presented at the Annual Meeting of the American Educational Research Association, San Diego, CA.
Lapadat, J. C., & Lindsay, A. C. (1999). Transcription in research and practice: From standardization of technique to interpretive positionings. *Qualitative Inquiry, 5*(1), 64–86.
Linton, S. (1998a). *Claiming Disability: Knowledge and Identity (Kindle Version)*. New York: New York University Press.
Linton, S. (1998b). Disability studies/Not disability studies. *Disability & Society, 13*(4), 525–539. doi: 10.1080/09687599826588
Madaus, J. W. (2008). Employment self-disclosure rates and rationales of university graduates with learning disabilities. *Journal of Learning Disabilities 41*(4), 291–299.
Markle, D., West, R., & Rich, P. (2011). Beyond transcription: Technology, change, and refinement of method. *Forum Qualitative Sozialforschung / Forum Qualitative Social Research, 12*(3). http://www.qualitative-research.net/index.php/fqs/article/view/1564/3249
Mullins, L., & Preyde, M. (2013). The lived experience of students with an invisible disability at a Canadian university. *Disability & Society, 28*(2), 147–160. doi: 10.1080/09687599.2012.752127
Oliver, M. (2009). The social model in context. In T. Titchkosky & R. Michalko (Eds.), *Rethinking Normalcy: A Disability Studies Reader* (pp. 19–30). Toronto: Canadian Scholars Press.
Peters, S. J., Johnstone, C., & Ferguson, P. (2005). A disability rights in education model for evaluating inclusive education. *International Journal of Inclusive Education, 9*(2), 139–160. doi: 10.1080/1360311042000320464

Poland, B. D. (1995). Transcription quality as an aspect of rigor in qualitative research. *Qualitative Inquiry, 1*(3), 290–310.

Poland, B. D. (2003). Transcription quality. In J. A. Holstein & J. F. Gubrium (Eds.), *Inside Interviewing: New Lenses, New Concerns* (pp. 267–287). Thousand Oaks: Sage.

Price, M., & Kerschbaum, S. L. (2016). Stories of methodology: Interviewing sideways, crooked and crip. *Canadian Journal of Disability Studies*, 5(3), 18–56.

Richardson, L., & St. Pierre, E. A. (2005). Writing: A method of inquiry. In N. Denzin & Y. Lincoln (Eds.), *Sage Handbook of Qualitative Research* (3rd ed., pp. 959–978). Thousand Oaks: Sage.

Ross, T. (2008). *Organizing Disability in Post-secondary Education: A Study of Exam Accommodation and Institutional Discourse.* (Unpublished Master's Thesis), University of New Brunswick, Fredericton, NB.

Roulstone, A., Thomas, C., & Watson, N. (2012). The changing terrain of disability studies. In N. Watson, A. Roulstone & C. Thomas (Eds.), *The Routledge Handbook of Disability Studies* (iBooks version). New York: Routledge.

Saldana, J. (2009). *The Coding Manual for Qualitative Researchers.* Thousand Oaks: Sage.

Shakespeare, T., & Watson, N. (2001). The social model of disability: An outdated ideology. In S. Barnartt & B. Altman (Eds.), *Exploring Theories and Expanding Methodologies: Where We Are and Where We Need To Go* (pp. 9–28). Oxford, Elsevier: JAI Press.

Shaw, S. F., Madaus, J. W., & Dukes, L. L. (2010). *Preparing Students with Disabilities for College Success: A Practical Guide to Transition Planning.* Retrieved from http://search.proquest.com/docview/742870507?accountid=8172

Test, D. W., Fowler, C. H., Wood, W. M., Brewer, D. M., & Eddy, S. (2005). A conceptual framework of self-advocacy for students with disabilities. *Remedial and Special Education*, 26(1), 43–54.

Titchkosky, T. (2007). *Reading and Writing Disability Differently: The Textured Life of Embodiment* (Kindle version). Toronto, ON: University of Toronto Press.

Titchkosky, T. (2011). *The Question of Access: Disability, Space, Meaning* (Kindle version). Toronto: University of Toronto Press.

Titchkosky, T., & Michalko, R. (2012). The body as the problem of individuality: A phenomenological disability studies approach. In D. Goodley, B. Hughes & L. Davis (Eds.), *Disability and Social Theory: New Developments and Directions* (pp. 127–142). London: Palgrave Macmillan.

Tremain, S. (2005). Foucault, governmentality, and critical disability theory: An introduction. In S. Tremain (Ed.), *Foucault and the Government of Disability* (pp. 1–26). Ann Arbor: University of Michigan Press.

Walker, A. R., & Test, D. w. (2011). Using a self-advocacy intervention on African American college students' ability to request academic accommodations *Learning Disabilities Research and Practice*, 26(3), 134–144.

Ware, L. (2005). Many possible futures, many different directions: Merging critical special education and disability studies. In S. L. Gabel & S. Danforth (Eds.), *Disability Studies in Education: Readings in Theory and Method* (pp. 103–124). New York: Peter Lang.

Warick, R. (2004). Visitors in the classroom: The academic experiences of students who are hard of hearing. In L. Andres & F. Finlay (Eds.), *Student Affairs: Experiencing Higher Education* (pp. 92–122). Vancouver, BC: UBC Press.

Chapter 9

Deaf research methodologies? Confronting epistemological silences and challenges in qualitative research

Bronagh Byrne and Michael Schwartz

Introduction

This chapter is based on the experiences of two deaf academics; one a profoundly deaf, oral lip-reader and hearing aid user based in the United Kingdom (Byrne) and the other a culturally Deaf sign language user based in the United States (Schwartz).[1] Both authors have doctorates, are based in leading universities and have longstanding experience of working on a wide range of qualitative projects, conducting interviews, focus groups and participatory research with a wide variety of subjects: people with and without disabilities; deaf and hearing people; sign language users; legal professionals; education professionals; policymakers; and children and young people. The extent of our research endeavours belies the ableist (Goodley 2014; Harpur 2012) and taken for granted norms on which the academy and empirical research frameworks are based. Despite the growing fields of disability studies, critical disability studies and Deaf studies which critically examine the myriad sites of social oppression (See for example, Bauman 2008; Goodley 2013; Oliver 1990), little has been written about the methodological implications and challenges of being a deaf researcher and the ways in which methodological frameworks can, in and of themselves, contribute to the subtle oppression of deaf researchers in the academy. Practically, there may be a temptation, particularly for early career researchers, to engage in a process of 'passing' in order to facilitate appropriate 'impression management' (Goffman 1959) and perform a so-called academic identity (Brown and Leigh, 2018; Inckle, 2018). We suggest, however, that just as academic institutions have an ethical responsibility to engage with, respond to and reflect the diverse societies and populations which are the focus of research and teaching, so too do they have a responsibility to recognise, listen to, learn from and respond to deaf researchers operating therein, and ultimately in bringing the diversity of 'being' and 'doing' within the academy to the fore. To this end, the authors seek to shine a light on the additional labours we are required to engage in to undertake academic research, due, not to the fact of our hearing loss, but to the endemic assumptions and legacy of 'hearingness' (Sutton-Spence and West 2011) that underpins methods and processes, and the assumed association between such 'hearingness' and academic ability. We suggest that this is necessary if we are to have a sociological future that is inclusive and social research methods that are universally accessible. Acknowledging the diversity of researcher experience and hearing our voices is a critical first step in this journey.

This chapter will address this gap by critically discussing our experiences and the challenges of using typical qualitative research methodologies that prioritise fluency in the spoken language. We will discuss the extent to which being deaf can be considered as either positive or negative – but rarely neutral – forms of symbolic capital depending on the research context. The chapter will present ways in which the authors have sought to overcome the challenges associated with taken for granted practices of communication in interviews and focus groups and the implications of these challenges for the recording, transcription and analysis of data. The chapter will end by outlining ways in which we can promote greater inclusiveness in social research methodologies for academics who are deaf.

A brief note on terminology and positioning

While most impairments generate extensive debate in relation to the use of what is deemed appropriate terminology, the case of deafness is unique given the centrality of linguistic difference (Bauman, 2008; Corker 1998; Gregory 1995; Ladd and John 1991; Padden 1980; Padden and Humphries 1988). Far from being merely a descriptive term, the word 'deaf' encompasses a range of identity locations:

> In terms of self-definition, deaf people are caught at different points in a linguistic and cultural web made up of spoken languages, sign languages, deafness and hearingness. Different locations in the web therefore become associated with different meanings of language and identity, and these meanings are not always static or consistent.
>
> (Corker 1998: 5)

Thus, to be 'deaf' does not imply a singular fixed identity. Both authors occupy different positions on the spectrum. Byrne is profoundly deaf and relies on a combination of lip-reading and hearing aids. Due to an oral educational background, she is not a fluent sign language user. In group interactions, she uses a personal loop system to supplement lip-reading. Byrne holds undergraduate and postgraduate degrees in Economics and Human Rights Law as well as a doctorate in Sociology and Social Policy with a focus on inclusive education. She has been Programme Director of the Bachelors Honours degree pathway in Social Policy and the Master's in Children's Rights pathway at Queen's University Belfast, Northern Ireland, UK. Her research passions and projects span the areas of disability rights and children's rights, the latter encompassing, but not exclusive to, children with disabilities. In respect of these, she co-directs two University research centres, one on disability research and one on children's rights and regularly engages with policymakers, national and international disability and children's rights organisations as well as working with people with disabilities (adults and children), including deaf people, children and young people in co-producing research.

Schwartz was born profoundly deaf and grew up in the oral tradition, learning at a very young age to speak, read and write English fluently without learning American Sign Language (ASL) until he was 22 years old. Growing up deaf, Schwartz brings lived experience and expertise with barriers that conditioned his thinking about disability (Murray, Klinger and McKinnon 2007). As a litigator, Schwartz developed a set of strategies for advocacy on behalf of the American Deaf community. These experiences sensitized him to the obstacles facing Deaf people around the world. While he is a superb lip-reader who can communicate with many hearing people in a one-on-one setting, he relies on sign language interpreters in group interactions with people who are not sign language users. Holder of five academic degrees, including a PhD in Education from Syracuse University in Syracuse, New York, Schwartz is a law professor and supervising attorney of the Disability Rights Clinic, Office of Clinical Legal Education, at Syracuse University College of Law. Schwartz wears two hats: disability rights litigator enforcing federal and state anti-discrimination law on behalf of people with disabilities, and sociological qualitative researcher focused on access to health care and justice under domestic and international law, including the United Nations Convention on the Rights of Persons with Disabilities. One of the four principals of Tangata Group, an international human rights NGO, Schwartz engages with a large coterie of people such as people with disabilities, employers, state and local government officials, including school boards and departments of corrections, private businesses open to the public, and national and international disability rights organisations. Schwartz's aim as a qualitative researcher is to afford an opportunity to people with disabilities, including those who are deaf, to have a say in the data gathering process. He and Byrne are mindful of the famous dictum, 'Nothing about us without us' (Charlton 2000). and have a particular commitment to research impact in a way that prioritises the voices of those involuntarily positioned at the margins.

It is important that social researchers reflect on their role in the research process. The need to be reflexive is relevant in instances where the researcher is perceived to occupy a place of difference – in this case being deaf. For Byrne, initial concerns of her role as a 'deaf researcher' conducting research on deaf issues raised the potential for accusations of bias. This questioning in the early stages of her research eventually led her to conclude that while accusations of bias may arise, this is, in essence, a natural consequence of researcher differences or similarities and inherent in the fact that researchers are 'human beings and not machines' (Brewer 2000; Gilbert 1993; Sellitz, Jahoda, Deutsch, and Cook 1965: 41). Both authors occupy an insider and outsider status, moving along and across the researcher-participant divide at different times and in different contexts (Ganga and Scott 2006). This is invariably the case when conducting research with other deaf people. An example of this is a joint project on access to justice for deaf people in the United Kingdom. This two-year project in partnership with the British

Deaf Association, is co-produced with a Deaf advisory group of sign language users. That both the researchers are deaf undoubtedly increases credibility with the Deaf community engaged in the project, demonstrating the advantageous position associated with being an 'insider' and how being deaf can act as a significant form of 'symbolic capital'. However, while the advantages and disadvantages of insider/outsider research are frequently espoused (Ganga and Scott 2006), there has been arguably less recognition of the complexity and fluidity that accompanies such positioning. Restricted or limited insider status can occur where it may be suggested that having a certain characteristic is advantageous, but where the precise nature of that characteristic does not align fully with the insider group in question. In the case of the access to justice project, for example, one of the authors (Byrne) is not a fluent sign language user and is thus not a full insider. Being able to communicate at a relatively basic level and/or with the support of an interpreter can mean that, for Byrne, the insider/outsider position is highly context-specific and transient.

So it is for Schwartz, too. ASL, the language he has known for the last 44 years, is not the same as British Sign Language (BSL).[2] While Schwartz can converse with BSL users in a colloquial setting, he finds interviewing BSL users more challenging because of the language difference. Even though Schwartz has been studying BSL for the last 36 years, BSL is not his native sign language. The interaction between Schwartz and Northern Irish BSL users is made more complicated by the fact people in Northern Ireland are surprised or amazed to learn that Schwartz is a practising lawyer. So, like Byrne, while Schwartz is an insider, he is also an outsider. Clearly, the delineation between insider and outsider status is far from straightforward.

Uncovering methodological barriers

The form of academic discourse adopted within a study carries with it particular consequences for thinking about theoretical and methodological issues. The epistemological framework that is developed 'dictates not only the general perception of reality and social relations, but … the types of methods and techniques available to researchers and the motives and aims of social research' (Sarantakos 1998: 15). Whilst the methodological implications of a theoretical framework in uncovering practices of oppression, power and privilege is commonly recognised, that is, researchers need to practice epistemological vigilance (Bourdieu 1984: 15), the concealment of power under the guise of value-free, robust and valid research methods is rarely considered. Research methods that claim to be 'value-free' run the risk of reaffirming the status quo by rendering silent the ableist rules that are taken for granted. Indeed, qualitative methodologies replicate social relations of power through which deaf researchers are unquestionably disadvantaged. Methodological frameworks, tools and means of analysis have been developed and controlled by and for researchers based on assumptions of full 'hearingness' whereby the academy legitimates qualitative methodologies grounded in oral and auditory intelligence. We can relate this to Bourdieu's argument that '...any language that can command attention is an 'authorised' language', invested with the authority of a group; the things it designates are not simply expressed but also authorised and legitimated' (Bourdieu 1977: 170), and in so doing become objectified. That the deaf researchers need to undertake additional labours, incur extra financial costs and make adjustments so that the chosen research method is accessible to themselves and their deaf subjects, is indicative of the hearing-exclusivity that has endured and continues to endure. These additional labours, costs and adjustments include the booking of in-demand and highly expensive sign language interpreters; the purchase, charging and transportation of expensive personal loop systems, ensuring that research spaces have adequate lighting for lip-reading and space for interpreters, and, in some situations, the booking of electronic notetakers or CART (Communication Access Real Time Translation). In each case it is the deaf researcher that carries the burden of these additional labours and is required to source funding. Where no institutional or government funding is available, it is again the deaf researcher that incurs the extra costs. Here we outline further examples of these barriers across research processes.

Interviews and focus groups

Interviews and focus groups are the bedrock of qualitative methodologies. Before embarking on any fieldwork, as deaf researchers, we are required to engage in thorough planning. While some of this planning is the same as for any researcher irrespective of background (recruitment, ethical approval, obtaining consent and determining when and where to meet), other aspects are unique and require forethought and anticipation of potential barriers. The extent of planning will also be determined by the characteristics of the research sample. For Byrne and Schwartz, regular engagement with hearing policymakers and representatives from non-governmental organisations in research projects brings a number of factors into consideration. Making initial contact for study recruitment is always filled with trepidation for a researcher – will they or will they not agree to take part? What kind of questions will they have? Added to the mix is the need for a deaf researcher to inform the potential participant that they are deaf and require a certain format for initial answers prior to face to face interviews: for Byrne, email works best, while Schwartz can use a sign language interpreter to speak with the participant by telephone. Disclosure of information on disability introduces an 'unknown' to fieldwork dynamics. On the one hand, it places a burden on the deaf researcher to disclose highly personal information, on the other, it provides potential participants with additional consideration and may bring to the fore, consciously or subconsciously, their own perceptions around deafness and perceived ability to communicate with a deaf researcher. While disclosure of deafness helps in building a rapport with deaf participants, for Byrne, research projects are not exclusively with deaf people or on deaf issues and can encompass projects that have no relation to deafness or disability at all. It is not known whether decisions not to take part in research studies are due to perceptions around deafness or for some other reason. While entirely within the power of the potential participant, the added dynamic of communicating with a deaf researcher needs to be considered. Further issues arise when meeting with hearing participants, particularly those in positions of power. At a fundamental level, accessing an interview venue with an intercom at the entrance can be immediately exclusionary and result in delays in getting to an interview or focus group, creating tensions from the outset. In interviews and focus groups, Byrne uses a personal radio aid system which resembles a silver pen. At the beginning of each interview or focus group, Byrne faces the task of explaining and raising awareness of accessible communication – that is, lip-reading, good lighting – and how the microphone should be used. This is particularly complex in group interviews due to the need to pass round the microphone, while in individual interviews the microphone can be placed on a desk or table and is essentially 'forgotten', thus minimising subsequent impacts. The passing round and use of the microphone in focus group situations introduces an added dynamic for Byrne. While doing so makes the scenario accessible for Byrne, it would naïve to suggest it does not impact on the nature of the exchange. Reminding participants to pass it to the next speaker, ensuring they hold the microphone the right way up and waiting while this occurs adds time to the focus group length and requires patience from all parties. There is also the risk that some participants will not want to engage with the microphone, feel uncomfortable, awkward or would rather not use it which impacts on the information understood by Byrne and the kinds of prompts that follow. This has happened on some occasions and requires additional concentration and energy in an attempt to follow a discussion where the equipment is not being properly used. In this sense, the use of one-to-one interviews can be considerably easier and more straightforward. While familiarity with 'hearingness' and competence in fluent oral communication is assumed – both by society and by the academy and research textbooks, familiarity with deaf ways of being and doing is an exception and perceived as strange, abnormal, even unnecessary. Discussion of these important practical issues is resoundingly invisible in major research texts. Deaf researchers, lacking the so-called navigational capital (Listman and Dingus-Eason 2018) that is deemed necessary to facilitate 'robust' and 'valid' verbal interactions and/or to interpret verbal cues, are positioned neither as 'one of them' (research subject) nor as 'one of us' (academic researcher).

When Schwartz interviews American deaf subjects in ASL, he has a recording device and an ASL interpreter on hand (no pun intended) to voice the signs of both interviewer and interviewee. Once the interview is over, Schwartz forwards the tape to a transcriptionist who produces a transcript of the interview. The limitation of this process is that because Schwartz is deaf, he cannot determine if the ASL interpreter is voicing accurately for the tape recorder. This is why Schwartz is careful to retain high-quality interpreters who he has worked with for years. He has confidence in these interpreters that the transcript will accurately reflect the dialogue between Schwartz and his interviewees.

The setting for Schwartz's interviews of deaf subjects in BSL is different simply because it is not the same as ASL. However, having visited Northern Ireland at least 25 times over the last 36 years, Schwartz has developed a comfortable familiarity with BSL. A former mime and actor with the renowned National Theatre of the Deaf in the United States, Schwartz has the ability to communicate his questions to his Northern Irish interviewees in a clear and compelling manner. But given the fact Schwartz did not grow up with BSL, he is cognisant of the risk in handling the interview on his own. He recognises that his fluency in BSL does not match his fluency in ASL. Thus, he retains two interpreters, one an ASL interpreter and the other a BSL interpreter. Schwartz signs in ASL, the ASL interpreter voices his signs, the BSL interpreter signs what he or she hears from the ASL interpreter, and the BSL interpreter voices the deaf interviewee's signs. The voices of the ASL and BSL interpreters are recorded and sent for transcription. Again, the limitation is the same: Schwartz cannot tell if the interpreters are voicing the questions he is asking. Aside from being as clear as he can be in his questioning, Schwartz shares his questions with the interpreters so they are familiar with the subject matter and the questions to be asked. He is also careful to retain only the best-qualified interpreters for his interviews.

For Schwartz, the level of comfort while interviewing deaf subjects, whether American or Northern Irish, is largely absent when interviewing hearing people. For the interviews in the United States, Schwartz retains an ASL interpreter, and the process as described above is the same: he signs to the interviewee, the ASL interpreter voices his signs, the interviewee responds in spoken English, and the ASL interpreter signs the responses. If the interviewee is uncomfortable watching Schwartz's signs and/or listening to the interpreter, or if the interviewee is confused as to who to look at, Schwartz or the interpreter, then that makes for an uncomfortable interview. The problem is compounded by Schwartz's need to look at the interpreter, not the interviewee, when the interviewee is talking. This disconnect in eye contact can be a problem for a successful interview. A way to alleviate this discomfort Schwartz has found effective is to fully explain the process to the interviewee and take the time to answer the person's questions about the process. Another mechanism is to pause the interview and ask if the person is comfortable. This approach is similar to the interviews of people with typical hearing in Northern Ireland.

In research focused on deaf or disability issues, we have had a concern that some stakeholders would view us as a 'threat' or an 'intruder' and would perhaps 'hold back' or seek 'social approval' (Brewer 2000). This has occurred in some interviews; nonetheless, Byrne feels that her 'insider' status has facilitated rather than hindered the acquisition of rich data. In some cases, stakeholder interviewees asked Byrne if she required any further support, and in one instance, a portable loop system had been set up for the meeting. In such instances, it is not beyond the realm of possibility to suggest that some people made an attempt to make a good impression. Most interviewees are keen to inform the deaf researcher of progress in a particular area. In this way, researcher presentation as a deaf person has its benefits, not just in terms of the verbal content and the context in which this was produced, but arguably also in terms of 'impression management' (Goffman 1959). It is interesting to consider if the same outcomes would have emerged had the researcher not been deaf. In other instances, it is clear that engaging with a deaf researcher has unintended impacts. For example, in a study on access to deaf justice, the very fact that two of the three researchers were deaf prompted policymakers and legal professionals to be more alert to the need for and importance of deaf equality training for staff and lent credibility to the overall project. Indeed, in a research project led by Byrne on post-16 education for students with disabilities, it was interesting to note that a post-16 educational establishment had previously declined to participate in a piece of disability research carried out by a non-disabled researcher, yet had agreed to participate in Byrne's research. Such interactions also provide an interesting insight into hearing people's perceptions of deafness. For example, in a non-disability related research project involving policymakers, some interviewees informed Byrne after the interview that she had 'really good' or 'excellent' speech for a deaf person, raising concern on what exactly they expected a deaf person to be like. The authors feel compelled to explain to these people that the deaf community is not monolithic, that there are profoundly deaf people with good speech and there are hard of hearing people who choose to sign rather than speak. Deaf researchers often find themselves in the position of having to educate people outside the scope of the research project.

Byrne also has experience in conducting interviews and focus groups with young deaf people and young people with visual impairments who are students (Byrne 2014, 2017). When meeting them for the first time, disclosing her deafness had a positive impact on readdressing the social relations of research production. Students ultimately became less guarded and were able to identify with both her impairment and disabling experiences. Likewise, Schwartz finds that when he interviews deaf people in the United States, they are comfortable with him in a way they are not with a hearing interviewer. Interviewing individuals with similar experiences also has the benefits of enabled empathy, openness and the acquisition of rich, deep data (Leicester 1999). This is not unique but has been an ongoing feature of those studies where the leading researcher has a disability. For example, Shah (2005) in her doctoral study of 'disabled high flyers', found that 'the acquisition of rich quality data…was facilitated by the fact that the interviewer and the participants came from the same minority group, that is, both parties shared experiences of physical impairment and life development' (Shah 2005: 14).

The emergence of new methods and approaches is reflective of the evolving nature of research methodologies. The use of online forums and social media can contribute to the provision of more inclusive research spaces for deaf researchers, minimizing the need for oral communication and creating a more level playing field. This is not the case for all 'new' possibilities. The emergence of 'participatory' research methods for children and young people is one such example (see, for example, Christensen and James, 2017; Groundswater-Smith et al. 2014). For Byrne, the use of such methods is fundamental to facilitating the voices of children and young people in child-friendly ways. Yet this can create a tension between ensuring methods are participatory enough for children and young people, allowing for engagement, perhaps through the use of drawing, painting, Photovoice or guided tours (see, for example, MacDougall et al. 2009), and ensuring that they are accessible for a deaf researcher. Allowing children and young people to express themselves in ways that make them feel comfortable whilst engaging is only one part of the equation. Young children in particular may not be deaf-aware and may not understand the importance of speaking one at a time or of looking at the researcher when speaking. Research texts on participatory methods do not reflect these considerations. This can place the onus on deaf researchers wanting to engage in such methods to consider how existing methods can be made accessible or to be creative in coming up with new methods or ways of obtaining data in participatory but accessible ways.

Doing data analysis and transcription

Recording of interviews and focus groups are critically important for deaf researchers. Both authors are unable to decipher audio material. Consent for recording data must be routinely sought. While this is generally unproblematic, particularly when explained, there is always a risk in any project of a voluntary nature that consent may not be provided. Equally, there is always a risk that recording equipment will not work or that batteries will run out during a session. This is made further problematic by being unable to listen to the device in advance for testing purposes or to know if the recording has been properly uploaded onto a computer. Interviewer transcription of data clearly has advantages in enhancing familiarity with the data (Marshall and Rossman 1989; Silverman 1985), however, given this is not possible for the authors, we rely on a transcriptionist. While many researchers may choose to get their data transcribed, they also have the option of listening to the recording to do a quality check on the transcription and to familiarise themselves with the data prior to analysis. For the authors, transcription incurs an unavoidable cost. This entails seeking resourcing which may not always be available. Postgraduate students who are deaf may be able to avail of funding available for students with disabilities. For those who are employed in a university, funding may be sought as part of a reasonable adjustment or incorporated as part of a research grant application. There are other ways of getting to grips with the data such as recording a research diary after each interview or focus group in which to record any initial feelings, thoughts and ideas. This can compensate for not being able to take notes during an interview due to the need to lip-read. This has not proved to be a disadvantage since the characteristic of 'active listening' in any research is maintained by direct eye contact with the interviewee (Lofland and Lofland 1995), particularly with those who are deaf and for whom lip-reading or body language/facial expression is vital.

Arksey and Knight (1999) assert that transcriptions are neither neutral nor value-free, but

> what passes from tape to paper is the result of decisions about what ought to go on paper.... Sometimes, a typist decides to type only words, not pauses.... Similarly, there is the notorious problem of how to punctuate speech: where should full stops, semi-colons and commas go? What about paragraph marks...?
>
> (Arksey and Knight 1999: 141)

These issues are arguably made more complex if the interviewer is not the typist. In other words, there is an added need to consider the problem of transcriber reliability (Kvale 1996). In such cases, it is important at the outset to inform the typist what the researcher wishes to gain from the transcripts and by providing a copy of the interview guide or other relevant predictive content and terminology because: '[t]he quality of transcriptions can be improved by clear instructions about the procedures and purposes of the transcriptions' (Kvale 1996: 163). Ensuring that one person is transcribing the data means that any transcriber effect is constant. Finally, the confidentiality of interview data should be strongly emphasised as should the identity of each interviewee or anyone else discussed during the course of the interview and who could possibly be identified.

Conclusion

Deaf researchers experience unique challenges in carrying out qualitative research. These challenges can be understood as a microcosm of the broader social relations of power and ableist discourses that are the focus of critical disability studies and Deaf studies. Contrary to popular belief, 'hearingness' is not a barometer for academic ability. Nor is the academy exempt from experiences of deafness. This can be understood literally in terms of the real possibilities for a broad spectrum of hearing loss among researchers, and metaphorically in the academy's long-standing reluctance to acknowledge, listen and effectively respond to the needs and rights of deaf researchers.

Qualitative research methodologies are resoundingly 'deaf' to the needs of their users, rendering silent the limitations of existing research tools. Methodologies that hearing researchers take for granted and can utilise with ease pose a myriad of challenges for deaf researchers. There is, however, no textbook on how deaf researchers should overcome the challenges they encounter. The additional labours and financial costs placed on deaf researchers seeking to engage in qualitative research must be acknowledged. So too, the extra energy expounded throughout the research process from intense concentration on lip-reading and/or using a sign language interpreter, as well as from the ongoing task of making research participants, funders, colleagues, policymakers and other stakeholders aware of how best to communicate with a deaf researcher. The authors hope that this chapter shines a spotlight on some of the barriers encountered and strategies that can be adopted to facilitate an inclusive sociological future. It is also the authors' hope that overcoming these barriers can be recognised as everyone's responsibility and not merely that of the individual deaf researcher. Patience, flexibility and understanding are key ingredients in adapting qualitative methodologies to accommodate the needs of parties, whether deaf or hearing. Alongside this there is a need for wider cultural change and discussion across the academy in determining what it means for qualitative research methodologies to be respectful and reflective of, as well as accessible to, the diverse research community it purports to represent.

Notes

1 Schwartz defines "culturally Deaf" as someone, whether profoundly deaf or hard of hearing, who identifies as part of the Deaf community and is fluent in a native sign language like American Sign Language or British Sign Language. Capitalising the letter "d" recognises deafness as a cultural and linguistic phenomenon whereas the lower case "d" signifies deafness as a hearing loss. Here, the authors use the word, "deaf," to include those who are hard of hearing.

2 The World Federation of the Deaf estimates there are over 200 sign languages around the world. Each country has its own sign, and indeed some larger countries have more than one sign language.

References

Arksey, H. and Knight, P. (1999) *Interviewing for Social Scientists*, London: Sage.

Bauman, H.-D.L. (2008) *Open Your Eyes: Deaf Studies Talking*. Minneapolis: University of Minnesota Press.

Bourdieu, P. (1977) *Outline of a Theory of Practice*, Cambridge: Cambridge University Press.

Bourdieu, P. (1984) *Distinction: A Social Critique of the Judgement of Taste*, Cambridge: Harvard University Press.

Brewer, J.D. (2000) *Ethnography*, Buckingham: Open University Press.

Brown, N. and Leigh, J. (2018) Ableism in academia: Where are the disabled and ill academics? *Disability & Society*, 33(6), 985–989.

Byrne, B. (2014) Getting in and getting on? The experiences of young people with visual impairments and hearing impairments in third level education, *International Journal of Disability, Development and Education*, 61(2), 119–133.

Byrne, B. (2017) Reconciling sameness and difference in disability rights ideology: The case of student identity. In G. Quinn & C. O'Mahony (eds.). *The United Nations Convention on the Rights of Persons with Disabilities*, Clarus Press.

Charlton, J. (2000) *Nothing about Us without Us: Disability Oppression and Empowerment*. London: University of California Press.

Christensen, P. and James, A. (2017) *Research with Children* (3rd ed.), London: Routledge.

Corker, M. (1998) *Deaf and Disabled or Deafness Disabled*, Buckingham: Open University Press.

Ganga and Scott (2006) Cultural 'Insiders' and the issue of positionality in qualitative migration research: Moving 'Across' and moving 'Along' researcher-participant divides,

FQS: Forum: Qualitative Research, 7(3). https://www.qualitative-research.net/index.php/fqs/article/view/134/289. Last accessed 17 September 2020.
Gilbert, N. (1993) *Researching Social Life*, London: Sage.
Goffman, E. (1959) *The Presentation of Self in Everyday Life*, New York: Anchor Books.
Goodley, D. (2013) Dis/entangling critical disability studies. *Disability and Society*, 28(5), 631–644.
Goodley, D. (2014) *Dis/ability Studies: Theorising Disablism and Ableism*, London: Routledge.
Gregory, S. (1995) *Deaf Futures Revisited*, Block 3, Unit 10, Course D251, Issues in Deafness, Milton Keynes: The Open University.
Groundswater-Smith, S., Dockett, S. and Bottrell, D. (2014) *Participatory Research with Children and Young People*, London: Sage.
Harpur (2012) From disability to ability: Changing the phrasing of the debate. *Disability and Society*, 27(3), 325–227.
Inckle, K. (2018) Unreasonable adjustments: The additional unpaid labour of academics with disabilities, *Disability and Society*, 33(8), 1372–1376.
Kvale, S. (1996) *Interviews*, London: Sage.
Ladd, P. and John, M. (1991) *Deaf People as a Minority Group: The Political Process* Block 3, Unit 9, Course D251, Issues in Deafness, Milton Keynes: The Open University.
Leicester, M. (1999) *Disability Voices: Towards an Enabling Education*, London: Jessica Kingsley.
Listman, J. and Dingus-Eason, J. (2018) How to be a deaf scientist: Building navigational capital. *Journal of Diversity in Higher Education*, 11(3), 279–294.
Lofland, J. and Lofland, L.H. (1995) *Analyzing Social Settings* (3rd ed.), London: Wadsworth.
MacDougall C., Schiller W. and Darbyshire P. (2009). What are our boundaries and where can we play? Perspectives from eight- to ten-year-old Australian metropolitan and rural children. *Early Child Development and Care*, 179(2), 189–204. doi:10.1080/03004430802667021
Marshall, C. and Rossman, G. (1989) *Designing Qualitative Research*, London: Sage.
Murray, J., Klinger, L. and McKinnon, C. (2007) The deaf: An exploration of their participation in community life, *OTJR: Occupation, Participation and Health*, 27(3), 113–120.
Oliver, M. (1990) *The Politics of Disablement*, London: Macmillan.
Padden, C. (1980) The deaf community and the culture of Deaf people. In Wilcox, S. (1989) (Ed.), *American Deaf Culture: An Anthology*, Silver Spring, MD: Linstok Press.
Padden, C. and Humphries, T. (1988) *Deaf in America: Voices from a Culture*, Cambridge: Harvard University Press.
Sarantakos, S. (1998) *Social Research* (2nd ed.), London: Palgrave Macmillan.
Sellitz, C., Jahoda, M., Deutsch, M. and Cook, S.W. (1965) *Research Methods in Social Relations*, Methuen: London.
Shah, S. (2005) *Career Success of Disabled High-Flyers*, London: Jessica Kingsley Publishers.
Silverman, D. (1985) *Qualitative Methodology and Sociology*, New York: Free Press.
Sutton-Spence, R. and West, D. (2011) Negotiating the Legacy of Hearingness, *Qualitative Inquiry*, 17(5), 422–432.

Chapter 10

"Repeat after me"

Gestalt, fluency and biographical research

Ciaran Burke

Introduction

Within social science research, identifying as a particular type of researcher carries with it certain assumptions about an individual's personality type and approach to knowledge – epistemology. A researcher who opts for a quantitative approach to data collection and analysis is often understood to be more "scientific" or "good with numbers", whereas the qualitative researcher is a "people person" who enjoys talking with people and getting to know their respondents on a personal level in pursuit of understanding rather than explaining a phenomenon. Thus, to be a qualitative researcher, the researcher is expected to enjoy talking and be able to talk on demand without hesitation or pause – in other words, be fluent. The friction that this chapter wishes to unpack is that between the assumption of ease of speech and dysfluency – in particular, stammering – in the context of life history research.

Life history research covers a broad range of approaches to data collection and analysis. However, a particularly clear and, at the same time, dogmatic approach within this school is the biographical narrative interview method (BNIM). Stemming from grounded theory, BNIM, developed by Fritz Schütze (1992, 2008) and Rosenthal (2003, 2005) and Miller (2000, 2005), has offered an opportunity to conduct ethnographic research within an interview setting (Burke, 2011). As outlined in many of these texts, the BNIM has a set of very strict rules which surround the principle of "gestalt" – essentially, preserving an individual's narration and protecting it for as long as possible from the researchers' interference. Two central rules which allow this to happen are:

- Once the initial narration question is asked, the researcher cannot interject or direct the narration, either verbally or physically.
- Once the initial narration has finished, the researcher can ask questions but must cover topics in the order the narration is presented to them and using the precise language used by the respondent.

It is this second rule which presents issues for researchers who have a disability that affects fluency of speech. In this chapter, I will first outline the sociological literature concerning speech dysfluency, building on the previous application of social theory to consider why stammering is such an issue within communication and why is it a site of ridicule and a marker of devaluation of that individual. I will then briefly set out the current landscape, within the UK, for academics who stammer. The chapter will then outline the specific mechanics of the BNIM and the rationale for its application within my own research. I will reflect on the issues I faced when balancing a lack of fluency and adhering to the strict rules of the BNIM. Also, I will discuss the general demands of fluency from qualitative research and ways in which the gestalt can be preserved within the BNIM and rigour more broadly within qualitative research, while not requiring researchers to keep to the strict language parameters the method currently demands. As such, I will provide guidelines for future researchers who wish to engage with this method but would initially feel unable to meet its demands.

Sociology and stammering

Speech is a crucial aspect of communication and interaction; what is of particular interest in the Sociology of Stammering is how those who stammer navigate a speech scenario in an attempt to pass as fluent.

> Stuttering is a speech disorder characterized by repetition of sounds, syllables, or words; prolongation of sounds; and interruptions in speech known as blocks. An individual who stutters exactly knows what he or she would like to say but has trouble producing a normal flow of speech.
>
> (NIH, 2017)

Acton and Hird (2004) comment on the resulting anxiety and stress a stammerer experiences when faced with an external speech situation, exacerbated by additional stress stemming from the context of the speech situation. The authors outline the main theories concerning stammering. These include stammering as a neurotic disorder where a stammer is a manifestation of a repressed memory or trauma, stammering as a learned behaviour and stammering as a physiological problem – however, the authors are quick to point out the physiological position is based on largely inconclusive research.

Focusing on interventions to "address" stammering, Acton and Hird (2004) unpack Gregory's (1979) identification of the two dominant approaches of "stutter more fluently" and "speak more fluently". The former model, which, among other things, encourages those who stammer to accept it as part of their identity and move beyond avoiding speech situations, can be seen within the contemporary academy. Within the UK there is the "silence on campus" campaign (STUC, 2018) to normalise stammering and support academic staff who stammer. This advocacy is presented on social media with the hashtag #itsokaytostammer. The latter approach of "speak more fluently" is much closer to the concept of "passing", where a stammerer conceals their speech dysfluency and rewards instances of fluent speech and admonishes periods of dysfluency. In terms of why dysfluency has not gained the same level of academic interest nor protection from ridicule, Acton and Hird discuss Lemert's (1970) assertion that, due to the relatively subtle manifestation of a stammer, the phenomena has been largely ignored by academic research and mocked by the public. While attempting to gather breath to tackle the next syllable is often both painful and shaming, the internal experience fosters little empirical interest and even less public empathy. It is then the mundane nature of dysfluency that removes protection from those attempting to speak but provides succour to those who gently mock.

Acton and Hird (2004) draw on Goffman's work on stigma and the friction between virtual social identity and actual social identity. The former is the identity that we construct for someone before we meet them – or, importantly for stammerers, before we talk to them – and the latter is an identity we construct for someone based on experience. The issue for someone who stammers is that, before an individual interacts with them, their social identity is based on a set of assumptions – in other words, a virtual form of social identity; these assumptions include fluency of speech. Returning to Goffman's concept of stigma, the authors comment that stammering falls under "discredited stigma" or a form of stigma which is immediately recognised. This issue is compounded by the strategies used by a discredited individual to ameliorate how others perceive them. In the specific case of stammers, this manifests in linguistic strategies such as limited vocal engagement or word replacement. Similarly, Butler (2013) examines how individuals with a stammer negotiate social space; these manoeuvres often involved "identity cloaking", including avoiding social situations, forestalling on a phrase and switching words. The respondents in Butler's study often tried to conceal their stammer in order to manage their stigma. The issue is that individuals will apply their own lay/spontaneous analysis on why an individual is applying such strategies, perhaps concluding that an individual is shy, inarticulate or uninformed. These are three qualities – shy, inarticulate and uninformed – that a social researcher, attempting to establish both rapport and command in an interview setting, would not want to project. A further contribution from Goffman when considering dysfluency is the "interaction order" (Goffman, 1983). Here, Goffman discusses the need for certain parameters and assumptions to be made to allow a constructive and meaningful interaction – again, an assumption within the interaction order is fluency.

Beyond the form of stigma and breakdown of interactions, it is important to unpack the sense of devalue via dysfluency. As discussed above, Butler (2013) outlines how her respondents would employ a number of different strategies to preserve the assumption of fluency. Here, I argue that thinking through Bourdieu's conceptual tools (1977, 1992, 2004) allows us to consider why preserving this assumption of fluency is so important to those who stammer and why it is a source of derision for the general population. Bourdieu's theoretical project of providing an account of social reality, which allows for the role of social structure and individual/group negotiation of these social spaces, is supported by a number of thinking tools – in particular, habitus, capital and field (Bourdieu and Wacquant, 1992). While the habitus has often been the leading focus of Bourdieusian research (Reay, 2004; Burke, 2016), it is the concepts field and capital which are most beneficial when considering dysfluency.

Bourdieu (1984) quite clearly argues that habitus and capital interact within different fields, and the success of this habitus/capital combination will be based on the tacit rules and expectations of that field, otherwise known as "doxa". While different fields have some unique and sometimes opposing rules, the expectation of communication and fluency is woven into the doxa of most fields. Within Bourdieu's concept of capital are three main forms: economic, social and cultural capital (2004); it is specifically cultural capital which is helpful when unpacking the devaluation associated with dysfluency. Within cultural capital, there are three sub-forms: institutional cultural capital, which stems from having attended a particular institution; objective cultural capital, which is demonstrated through possessing highly cultural artefacts, such as art or complex literature; embodied cultural capital, which is the demonstration of cultural mastery through the body and through knowledge via the inculcation of knowing how to act. It is within the final form for cultural capital (the embodied form) where we could arguably find the ability to communicate effectively and, certainly, the possession of fluent speech. As such, the lack of fluent speech suggests a lack of mastery or control within the field or social context an individual is trying to negotiate and limits the regions of social space an individual is intending to occupy. Also, due to a lower level of embodied cultural capital, the "field of the possibles" (1984: 110) – or an individual's expectations based on field position – will be reduced, preventing those who stammer from engaging in certain activities and professions.

The consequences of this perceived lack of embodied cultural capital can be seen when Butler (2013) discusses the "speech role fit" – or, rather, the consequences when there is a divergence from what is expected from the speech role. There was friction between the authority that stems from a particular role and the interpretation of an individual who stammers, stemming, I would argue, from a perceived lack of embodied cultural capital and, therefore, a lack of mastery. Respondents in Butler's study reported that the level to which their advice or instructions were followed was closely linked to levels of dysfluency: when fluency was high, so too was respect from co-workers and adherence to instructions. A further issue that stammerers face is the unpredictability of their dysfluency, which many suffer. Butler argues that stammerers often display no sign of dysfluency in situations where they are comfortable but unable to replicate this scenario:

> People who stammer encounter involuntary and intermittent disruptions in their ability to communicate fluently; their speech is inherently erratic throughout the day; and each episode of dysfluency is demonstrated to a differing degree.
>
> (2013: 1114)

Thinking about the unpredictability works against identity construction, and I am minded to revisit Jenkins' (1996) work on identity. However, the concept of emergent identity being structured by internal and external forces does not adequately account for the constant need to rewrite and rewrite how they present themselves based on minute-by-minute calculations of likely dysfluency.

Biographical narrative interview method: nuts and bolts

Biographical research, and life history research more broadly, has been a leading option for social researchers for over a century. Beginning with Thomas and Znaniecki's (1918/1996) *The Polish Peasant*, the method has enjoyed sustained application on both sides of the Atlantic within the Chicago School and Europe. For an overview of the broader life history research approach, Erben (1998) and Atkinson (1998) provide useful insights; however, this chapter is concerned with biographical research and, in particular, the specific mechanics of the BNIM, most notably attributed to Schütze (1992, 2008) and Rosenthal (2003, 2005).[1]

Rosenthal (2003, 2005) outlines the ideal (in a Weberian sense) or the "traditional" form of the biographical narrative interview – comprised of three distinct sub-sessions, each carrying a specific function and rules of protocol.

- Sub-session one: in this sub-session, the primary focus is on eliciting the initial or main narration. At the beginning of this sub-session, the "classic" biographical research question/prompt is given, often, "tell me about your life". During this stage of the research, the interviewer is instructed, by the rules of the method, to make minimum input or reaction to the respondent's narration – this includes both verbal and physical input (gestures, facial expressions). The rationale is that such interruptions or indications of interest can direct the narration and dilute the purity of the life history and, as such, interrupt the gestalt of the narration. What is allowed, however, are prompts, using a technique known as "parroting", where, if a respondent appears stuck or loses their train of thought, the interviewer can remind them what they were discussing – but the interviewer must use the precise terms the respondent has already used.
- Sub-session two: the second sub-session is generally conducted within the same sitting. During this sub-session, the researcher can ask for greater clarification or for the respondent to provide more information regarding areas or topics that the respondent has discussed. However, the rules of method dictate that the interviewer can only ask questions concerning topics that the respondent has discussed. Furthermore, the questions must be asked using the same language and phrasing that the respondent used, and the topics questioned must be presented in the order that the respondent discussed them. These rules, again, demonstrate the importance of maintaining a respondent's narration of maintaining the gestalt for as long as possible.

- Sub-session three: the third sub-session generally takes place at a later date. In the interim, transcription and preliminary analysis is conducted on the first two sub-sessions, and it is this analysis that will direct the focus and direction of the third sub-session. Unlike the previous sub-sessions, this stage of the interview does not carry as many rules and protocols. Instead, researchers are afforded much more freedom to discuss areas which may not have been discussed and apply a range of approaches to a qualitative interview. In some instances, the third sub-session is not conducted.

Miller (2000) outlines the various approaches or forms of the biographical interview: the realist, the neo-positivist and the narrative approach.[2] The realist approach applies an inductive approach to theory within the method, as such theory that should be built not imported. In order to achieve this type of theory as open an interview as possible is, therefore, required. The neo-positivist approach is, essentially, the other side of the coin, advocating for a deductive application of theory. This approach uses theoretically influenced interpretations of data to test a pre-determined hypothesis, employing semi-structured interviews. The final form that Miller discusses, the narrative approach, is a much more flexible way of conducting a biographical narrative interview, with the focus on "the ongoing development of the researcher's viewpoint during the telling of a life or family 'story'" (Miller, 2000: 12). While there are highly contrasting epistemological points of departure for biographical researchers, the fundamental rules of the method outlined above are required for each form of biographical research project.

Applying the method in practice

Reflecting on the quite strict rules of method, a legitimate question is why I would employ this form of data collection. Perhaps this question gains traction through the admission that I did not use the BNIM for its usual or intended purpose. Rather than inductively constructing an individual's biography, I was conducting a theoretically informed/hypothesis-testing project. I used this particular form of empirical inquiry to examine the role of social class on UK graduate employment trajectories (Burke, 2016). The rationale was that I was attempting to recreate the closeness and purity of data that is more closely associated with longitudinal participant observation. Due to the practical limitations of the research, which was my doctoral research, I opted to approach the BNIM as a form of ethnographic interview focusing on longitudinal processes and influences. Traditionally, within the BNIM canon, social theory is reserved for the later stages of data collection; for example, Merrill and West suggest the application of theory within biographical research can be found within the data analysis. Theory, within this context, is "middle range and experimentally driven" (2009: 184). However, I followed Bourdieu et al.'s (1991) assertion that social theory – in the pursuit of the epistemological break – will be present in all aspects of the research process and not only during analysis.

In my application of the research tool, I kept to the strict conventions of the method. Rather than having a very broad "tell me about your life" biographical question, I took on Rosenthal's (2005) advice on the varying levels of specificity initial narration questions are allowed. She discusses instances where a greater focus is required; she suggests that researchers attempt to find a middle ground with respondents. Interviewers may explain what they are researching, but they should make it clear to the respondent that they are interested in his/her whole life. Rosenthal comments that this approach will ensure the respondent will discuss the topic or area of interest while providing a rich narrative. As such, I began each interview with the same initial narration prompt:

> The focus of this research is to look at pathways in education and employment, but, to really understand this, you need to look at someone's whole life story, to look at the subtle processes that have influenced these pathways. Everything you say is relevant.
> I'm not going to speak that much during this part of the interview. I'm just going to make a few notes, if that's okay.
> Would you tell me your life story – all the events and experiences which are important to you? Start wherever you like.

In my research, the first two sub-sessions of the biographical interview were completed within the same sitting. Similar to sub-session one, in the second sub-session, I applied the strict rules of convention in only asking about topics in the order in which they were presented and using the precise language used by my respondents. After some initial analysis, the third sub-session was completed using a more standard semi-structured interview.

Can we move beyond prescriptive rules?

As an author, and an editor, of this collection, I accept it is counter-intuitive – or, dare I say, hypocritical – to present academic literature on speech dysfluency, outline a popular approach to data collection which carries many issues for those who do not have fluency of speech and then conclude that I still followed the strict protocols of the research method. In my part, it is this adherence to the rules despite personal damage that inspired this chapter: it was the understanding that I did not have a choice and had to meet the ableist requirements of research. As I discussed above, the rationale for using biographical research methods was as an effort to reproduce the conditions of ethnographic research and allow me to observe the interaction of structure and agency over the life course of my respondents. This pressure to fulfil the requirements of the method was increased due to it being my doctoral research, a period where, while an individual is becoming an independent academic, the mechanics of research protocol can be a reassuring anchor.

It's important here to make clear the issues such a prescriptive set of rules BNIM carries or, indeed, the broader focus on continuity within qualitative research.

Qualitative methods which require exact repetition of words and phrases, whether that is in the follow-up sub-sessions in the BNIM or an interview schedule within a semi-structured interview, demands not only fluency but what I would term precise fluency with no room for linguistic negotiation. There are strategies I used in order to "pass" as a fluent speaker; these included intercostal breathing techniques, keeping questions short (therefore reducing the number of words to say) and pre-empting a stammering "episode" with a forced stammer to let the respondent know that I have an issue with fluency. The reliance of such techniques means that not only is the dysfluent researcher entering research spaces with increased levels of anxiety but also delegitimises their identity as a researcher – in other words, if they are unable to pass as fluent, then they should not be doing the research.

There are I think two issues here: first, the rationale behind focusing on continuity with qualitative data collection more generally and, then, the preoccupation with preserving the gestalt within the BNIM approach – and I would like to unpack each in turn. The need for continuity within qualitative data collection, whether between one researcher and multiple respondents or multiple researchers and multiple respondents, in the first instance, is a sound demand from a method, a way of ensuring rigour within what is a highly subjective form of data collection. However, it is in how we understand rigour that issues arise; very often, we operationalise rigour as based on how well it can mirror methods within the natural sciences. As a discipline, the social sciences follow this logic in an effort to increase the level of reliability – essentially, the degree that research can be thought of as accurate and not due to other influential factors (Silverman, 2006: 282). The issue, again, is that these are quantitative expectations. It is in the hurry to often apologise for not meeting these standards – standards from a different epistemological position – that the discipline forgets (or, worse, sells out) researchers who cannot meet the ableist expectations of the method. There has been for some time a move toward a qualitative set of standards, including the trustworthiness of the respondent (Atkinson, 1998), and a shift away from reliability toward validity (Mason 1996). Within this shift, we see the focus on what a respondent has to say rather than on a researcher following a set of prescriptive mechanisms. It is within this school of qualitative research that researchers with a range of disabilities, including dysfluency, can be supported and recognised as legitimate actors within the field. This support and recognition are achievable through:

- Overtly shifting away from quantitative standards or measurements of rigour;
- Trusting researchers to reach the required endpoint of data collection through various routes;
- Allowing a researcher's identity, including disability, be part of the research process more generally.

Turning specifically to the BNIM and its commitment to maintaining the gestalt of a respondent's narration through quite rigid rules: again, in the first instance, this approach to a particular form of data collection appears to be a sound and logical way to conduct the various sub-sessions making up the interview. However, there are several points I would like to make questioning the veracity of such a position:

- A BNIM interview is essentially conducted in a vacuum or a sterile environment to keep away phenomena that could impact on the narration. The central strategy in this defence is the sub-session rules. However, the rules of the method do not appear to consider the impact of researcher identity, including ethnicity, gender or disability. The primary danger toward the gestalt appears to be audible rather than subtle cues and hints respondents pick-up or construct concerning their interviewer.
- People often choose their words carefully; in the context of my research on graduate employment, a respondent using the term "college" to mean a university could be a sign of youth, informality, globalisation or simply a preference. I would contend that a dysfluent researcher using a differing term for "college" allows the interview to continue and a partnership to develop between the researcher and respondent, more than piercing the gestalt. In other situations, the range of optional words will be narrow, but allowing the opportunity to reach for a different term while maintaining the focus of a respondent's narration increases support for dysfluent researchers.
- In the context of my particular application of the BNIM, as a form of ethnographic interview, we should remember that ethnographic research is not conducted under laboratory conditions, and, while measures are put in place to reduce the impact of the researcher, this does and will happen to an extent – the same can be said for the biographical interviewer.

The commitment toward continuity in qualitative research and the strict rules of the BNIM created, in many ways, a false economy. They are based on misplaced priorities and highly selective on what can and what cannot impact on the gestalt of a narrative. Researchers need to make a choice – and PhD/ECR researchers need to be supported in their choices – about the importance of following arbitrary rules when these rules limit researcher legitimacy and raise anxiety and self-doubt. We are asking questions; the order may be different at times, but, as researchers, we are still committed to faithfully representing individuals – just as we are at presenting our own ideas and argument. It just may not come out the way others expect.

Conclusion

As an academic who straddles both privilege and stigma, the former through ethnicity and gender and the latter (alongside my stammer) through my working-class background and national identity, I feel it is fundamental to articulate the experiences and challenges that disabled academics experience. Through this chapter, I have outlined an oft-overlooked disability both within the academy and the broader public life. The stigma stemming from speech dysfluency and the subsequent strategies employed by those who stammer to maintain the identity of a fluent individual are largely incompatible with current demands of qualitative research. While these issues are present within mainstream qualitative methods, I have focused on a specific form of data collection: biographical narrative interview method. I have attempted to outline the main stages and how the principle of gestalt places ableist demands on researchers – particularly, those who stammer. Echoing a central argument throughout this edited collection is that the reason for the strict rules of BNIM and preoccupation more generally within qualitative research is an insecurity towards its level of legitimacy. A reaction to this insecurity is to attempt to mirror natural sciences in terms of objectivity and standardisation of procedures. In the move to adopt such procedures, the wider academy has made a number of ableist assumptions and ableist requirements, without considering the impact that disabilities will have on being able to complete such requirements, and, more broadly, impacting on a sense of belonging a disabled researcher may have. This chapter has ended by advocating a set of principles for qualitative research to follow to support disabled researchers and asked a set of questions specifically focusing on the rigid demands of the BNIM.

Notes

1 In the UK context, a competing approach to BNIM comes from Tom Wengraph and Prue Chamberlin. At the level of most biographical researchers, there is little discernible difference between the authors; due to my training, I have used the original model from Shutze.

2 Miller consciously reminds his readers that these models are ideal types and can be used in part or combined.

References

Acton, C. and Hird, M.J. (2004) "Toward a Sociology of Stammering", *Sociology*, 38(3), 495–513.

Atkinson, R. (1998) *The Life Story Interview*. London: Sage Publications.

Bourdieu, P. (1977) *Outline of a Theory of Practice*. Cambridge: Cambridge University Press.

Bourdieu, P. (1984) *Distinction: A Social Critique of the Judgement of Taste*. London: Routledge and Kegan and Paul.

Bourdieu, P. (2004) "The Forms of Capital", In: Ball, S.J. (ed.) *The RouteledgeFalmer Reader in Sociology of Education*. London: RouteledgeFalmer. pp. 15–29.

Bourdieu, P., Chamboredon, J-C. and Passeron, J-C. (1991) *The Craft of Sociology: Epistemological Preliminaries*. New York: Walter de Gruyter.

Bourdieu, P. and Wacquant, L. (1992) *An Invitation to Reflexive Sociology*. Cambridge: Polity Press.

Burke, C.T. (2011) "The Biographical Illumination: A Bourdieusian Analysis of the Role of Theory in Educational Research", *Sociological Research Online*, 16(2), (online) Available from: http://www.socresonline.org.uk/16/2/9.html

Burke, C. (2016) *Culture, Capitals and Graduate Futures: Degrees of Class*. London: Routledge.
Butler, C. (2013) "Identity and Stammering: Negotiating Hesitation, Side-stepping Repetition, and Sometimes Avoiding Deviation", *Sociology of Health and Illness*, *35*(7), 1113–1127.
Erben, M. (1998) "Biography and Research Method", In: Erben, M. (ed.) *Biography and Education: A Reader*. London: Falmer Press. pp. 4–17.
Goffman, E (1983) "The Interaction Order", *American Sociological Review*, *48*(1), 1–17.
Gregory, H.H. (1979) "Controversial Issues: Statement and Review of the Literature", In: Gregory, H.H. (ed.) *Controversies about Stuttering Therapy*. Baltimore: University Park Press. pp. 1–62.
Jenkins, R. (1996) Social *Identity*. London: Routledge.
Lemert, E. (1970) "Sociological Perspective", In: Sheehan, J.G. (ed.) *Stuttering: Research and therapy*. New York: Harper & Row. pp. 170–187.
Mason, J. (1996) *Qualitative Researching*. London: Sage Publications.
Merrill, B. and West, L. (2009) *Using Biographical Methods in Social Research*. London: Sage Publications.
Miller, R. L. (2000) *Researching Life Stories and Family Histories*. London: Sage Publications.
Miller, R.L. (ed.) (2005) *Biographical Research Methods Volume I–IV*. London: Sage Publications.
NIH (2017) *Stuttering*, (online) Available from: https://www.nidcd.nih.gov/health/stuttering
Reay, D. (2004) "It's All Becoming a Habitus: Beyond the Habitual Use of Habitus in Educational Research", *British Journal of Sociology of Education*, *25*(4), 431–444.
Rosenthal, G. (2003) "The Healing Effects of Storytelling: On the Conditions of Curative Storytelling in the Context of Research and Counselling", *Qualitative Inquiry*, 9(6), 915–933.
Rosenthal, G. (2005) "Biographical Research", In: Miller, R.L. (ed.) *Biographical Research Methods Volume III*. London: Sage Publications. pp. 25–58.
Schütze, F. (1992) "Pressure and Guilt: The Experience of a Young German Solider in World War Two and Its Biographical Implications", *International Sociology*, *7*(2), 187–208; *7*(3), 347–367.
Schütze, F. (2008) Biography Analysis on the Empirical Base of Autobiographical Narratives: How to Analyse Autobiographical Narrative Interviews – Part I, (online) Available from: http://www.biographicalcounselling.com/download/B2.1.pdf
Silverman, D. (2006) *Interpreting Qualitative Data: Methods for Analysing Talk, Text and Interaction* (3rd ed.). London: Sage Publications.
STUC (2018) *Stammering through University Consultancy*, (online) Available from: https://www.stuc-uk.org/
Thomas, W.I. and Znaniecki, F. (1918/1996) *The Polish Peasant in Europe and America*. (edited by Zaretsky, E.). Champaign: University of Illinois Press.

Editorial reflections

Bronagh Byrne and Ciaran Burke

This book has been borne out of a desire by the editors to uncover ways of being and doing in the academy that have been predominantly hidden and silenced. Disabled people have been positioned, at best, as the subject of research, but never as the instigator, investigator or 'doer' of research. As is evident throughout this text, disabled academics are not in a minority of one. Yet the tendency of the academy to treat those with any kind of impairment as chronically unexpected or disruptive has relegated the working lives of disabled academics to the margins. In bringing together research-academics who identify as 'disabled', this book centralises or 'normalises' disabled researchers and positions the social sciences as the key issue of inquiry. It is clear that the methodologies upon which the social sciences have made its name has not been designed for (or indeed by) researchers who happen to fall outside of corporeal norms. Nor has this shortcoming been offset by the emergence of so-called innovative methodologies that look set to shape the academy of the 21st century. Together, the editors and contributors of the book call upon all research funders, Higher Education Institutions, faculties, departments, schools, supervisors and colleagues in the social sciences to work together to create meaningfully inclusive research spaces. The following recommendations are made in light of the common themes that have emerged throughout.

Acknowledgement

Disabled researchers' struggle for acknowledgement and respect is not unique. Nor is it unique to the academy, having been the driving force behind the global disability movement since the 1960s. The presence of disabled researchers throughout the social sciences must be recognised and respected as a valued identity category on an equal basis along with other identity categories. This challenges our colleagues, employers and funders to view disability, not as a deficit to be overcome, but simply as a difference in the same way as gender, race, ethnicity and sexuality. It calls on all to positively engage with that difference and to acknowledge the commonalities of oppression. In particular, we call on academics to consider and reflect the lived experiences of disability in developing or thinking through theory and in developing, designing or amending new or existing methodologies.

Accessibility

Accessibility is not limited to the immediate physical working environment. It extends to all research facilities and the environment in which fieldwork is being conducted. We are not arguing for the academy to remove all barriers from the entire society in which we live given its potential to be subject to fieldwork at any time. What is critical, however, is that the academy leads by example. In creating a working environment and research facilities (whether that be a seminar or teaching rooms, libraries, computer suites, computer software and hardware including qualitative and quantitative data analysis packages) that are physically accessible, institutional commitment to equality and diversity is being actively demonstrated and not merely consigned to a tick box exercise. This also transmits clear messages to all students, including students with disabilities, of what we can expect our world to be like. Nowhere is there greater potential for this than the social sciences with its associated underlying values.

Additional labours

The chapters in this book speak resoundingly to the additional labours a disabled researcher has to undertake to make inaccessible methodologies accessible. This incurs additional time, energy and stresses in the research process over and above that which might be experienced by a non-disabled researcher. Yet such endeavours are rarely acknowledged or referred to in research texts, funding applications or accounted for by institutional processes. This can result in disabled researchers, particularly student and early career researchers, feeling isolated and demoralised in the face of what might appear to be insurmountable obstacles. Creating spaces for discussion of identified additional labours recognises that it is not the individual that is perceived at fault, but the normative basis on which social science methodologies and related processes have been founded. In the same way that flexibility is being promoted in the context of family life and work-life balance policies, the realities of additional labours for disabled staff need to be given a voice. Better still, the inaccessible features of research methodologies and the limited resources that necessitate additional labours should be explicitly unpacked and confronted.

Actions

It would be naive to assume that the issues highlighted in this book are the sole responsibility of non-disabled actors whether a funder, a Higher Education Institution (HEI) policymaker, the management or a faculty colleague. It would equally be naive to conclude that the issues can only be resolved by disabled researchers. The themes uncovered in this text are symptomatic of an ableist academy which has developed over time and which has become legitimised and subsequently taken for granted through the actions of multiple actors. It is only through collaborative actions that the shackles of ableism will become, at first, loosened, and finally removed. It is the responsibility of funders, HEIs, faculties, departments, supervisors and colleagues to address the structural inaccessibilities that have been uncovered. This must, however, be done in partnership with disabled researchers. Only then can we create a Sociological Future that is inclusive of everyone.

Index

For Product Safety Concerns and Information please contact our EU
representative GPSR@taylorandfrancis.com
Taylor & Francis Verlag GmbH, Kaufingerstraße 24, 80331 München, Germany

www.ingramcontent.com/pod-product-compliance
Ingram Content Group UK Ltd.
Pitfield, Milton Keynes, MK11 3LW, UK
UKHW020003200926
475702UK00015B/2446

9780367681586